WANDERLUST

WANDERLUST

THE AMAZING
IDA PFEIFFER

The First Female Tourist

JOHN VAN WYHE

RIDGE BOOKS
SINGAPORE

© 2019 John van Wyhe

Published under the Ridge Books imprint by:

NUS Press
National University of Singapore
AS3-01-02, 3 Arts Link
Singapore 117569

Fax: (65) 6774-0652
E-mail: nusbooks@nus.edu.sg
Website: http://nuspress.nus.edu.sg

ISBN 978-981-3250-76-5 (paper)

National Library Board, Singapore Cataloguing in Publication Data

Name: Van Wyhe, John, 1971-
Title: Wanderlust : the amazing Ida Pfeiffer, the first female tourist / by John van Wyhe.
Description: Singapore : NUS Press, [2019] | Includes bibliographical references.
Identifier(s): OCN 1096384476 | ISBN 978-981-32-5076-5 (paperback)
Subject(s): LCSH: Pfeiffer, Ida, 1797-1858--Travel. | Women travelers--Austria--Biography. | Women explorers--Austria--Biography. | Voyages around the world.
Classification: DDC 910.41--dc23

Printed by: Markono Print Media Pte Ltd

Ich bin mit dieser Reise- und Wanderlust geboren worden.

Ida Pfeiffer, 1856

CONTENTS

ACKNOWLEDGMENTS

I am indebted to the many people who have helped with the research for and writing of this book. My assistant and collaborator of many years, Kees Rookmaaker, was an enormous help as always. I am no less grateful to the following for helping in various ways, including David Clifford, Gerrell M. Drawhorn, Pei Rong Cheo, Gordon Chancellor, Antranig Basman, David Bickford, Elaine Sam, Christine Chua, Ashley Toh, Gerda Bleckwedel, Ann Mitchell and Posman Manurung. The foremost expert on Pfeiffer, Hiltgund Jehle, was exceedingly generous in sharing suggestions, information and results from her many years of indefatigable research on Pfeiffer. I also owe a debt to the many people who assisted me in my journeys to the places visited by Pfeiffer. In most cases I did not record their names, but without the help of local drivers, guides, translators and local residents, many interesting details would have remained unknown or misunderstood by me. I also thank my students from Tembusu College and the National University of Singapore who have accompanied me on several expeditions to study the state of nature conservation that covered some of the same ground as Pfeiffer and Wallace in Southeast Asia. The audiences at various venues where I have given talks on Pfeiffer have also contributed by asking questions that sometimes suggested new aspects of her story. I am indebted as ever to the staff of Cambridge University Library's rare books and manuscripts reading rooms.

I also owe many thanks to Peter Schoppert and Lindsay Davis at NUS Press for seeing promise in a book about Pfeiffer and helping the book through to completion. I am also indebted to two anonymous referees for surprisingly supportive and detailed suggestions and feedback. I gratefully acknowledge the permission of the editors of *Terra Mater* to reproduce photographs of Pfeiffer objects in a private collection. This too was brought to my attention and made possible by Hiltgund Jehle.

EDITORIAL NOTE

Pfeiffer not only used now archaic spellings but very often misspelled the names of people, ships and places – often unrecognisably. Presumably she just wrote down what she thought she heard. For example, she called the Kallang river in Singapore the "Gallon". Others may be transcription errors made by the printers from her handwritten diaries such as a steamer captain named "Fronson" in her book who was in fact Tronson. Her English translators made further errors. The Singapore merchant Mr Behn became Mr Behu and Danau in Sumatra became Donan. I have silently corrected these where possible. Very often Pfeiffer gave no name at all or only a title or surname. In many cases I have identified the person she met or referred to and supplied the name.

I have used modern place names in almost all cases for the sake of simplicity. Some others, such as Constantinople, Canton, Benares and Bombay have been retained since they were used at the time in which this story takes place and no one will be misled by the historical names of these famous cities. All English quotations from German language sources are my own. The terms "German" (as in a person) and "Germany" were used in the nineteenth century long before the unification of Germany in 1871, and Pfeiffer was of course Austrian. Nevertheless, the terms were commonly used to refer to German speakers and the German-speaking lands respectively. These terms are used in this way in this book. When multiple quotations come from the same page of the same source, a note is given only for the final quotation from that page.

PRELUDE

In the brisk and tumultuous winter of 1809 the triumphant Emperor Napoleon Bonaparte entered Vienna, the capital of the Austro-Hungarian Empire he had conquered along with much of Europe. Arguably the most powerful man in the world, Napoleon took up residence in the magnificent rococo Schönbrunn Palace, where the young Mozart had played for Maria Theresia. Napoleon, along with his marshals and generals, strutted in pomp and splendour as they reviewed their troops before the palace. The assembled well-to-do Viennese lined the road, eager to see their conqueror. The vivid blue coats, black felt bicornes and clanking sabres combined with the smell and stamp of the horses, created an atmosphere full of energy. It felt like a new era. Some Austrians could not help feeling a begrudging admiration for the French display.

But one Austrian patriot in the crowd of onlookers felt differently. This was an eccentric twelve-year-old girl named Ida Laura Reyer. Although she was a girl, she despised feminine clothing. Despite strong disapproval from her mother, Ida wore boys' clothes. As she stood shuddering in the bracing morning air, Ida suddenly heard someone nearby say that the Emperor was about to ride past. To express her defiant contempt for the invader, Ida turned her back as some horses clopped slowly past. Horrified at this public display of disrespect, and perhaps also frightened of the consequences, her mother gave her a smart box on the ears. But it was only some generals that had ridden past, not the Emperor. Ida's hatred was so intense that she declared that she would assassinate Napoleon, if only she had the chance. A short while later, as Napoleon himself rode up, the spirited Ida was held firmly by the shoulders by her mother. All that remained to Ida was to tightly shut her eyes and avoid the sight of the hated tyrant who had conquered the fatherland. This youthful show of obstinate defiance was the opening act of an extraordinary life. Someday Ida would be able to go her own way and when she did, she would shock the world.

A FATAL ATTRACTION

"As for me, I am tormented with an everlasting itch for
things remote.
I love to sail forbidden seas, and land on barbarous coasts."
Herman Melville, *Moby-Dick* **(1851)**

The early nineteenth century was the last great age of heroic
explorers, discoverers and adventurers. There were circumnavigation
expeditions like those of Freycinet, de Alava, von Krusenstern,
Bellingshausen and FitzRoy, Commander of HMS *Beagle*.
Alexander von Humboldt explored and investigated South America
and Cuba, von Spix and von Martius explored Brazil, Basil Hall
the western coast of South America and Mexico, Abel Clarke in
China, von Buch in Scandinavia and Burchell in South Africa. And
they were all men.

Today she is forgotten. But in the middle of the nineteenth
century, Ida Pfeiffer was one of the most famous women in the
world. One Austrian magazine called her "the strangest female
traveller of the nineteenth century".[1] Even ten years after her death,
one writer in 1868 described her as "one of the most remarkable
women of modern times".[2] *The London Review* went so far as to
declare her "one of the most extraordinary women that ever lived".[3]
She was renowned, even notorious, as the lady who travelled the

world all by herself. One could almost imagine her as the Amelia Earhart of the Victorian age.

Pfeiffer travelled further than Marco Polo, Ibn Battuta and Captain Cook. During her five great journeys she circled the globe twice. This made her both the first woman to circle the globe alone and the first to do so twice. What was just as remarkable was that she had no wealth or connections and travelled by her wits and serendipity.

Pfeiffer was an unlikely heroine or celebrity, a middle-aged housewife who wasn't glamorous or beautiful or rich. She was no scholar and made no pretensions to any type of learning or expertise. Yet she collected a treasure trove of natural history specimens and made valuable contributions to science. The hardships she endured would turn back or cripple most people. She was constantly confronted with resistance, opposition and incredulity. But despite the powerful constraints of her society, she followed her dreams to see more of the world than any woman who had ever lived.

Her contemporaries were perplexed by Pfeiffer not just because what she did was unprecedented, but why she did so was difficult to comprehend. To travel for business, government, pilgrimage or as a companion was understandable – especially for a man. But to travel vast distances, and to immerse oneself in foreign cultures where one did not speak the language, just to see and experience for oneself smacked of unbalanced self-indulgence. "Who does she think she is?" some contemporaries contemptuously sneered. What purpose does she fulfil? What type of person does this? Some asked questions that could still be asked of tourists today: what good does it do to go and visit faraway places when one is not an expert? One really cannot understand what one sees. To travel only to experience the world, just because she wanted to, seemed to be a radical severing of the ties, expectations and constraints of a nineteenth-century woman.

And yet Pfeiffer was decidedly not a feminist. She chided American women who called themselves "emancipated". As her unnamed biographer would later note, "Ida Pfeiffer did not give those who saw her the impression of an emancipated, strong-minded, or masculine woman. On the contrary ... In her whole appearance and manners there was a quiet staidness that seemed to indicate a practical housewife, with no enthusiastic thought beyond her domestic concerns."[4] Who was this extraordinary person?

When it came to her travel books, she was not always treated gently because she was of the softer sex. One writer in the *Dublin Review* in 1852 thought that although "there is a certain equality in the republic of letters":

> When a lady takes pen in hand, and appears before the world as an authoress ... the critic praises or blames as freely as when reviewing the literary productions of his fellow-men. ... When, however, a talented female writer describes scenes or personages in foreign lands, we are immediately interested and attentive, for we know that they have been viewed and considered from different points from those on which we take our stand, and often under such circumstances of time and place, as we ourselves could not hope to enjoy.

Pfeiffer did not just undertake one great journey. There were five. She just couldn't stop. She was driven by a longing for faraway lands. Pfeiffer had a fatal attraction to travelling. This was a type of what in German is so fittingly called *Wanderlust* – a passion, a lust, for travel.

And yet in part, Pfeiffer did what today no one would think at all remarkable – she was a tourist. Or perhaps more accurately she should be called a proto-tourist since the very idea of a tourist was just then emerging and evolving. In the 1840s and 1850s, unless one was extremely wealthy or state-financed, it was almost unthinkable to travel just because one wanted to see distant lands. And for a woman of her age (between forty-five and sixty-one) to do so was nothing short of shocking. The people she met along the way simply could not believe what she was up to.

In the preface to one of her travel books, Pfeiffer declared that she was no tourist.

> I have been called in many newspapers a *tourist*; but this name is unfortunately not correct for me according to its usual meaning. On the one hand I possess too little wit and humour to write entertainingly, and on the other hand too little knowledge to judge rightly what I have experienced.[5]

Yet although Pfeiffer explicitly denied that she was a "tourist" her definition was clearly a very early and narrow one that would not at all match what is meant by tourist today.

In previous generations a travelling person (a man of course) was simply called a traveller. But around the turn of the nineteenth century some travellers came to be called by a new term, tourist. Today the *Oxford English Dictionary* defines a tourist as "one who travels for pleasure". We have forgotten how recent this idea really is.

As they gradually emerged as a recognisable type of person, tourists were at first a small and privileged set. They were the social elite who had the means and inclination to travel before the age of cheap long-distance travel. The Grand Tour emerged at the start of the eighteenth century as a traditional right of passage for upper-class gentlemen. They travelled leisurely through Europe to take in the cultural highlights of Italy and Germany. With the rise of romanticism, taking in grand views, landscapes and ancient ruins became de rigueur. The primitive was preferred over the modern. The thing to do was to become immersed in foreign places, to witness the exotic and strange and lose oneself in the sublime. Along with this went art and sketching and, of course, writing about and describing the foreign or natural spectacle. The tourist had the luxury of skipping over the boring and unremarkable, and focusing on the striking or noteworthy. As one writer put it in 1824: "the tourist has higher privileges and a happier avocation; like a bird upon the wing, he explores a wide horizon, flits over all that is uninviting, and rests only on pleasant places."[6]

In the first half of the nineteenth century, travel was primarily the reserve of the well-off. Places on trains and steamships were almost all first class, with only a few places for second-class or third-class passengers. This is exactly the reverse of today when almost all places are "economy" (some would say cattle class) and very few are first class. Over the course of the century, as the industrial revolution matured and middle classes burgeoned, railways and steamships stitched and pulled the world ever more tightly together.

From the 1830s John Murray in London and Karl Baedeker in Koblenz began publishing handbooks for tourists. Baedeker's name would eventually become synonymous with guidebook. Tourists became ever more and more numerous. Almost 1,000 editions of Baedeker were published by the First World War.

What locals once felt as the honour of a visit by an elite gentleman from another country became the repellent smothering crowd of an ignorant mass of tourists. By the end of the century new expressions such as "tourist mobbed" and "tourist ridden" came into use.

The Italophile novelist Miss Lavish snootily remarks in E. M. Forster's *A Room with a View* (1908): "They walk through my Italy like a pair of cows. It's very naughty of me, but I would like to set an examination paper at Dover, and turn back every tourist who couldn't pass it."[7] Today annual tourist arrivals total more than a billion a year. International tourism receipts are well over a trillion dollars. Pfeiffer blazed the trail for modern tourists – in some cases literally.

The splendour, fame or the remote beauty and isolation of foreign sights has led many to be swamped with tourists whose crushing weight of numbers, graffiti, rubbish and sewage choked and polluted the places they descended upon. Given enough numbers and time, even mundane and apparently harmless activity gradually destroys tourist sites. Endless footsteps wear away Roman marble and mosaic floors or the intricately laid parquet flooring of stately homes. Even stone steps are gradually worn away by countless footsteps. In caves with painted ceilings, or precious works of art hung in beautiful frames, even the breath of tourists leads to the devastation of the very things they come to see. These processes still continue. Eco-tourists travel to beautiful tropical islands such as Tioman in the South China Sea. They are attracted by photos of the dazzling and vibrant coral reefs and their visits eventually destroy the beautiful things that brought them there. And so a new island is promoted as pure and untrammelled. And the process begins all over again.

What made Pfeiffer famous then would be almost unworthy of remark today. But travelling by herself at a time when it was unthinkable for a woman to do so was not her only claim to fame. And her sex should not be the focus of her story anyway. It is not the unconventionality of a female traveller, or even the formidable social obstacles she had to overcome that is worth our attention. Above all else – it is what she did and what she wrote that remains extraordinary. The extent of her travels is astonishing, even by today's standards. She travelled an estimated 32,000 kilometres by land and 240,000 kilometres by sea. She fearlessly visited peoples and places that no European had ever seen, let alone a European woman. Along the way she had some harrowing adventures. She encountered storms at sea, ships that ran aground, plague, murderers, headhunters and cannibals. She braved tigers, snakes, pirates, robbers, jungles and deserts. Unable to swim, she almost drowned when she fell off a boat in Ecuador. And she was not afraid of brandishing her horsewhip if she was cheated or imposed upon. We owe all of these images to her delightful books. Her writings have a vividness of observation and description that still stirs, still strikes a chord.

Her travels remain as fascinating now as they were when they first gripped the nineteenth-century literary world. Indeed, today they hold a special fascination as her lucid descriptions captured scenes of a world that is lost. It was a world on the cusp of our modernity, the mid nineteenth century when railways and steamships were opening up the world in a new way. In their wake would come ever-increasing cultural homogenisation. Out of these international arteries a new species evolved which most of us have, at one time or another, belonged, *Homo touristicus*.

But Pfeiffer was not just a tourist, she was an explorer, ethnographer and naturalist. Wherever she travelled, she collected minerals, beetles, butterflies, shells and plants, discovered hundreds of new species and enriched the museums of Britain and Europe.

Although she has been called the first "hippie traveller", a more fitting way of describing her would be as the first budget traveller.[8] Her unconventional means of travel were almost as shocking to her contemporaries as the fact that she was a woman. She did not ride in fine railway carriages or wood-panelled first-class steamship cabins. She travelled second or even third class – something that was then only for servants or natives. She sailed in Malay proas and Chinese junks where other Europeans never did. She rode horses through rainy meadows, joined camel caravans plodding slowly across scorching deserts and trekked through entangling rainforests swarming with leeches and malarial mosquitoes. She ate local foods that were revolting to Europeans. She slept in the houses of local peoples or on the bare ground. In Borneo there were freshly severed human heads drying in the longhouse near where she slept. She risked her life on countless occasions and had several very close calls. She was stabbed in Brazil, threatened with decapitation in Persia and Sumatra and kidnapped by a Cossack in Russia. In Madagascar she was almost executed. And perhaps, in the end, she was.

All of this and yet she never went to school or university. But the world would have known none of it if she had not also written about her experiences. Her travel diaries were published to the astonishment of the public. To her surprise, Pfeiffer became a best-selling authoress. Her books were translated into at least seven languages. Her fame grew rapidly until the great and good, learned men and scientific societies and even the crowned heads of Europe vied to meet and honour her. Inevitably such an eccentric and unconventional woman also became the subject of ridicule. For example, one rather thankfully forgotten British poet penned:

> Except Ida Pfeiffer, that wonder, who can
> With umbrella and tooth-brush, reach far Yucatan[9]

As she travelled from island to island or country to country, her exploits were reported in newspapers around the world. The public eagerly awaited the next volume of incredible stories from Madame Pfeiffer, as she was usually known in English publications. But it was not to last. Her final voyage was too much for her. After her tragic and premature death in 1858 her fame gradually waned and her memory eventually vanished into obscurity.

I came across Ida Pfeiffer almost by accident. As a historian of science, I specialise in the Victorian evolutionists Charles Darwin and Alfred Russel Wallace. While conducting research for my book on Wallace and Darwin, *Dispelling the Darkness* (2013), I first encountered Pfeiffer. Many accounts had been written about the voyage of Wallace through Southeast Asia using little more than his own book as a source. Unsurprisingly, they said exactly the same things and perpetuated many myths. I wanted to explore the entire story afresh from the ground up, and to tell the story based on the largest evidence base I could assemble. For example, Wallace only said so much about each island he visited. But vastly more information and detail could be found in the accounts of other writers who visited these places around the same time. A far more complete picture could be reconstructed by using what others had recorded to fill in blanks in Wallace's account. So I set myself the task of reading the books of other travellers who came through Southeast Asia around the same time. One of these was Ida Pfeiffer. She visited Singapore on both of her round-the-world journeys and much of her route through the islands of present-day Indonesia was later followed by Wallace.

Even more striking was the fact that she also collected and sold natural history specimens, which Wallace would later do, and some of hers were even sold through the same London agent and auctioneer, Samuel Stevens. In his letters home, Wallace occasionally mentioned Pfeiffer.[10] He knew well the value of the specimens she had collected on certain islands. He would later make these islands some of his main destinations. And yet, strangely, he never mentioned her in his travel book or articles.

And in a final stroke of coincidence, if that is what it was, Wallace advised Stevens in 1855 to recommend Madagascar as Pfeiffer's next destination. Wallace thought that it would prove a very profitable locale for collecting. Pfeiffer's next destination, in 1856, was indeed Madagascar. Unfortunately, it ultimately proved fatal. Had my protagonist inadvertently killed off Ida Pfeiffer? There was no way to tell. At any rate, reading her works one finds that her travels were far wider ranging, her adventures far more hair-raising and her descriptions of many of the places I knew from Wallace's writings, were often far more detailed. Her story and adventures were incredible. And yet she seems to be totally forgotten and unknown today. In my book on Wallace and Darwin I could only note: "Pfeiffer might be called the dark lady of Wallace's Eastern archipelago as she has been lost from the story as the biophysicist Rosalind Franklin, overshadowed by Watson and Crick, has been called the dark lady of DNA."[11]

I was intrigued to know more about this enigmatic lady who refused to be hemmed in by societal constraints and chose to go her own way. I have been fortunate enough to retrace some of her footsteps in Vienna, London, Singapore, Penang, Sarawak, Tahiti, Java, Sumatra, Sulawesi and Ternate. Her story is endlessly fascinating and deserves to be remembered. This book is intended to bring her to an English-speaking audience.

CHAPTER 1

BRINGING UP IDA

"I was born with this travel- and wanderlust."
Ida Pfeiffer, 1856

Ida was born in October 1797 in Vienna the third child of Aloys and Anna Reyer. Her father was a wealthy textile manufacturer and exporter. Ida and her elder brothers Karl and Gustav were joined in the following years by another three brothers. Until her ninth year, Ida was the only girl in a family of five boys. A sister, Marie, would be the last child.

This environment may have allowed Ida's somewhat wild and independent nature to flourish more freely than it might otherwise have done. "I was not shy," she recalled, "but wild as a boy, and bolder and more forward than my elder brothers."[12] We have to rely on her later autobiographical account for many details, even though, of course, retrospective self-reporting is fraught with problems, biases and inaccuracies.

She was without doubt a tomboy. She wore boys' clothing and abhorred the idea of wearing a dress or pursuing feminine pastimes. Instead she played with toy swords and rifles with her brothers. When the Napoleonic wars erupted across Europe, she regretted her young age, rather than her sex, which she naively believed was the only thing that kept her from taking part in fighting for her country.

These fantasies may have been encouraged by her otherwise strict father who, perhaps facetiously, declared that Ida should be raised in the same manner as her brothers. As a stern father, Reyer refused to spoil his children with luxuries. They were served only the simplest meals while the adults dined sumptuously. Special favours or complaints about harsh treatment were taboo. Such measures were meant to teach his children to endure hardship. This would turn out to be good training for Ida. And, in retrospect, the strict but indulgent regime of her father was a sort of utopia, in the original sense of the word.

In 1806 Herr Reyer died aged only forty-three. For young Ida this meant not only the loss of a parent, but the loss of the tolerant phase of her childhood when wearing boys' clothes and abstaining from learning the feminine arts were tolerated. After a few months her mother insisted that it was time for Ida to wear dresses and adopt womanly ways. The result was a massive act of passive protest by Ida. She fell dangerously ill. It was probably a form of deep depression. The doctors advised that Ida be allowed to resume her masculine garb for a little while longer. It worked and she recovered.

Eventually Ida reluctantly had to give in to the pressure. Although it cost her many tears, at thirteen she had to put on a dress again. Along with proper attire came the other expected female activities for a young lady of her class. There were the trappings of middle-class learning, piano, foreign languages, literature, household management and social skills. Transforming into what she had abhorred must have cost her more than a pang. Perhaps a part of her died and a new Ida emerged. Or perhaps the new Ida was a hybrid. Maybe the independent rebel still lurked inside, like a seed silently awaiting the right circumstances to sprout and grow.

Vienna was the capital of the Austro-Hungarian Empire, one of the great powers of Europe and exceeded in size only by the

Russian Empire. The elegant capital city along the gentle Danube was surrounded by beautiful and fertile fields, to the west the imposing spectacle of the mountains and to the east a vast fertile plain all the way to Hungary. Mountains in the background would prescribe Ida's idea of a beautiful view for the rest of her life. Firmly Roman Catholic, Vienna's trademark building then as now was the charming gothic monument of St. Stephen's Cathedral whose bright Romanesque roof tiles and spire towered above all other structures in the city. From these heights stone gargoyles overlooked the city.

English-speaking readers will tend to think of Pfeiffer as Victorian, but Ida grew up during what German speakers know as the Biedermeier period, including the years after the fall of Napoleon in 1815 to the revolutions of 1848. The name itself is a later caricature derived from a fictional character designed to make fun of the domestically obsessed and tamely depoliticised middle classes of the era. Historian E. H. Gombrich called it the "period of tranquillity and leisure ... of the administrative or professional middle-class citizen".[13] Thomas Mann's novel *Buddenbrooks* (1901) remains a quintessential portrayal of the age.

In the aftermath of the French revolution and the Napoleonic wars, the re-established European monarchies, and in particular that of the Austro-Hungarian Empire ruled by Francis I and his ruthless Foreign Minister, Prince von Metternich, reigned with great strictness and suspicion. Secret intelligence agencies and press censorship were mercilessly employed to protect the status quo. Clubs and social societies were closed and some of their leaders imprisoned.

With the public and social spheres so curtailed and under surveillance, more time and attention were focused on the home and the private sphere. At the same time burgeoning numbers of middle-class families had money to spend. Although they tried to emulate the untouchable aristocracy above them, their own culture developed into the distinctive Biedermeier style of interior design, furniture, music and art. A well-appointed living room was the centre of much attention and scrutiny by visitors. And no *haute bourgeois* household such as the Reyer's was complete without fine furniture, elegant wallpaper, a piano and windows festooned with elegant lace curtains. From 1826 the popular waltzes and polkas of Johann Strauss were to become the background music to this world.

Biedermeier society also involved the meticulous scrutiny of dress, manners and behaviour. Social etiquette and polite social intercourse involved many rules about meeting and greeting, conversation, invitations, dining and so forth. Virtues such as diligence, modesty, order and cleanliness were the most highly praised. The latter was to become a particular favourite of Ida's. When she later travelled to distant places, it was through Biedermeier spectacles that Ida would perceive the world.

Don't stand so close to me

The year after Ida's brief encounter with Napoleon, a handsome tutor named Franz Josef Trimmel, twenty-three, was engaged to educate the Reyer children, including the eccentric Ida, now thirteen. In his free time Trimmel was an enthusiastic traveller, if only regionally. He even wrote poetry about travel. Trimmel taught Ida history and geography and to appreciate nature from the then fashionable romantic perspective. Trimmel succeeded in passing on his enthusiasm for reading books of travel to his recalcitrant young pupil. Ida was soon inspired above all by the idea of visiting far-off lands. She envied "every navigator and naturalist" who was lucky enough to travel.[14]

The great Prussian naturalist-explorer Alexander von Humboldt was an obvious favourite. His writings ignited the imaginations of generations of scientific travellers.[15] Charles Darwin was only one of his scientific offspring. The remotely set fantasy of *Robinson Crusoe* was another of her favourites. Reading about distant lands was not only part of the fashionable romantic longing for places remote, but for Ida it was also an escape from her uncomfortable position in both home and society – where she was a misfit, barely tolerated, and felt unloved. Surely in distant countries one could be free.

Trimmel treated her with a kindness and sympathy she found nowhere else. Ida soon developed a crush on him. For his sake she undertook the training in feminine arts that she had so long resisted and so deeply despised. Such contemptible domestic activities as sewing, knitting and cooking were mastered. Even the stereotypical middle-class piano playing was taken up. To please him she tried to succeed at all the tasks he set. After three or four years the "wild boy" had become an unassuming young lady.

Perhaps unsurprisingly, her feelings for Trimmel soon turned from a crush to an enflamed "gushing love for him".[16] Eleven years older than Ida, Trimmel sensed the invisible sparks and felt something for her too. But it seems that, for now, such feelings were kept secret by both parties.

After tutoring Ida, Trimmel moved on to become a modestly well-paid civil servant in the Ministry of the Interior. Yet he remained such a close friend of the family that Frau Reyer jokingly referred to him as "her dear sixth son".[17] Ida later recalled:

> He was at every party in our house, and went with us wherever we accepted an invitation; always accompanying us to theatres, in our walks, and so on. What was more natural than that we should both persuade ourselves that my mother had intended us for each other, and would perhaps only stipulate for our waiting till I had attained my twentieth year, and T[rimmel] had a better appointment?[18]

In 1814, when Ida was seventeen, a wealthy Greek gentleman asked her mother for permission to marry Ida. This was declined because the Greek was not a Catholic and her mother thought it indecorous for a lady under twenty to marry. Perhaps people always want what seems hard to get. The Greek's proposal had two dramatic consequences. First, it awoke in Ida more passionate and heart-rending feelings for Trimmel than she had recognised before. "I had hitherto had no idea of the powerful passion which makes mortals the happiest or the most miserable of beings ... I felt that I could love no one but T[rimmel]."[19]

The second effect was on Trimmel. He had heard about the proposal. Suddenly spurred by the fear of losing Ida, Trimmel confessed his love to her. The two were of one mind. They wanted to marry. Trimmel had only to ask Frau Reyer for Ida's hand. Bad idea.

This was no Jane Austen romance – although exactly contemporary. Yet Ida, plain but intelligent, could have been an Austen heroine. But Trimmel was no Darcy. He was a love match to be sure but he was of lower social status and wealth. Frau Reyer was horrified at this unperceived wolf in sheep's clothing in their midst. He was not even close to the social level she expected for Ida. Frau Reyer not only refused his request but Trimmel was banned from the house and from seeing Ida ever again.

Ida was as obstinate as ever. She declared that if she could not be with Trimmel, she would not marry. Frau Reyer took Ida to a priest to talk some sense into her about the duty of children to be obedient to their parents. Her mother and the priest pressured Ida to swear a solemn oath on a crucifix that she would not secretly see Trimmel or ever write to him. Ida refused to take the oath but was finally persuaded to promise to do as she was bidden, but on one condition, that she could write him one last letter explaining what had happened. In the letter, she begged him not to believe anything he might hear about her from other people. Since she would be obliged to marry a suitor of her mother's choice, Ida vowed to write and tell Trimmel if she became engaged.

Trimmel replied with a brief letter full of bitter sorrow. He knew her mother and understood the circumstances and accepted that there was no way out. He resigned himself to the inevitable. With all his hopes smashed, he declared that he would never marry.

Ida recalled that "three long, sorrowful years passed away without my seeing him, and without any change in my feelings or position". Then one day while Ida was out walking with a friend of her mother's, she ran into Trimmel. They both froze. There was a long awkward pause. Neither could utter a word until Trimmel enquired after her health. "I was too deeply moved to be able to reply," she recalled, "my knees trembled, and I felt ready to sink into the earth. I seized my companion by the arm and drew her away with me, and rushed home, scarcely conscious of what I was doing. Two days afterward I was stretched on my couch in a burning fever."[20]

Literally heartbroken, Ida fell into a terrible illness. It was believed that her life was in danger. However, one day a gossipy nurse let drop that the family expected Ida to die. The effect was extraordinary. Ida fell into a deep slumber and awoke refreshed and recovered. Perhaps knowing her protest wasn't working had some unconscious effect.

As the family was wealthy, there was no shortage of suitors, circling like vultures. But Ida rejected every offer. With each refusal her position at home became more difficult. In the end her home life became so unbearable that she decided it would be better to marry to escape it. So she promised to accept the next proposal provided that the gentleman was of advancing years. This would at least show Trimmel that she had been coerced into marriage. Maybe she also hoped that she would soon be a widow.

In 1819 Dr Mark Anton Pfeiffer visited Vienna on business. Originally from Switzerland, he was one of the most distinguished advocates in Lemberg, the capital of Austrian Poland (now Lviv, Ukraine). He was a widower whose grown son was studying law at the University of Vienna. Having been introduced socially to the Reyers, Dr Pfeiffer returned home after a few days.

A few weeks later an extraordinary letter from Dr Pfeiffer arrived in Vienna. It contained a formal proposal to marry Ida. She could hardly believe it. They had exchanged only a few words on trivial subjects. But her mother reminded Ida of her promise to marry the next suitor. Ida considered the matter. Dr Pfeiffer seemed kind and was intelligent and well educated. But even more importantly for Ida's calculations was the fact that he was twenty-four years her senior and lived 800 kilometres away. This would take her far out of the reach of her mother's repressive control. Dr Pfeiffer ticked all the boxes available to her.

And so Ida consented – on one condition. She was to be allowed to inform Dr Pfeiffer of her past and her true feelings. This was granted. She wrote him her full story in a letter and confessed her feelings for Trimmel. Perhaps she secretly hoped that Dr Pfeiffer would lose interest. Instead, Dr Pfeiffer replied that he was not in the least surprised that a young lady of twenty-two had already fallen in love and that he respected her all the more for confessing her feelings so fully. And so the deal was done. Ida was obliged to write to Trimmel with the news. He replied as before that he would never forget her, and never marry. He never did.

The hard years

Ida Reyer married Dr Pfeiffer on 1 May 1820 in Vienna. A week later the couple left for Lemberg. If it did not awaken any romantic feelings in her heart, the 500 mile journey did fan the old embers of Ida Pfeiffer's dreams of travel. In the first month of her marriage she became pregnant. Undeterred, she nevertheless took every opportunity to make numerous little trips.

But all was about to change for Dr Pfeiffer. This, at least, is how Ida Pfeiffer later explained her husband's loss of fortune. In the course of bringing an important lawsuit to a successful conclusion, he uncovered serious bribery amongst senior government officials. Although he foresaw that exposing them might lead to unpleasant consequences, true to his noble character, he bravely reported the bribery to the government in Vienna. An investigation was ordered into the accusations. As a result several officials were sacked.

Alas foreseeing dire consequences does not prevent them, and soon Dr Pfeiffer was made to suffer. The old-boy network closed ranks about him. The gossip and snubs grew ever more oppressive and widespread until they were too much to bear. His reputation was so tarnished that he felt he was a liability to his clients. He resigned from his appointment as councillor.

And so in 1821 the family moved to Vienna where Dr Pfeiffer expected to find new employment. Being heavily pregnant did not keep Pfeiffer from making the long journey. Two weeks later she bore a son, Alfred.

But Dr Pfeiffer's enemies had been busy and his reputation as a troublemaker and enemy of the comfortable if corrupt status quo was too widely spread. His job applications were all unsuccessful. The same posts were instead given to more junior and untalented people thus adding insult to injury.

The Pfeiffers' financial condition became serious. At Lemberg Dr Pfeiffer had been a wealthy man and kept horses, carriages, servants and so forth. With such an ample income he had not thought of investing for the future. Even Ida's inheritance had been lost. Dr Pfeiffer had lent it to a friend in financial difficulties. The friend went bankrupt and the inheritance was lost.

Ignominious poverty was the result. Pfeiffer had been accustomed to a privileged bourgeois lifestyle with servants to do the hard work. Now she had to perform all the household labours herself. Worse, for someone of her station, she had to secretly find ways to earn money. She was too ashamed that anyone should know her condition. Secretly giving lessons in drawing and music earned a few guilders. But it was not enough. Her little family suffered from the cold and on many days she could provide them with nothing more than dry bread.

In May 1822 the next disaster struck. In her parent's house Pfeiffer was delivered of a baby daughter they named Bertha. But the baby lived only eighteen hours. Constantly seeking employment, the Pfeiffers moved back and forth between Lemberg and Vienna where their last child, Oscar, was born on 22 October 1824.

Her mother and brothers could have helped but Pfeiffer was too proud to appeal to them. Considering how her mother had pressured her into the marriage in the first place, one wishes she had. As the years of bitter poverty dragged on, compounded by the need to conceal the urgency of her situation, only the thought of her children kept Pfeiffer from considering suicide. Finally things became too desperate and she was forced to ask her brothers for money. The shame must have been almost unbearable. She would later recall, "Heaven only knows what I suffered during eighteen years of my married life."[21]

In October 1830 Pfeiffer returned with Oscar to Vienna to tend her mother during a lengthy illness. Frau Reyer died in October 1831 leaving Pfeiffer just enough money to end the years of real hardship, though she could never return to the lifestyle she had once known. Dr Pfeiffer wrote from Lemberg announcing he would soon again have gainful employment. But it was all a delusion. With the various moves between Lemberg and Vienna and further afield, Pfeiffer took several opportunities to live away from Dr Pfeiffer during these years.

In 1833 she took the boys once and for all back to Vienna where she would live on her own and continue her sons' education. Dr Pfeiffer remained in Lemberg. Oscar in particular showed considerable talent as a composer and pianist and Pfeiffer did her best to further his education. She was now, as we would say, amicably separated from Dr Pfeiffer. But in those days such things were not openly acknowledged or announced.

After this Dr Pfeiffer mysteriously vanishes from the record. Ida made no further reference to him and even in the posthumously published biographical memoir by Oscar, Dr Pfeiffer's fate is not revealed. Pfeiffer's remark about eighteen years of marriage might suggest that he died in 1838. (Or she simply meant that she suffered during eighteen years of the marriage.) Some contemporary sources reported that her husband died before her first journey. The London *Literary Gazette* (1851) referred to her being widowed before she began travelling. The Augsburg newspaper *Der Sammler* reported in 1854 that it had received a long series of travel reports from Pfeiffer during her latest journey. *Der Sammler* repeated the well-known story of how Pfeiffer could only begin her new life of international travel after her sons had been educated and found employment. But it also added another detail, that it was settling her sons and the death of her husband that had made Pfeiffer free to travel.[22] But press reports are notoriously unreliable. Pfeiffer biographer Hiltgund Jehle quoted a letter in which Pfeiffer asked her first publisher, in 1842, to return her travel diary so that it could be checked by her siblings and "husband". And in another letter Pfeiffer wrote in 1848 that she had not written to her husband for some time.[23] His fate remains a mystery.

A new hope

In July 1836 Pfeiffer and Oscar travelled 480 kilometres southwest to the port city of Trieste on the Adriatic coast where her aunt and uncle von Reyer lived. Pfeiffer wanted to give her twelve-year-old son some sea bathing and no doubt she was keen to travel.

Her first sight of the sea sent a shudder through her which would change her life forever. It's reminiscent of the warning that Galadriel gave to Legolas in J. R. R. Tolkien's *The Two Towers* (1954):

> Legolas Greenleaf, long under tree
> In joy thou hast lived. Beware of the Sea!
> If thou hearest the cry of the gull on the shore,
> Thy heart shall then rest in the forest no more

Her youthful longing to travel came rushing back. She was infected with what in German is so aptly called, *Fernweh* – a painful longing for distant lands. Now more than ever to travel, to escape, would be a balm to all that had hurt and hindered her. If it hadn't been for Oscar she would have boarded the next ship to travel over the horizon into the mysterious blue world beyond.

Although Pfeiffer now longed to travel, her sons still needed her. She would later recall that "as long as homely duties bound me, I forced back this longing to travel."[24] After two months she returned to Vienna, grateful to be out of sight of temptation. But the romantic yearning to see distant lands was growing. In 1841 she would make a short trip back to Trieste and, with her brother Adolf, visit Venice and Padua, then both part of the Austro-Hungarian Empire. From there, at the end of August, she travelled back to Vienna alone. She could make her own way.

CHAPTER 2

A SECRET JOURNEY (1842)

"My heart is longing day and night for voyages to faraway lands."
Jan Huyghen van Linschoten, 1584

On the surface Ida Pfeiffer was quiet and demure, which seemed to fit her petite stature and unprepossessing appearance. She was described as "small and slight of figure, rather plain in countenance".[25] Her slightly protruding dark brown eyes, her sunken cheeks and prominent cheekbones gave her a somewhat cadaverous appearance and her overbite was pronounced. But looks can be and often are deceiving. Beneath this unassuming exterior was a strong-willed, driven, immensely ambitious, impatient and sometimes headstrong character.

By 1842 her sons were both settled in secure employment. Alfred had become a civil servant and Oscar a promising musician. In November 1844 Oscar would make his public debut in Vienna at the Society of Friends of Music.[26] At last Ida Pfeiffer was free to pursue the longing of a lifetime: to travel. She recalled how at this juncture in her life, "I thought of strange manners and customs, of distant regions, where a new sky would be above me, and new ground beneath my feet."[27] And, curiously, it was a longing to travel alone.

As Pfeiffer laid her plans, she was well aware of the most likely reaction others would have: "that I, a woman, should venture into the world alone" would be considered an utterly fatal objection. She had three answers in mind. First her age, she was now forty-five years old and not remotely handsome and so not a likely target for predatory men, and also at an age when a woman was normally allowed more autonomy. Secondly, there was her innate courage and thirdly, her self-reliance which she had acquired during the years of impoverished hardship. "As regarded money," she thought, "I was determined to practice the most rigid economy. Privation and discomfort had no terrors for me. I had endured them long enough by compulsion, and considered that they would be much easier to bear if I encountered them voluntarily with a fixed object in view."[28]

Other women before Pfeiffer had of course travelled, but very few without male companions. One pioneer was the German-born naturalist and artist Maria Merian, fifty-two, who sailed with her daughter on Dutch government funding to Suriname in 1699 to study insects and plants. Merian was a great early entomologist and her illustrations of plants and insects remain astonishingly fresh and vibrant works of art. Unfortunately a case of what must have been malaria forced her to return to Europe after two years.

A century later Lady Hester Stanhope travelled extensively in the Near and Middle East from 1810 and stayed until her death in 1839. While she did at times wear oriental dress, she did not travel alone and was very, very rich. She became well known from books that appeared after Pfeiffer's first book. Another was the Wagnerian-sounding Wolfradine Minutoli, who accompanied her Prussian husband to Egypt on a scientific expedition and published an account of the journey in 1826.

Lady Mary Montagu was the wife of the British ambassador to the Ottoman Empire at Constantinople. Her *Turkish Embassy Letters* (1763) is often credited with inspiring later female travellers to the Middle East. Lady Mary died in 1762 after transferring the idea of smallpox vaccination to Britain. Some of her more exciting exploits are echoed in Pfeiffer's writings. Lady Mary too was allowed to go where no man would be suffered to enter, such as Turkish harems to see the secret fleshly beauties ensconced within. Lady Mary praised the comparative freedom of women in Turkey, claiming they were better off than the women of Europe. She became a staunch critic of the condition of women in western society.

A direct contemporary of Pfeiffer's was the Prussian Countess Ida Hahn-Hahn. After divorcing her husband in 1829 (a cousin who gave her the double-barrelled name), she travelled in Europe and the Near East with a male partner in the mid 1840s. Her travel books became hugely popular in aristocratic circles. So women travellers were not unprecedented, but they were very rare and unusual. Those women who did travel were wealthy. And they almost never travelled alone.

Two exotic destinations had long been at the top of Ida Pfeiffer's wish list – the Holy Land and Iceland. If she could manage it, the former would be her first destination. She could not help mentioning to friends that she wished to visit Jerusalem. They looked at her as if she were crazy. No one believed for a second that she could actually be serious. A middle-aged woman, travel to Jerusalem alone? Impossible! Her friends told her that even men "were obliged gravely to consider if they had physical strength to endure the fatigues of such a journey, and strength of mind bravely to face the dangers of the plague, the climate, the attacks of insects, bad diet, etc". In her friends' opinion "to think of a woman's venturing alone, without protection of any kind, into the wide world, across sea and mountain and plain,—it was quite preposterous".[29]

Pfeiffer was determined not to let this stop her. She decided to keep her plans a secret. Instead, she let it be known that she was going to visit a friend in Constantinople (Istanbul), capital of the Ottoman Empire. That alone was an enormous journey of 1,730 kilometres, much further than she had ever travelled before. But it could be managed by booking tickets with commercial steamship companies. As she packed, she kept her true destination, as well as her passport, concealed. Since it was known that she was going abroad, why hide her passport? In her day a passport was a certificate by the government in response to a request to travel to specific countries. Hence her passport was kept hidden because it listed her true destination. Amongst her things were fourteen notebooks in which she would record her travel diary.

The 22nd of March 1842 was a mild spring day along the banks of the salubrious Danube. Ida Pfeiffer arrived at the steamer office with her portmanteau and boarded the small paddle steamer *Marianne* with a second-class ticket. She waved goodbye to her sons and a few friends as the steamer puffed and churned its way down the Danube towards Budapest. Such a long journey could take a year to complete. Indeed it was quite possible that she would not make it back alive. Consequently she had made out her will and put her affairs in order before departing.

A female passenger travelling all the way to Constantinople was unprecedented. The steamer captain announced the curious fact to the small number of passengers – there was a lady on board intending to travel so far alone. The inquisitive immediately surrounded her full of questions and eager to stare at such an oddity. Pfeiffer's new life as a living curiosity had begun. One of the onlookers stepped forward and said he was also heading to Constantinople and offered his services should she require assistance. This too would be a key to Pfeiffer's future success. By simply taking the plunge and throwing herself into wild and unpredictable circumstances, she usually found people moved to assist her.

The primitive little paddle steamers that then plied major European waterways made frequent stops and from time to time one had to change steamer to continue onwards. At some stops one stayed in a hotel or inn for the night before continuing the journey the following morning. There were six changes of vessel between Vienna and Constantinople. The last steamer, the *Ferdinand*, exited the Danube and entered the broad expanse of the Black Sea on 3 April 1842. Pfeiffer noted in her journal how uncomfortable the steamer's plain wooden benches were – and these were not just for sitting on but also for sleeping as there were no bunks.

A storm arose that tossed the tiny ship about and made all the passengers seasick. All they could do was lie on their benches and hold on tight. Some were too weak and fell off as the ship pitched back and forth. Undaunted, Pfeiffer went on deck "to enjoy the aspect of that grandest of nature's phenomena—a storm at sea".[30] The ship rushed down into the immense valley of a trough between waves and then rose up again onto the mountain-like peak of the next wave. Water crashed over the deck again and again. Pfeiffer simply held tight in order to witness it. Even though she was soaked through, the sight thrilled and intrigued her and she forgot all about her seasickness.

At 3 a.m. on Tuesday 6 April the tiny ship steamed up to Constantinople and dropped anchor. Almost everyone on board was asleep at this late hour, but not Ida Pfeiffer. She stood watch on deck eager to see the first glow of sunrise over the historic city. As the crisp spring day slowly dawned, she eagerly feasted her eyes on the exotic sight before her with its "beautiful mosques, with their graceful minarets—the palaces and harems, kiosks and great barracks—the gardens, shrubberies, and cypress-woods—the gaily painted houses, among which single cypresses often rear their slender heads,—these, together with the immense forest of masts, combine to form an indescribably striking spectacle."[31]

Although she had brought letters of introduction to some prominent Austrian residents in Constantinople, "not being fortunate enough to travel in great pomp or with a great name, my countrymen did not consider it worth while to trouble themselves about me".[32] Budget travel had its ups and downs then as it still does.

As was the custom at the time in polite society, Pfeiffer always brought letters of introduction to new acquaintances. Books of etiquette at the time advised: "Letters of Introduction are to be considered as certificates of respectability—as proofs that you are known by the introducer to be a proper person to be admitted into the friendly circle of him to whom you are recommended, without the risk, in these days of elegant exterior, of his harbouring a swindler, or losing his silver spoons."[33] Letters of introduction were to be brief and refer to the occupation of the person presented and might include a polite request that the recipient extend assistance and friendship. Such letters were never sealed, as this would have been considered very impolite. The bearer was always permitted to read the letter. It was considered good breeding to acknowledge the receipt of such letters, even if one was unable to immediately receive or call on the visitor. On the continent it was normal for a visitor to call on local residents whereas in Britain it was the reverse and established residents were expected to call on newcomers. To push oneself on the attention of residents was considered discourteous.

There was far worse than an outbreak of impoliteness in Constantinople. There was yet another outbreak of plague in the city. One needed a safe place to stay. Fortunately, a fellow passenger from the *Ferdinand* recommended one of the better boarding houses, run by Madame Giuseppini Balbiani, where rooms as well as coffee, breakfast and lunch, cost only 40 piastres a day or 4 guilders. A German by birth, and recently widowed, Madame

Balbiani took a particular interest in and care of Pfeiffer who found the accommodation excellent in all respects.

From this safe base on a hilltop at Pera, where the Europeans dwelled, Pfeiffer was able to explore the city and its environs. She toured many beautiful local mosques, including, of course, the great Hagia Sophia, the grand bazaar and Turkish coffee houses. She found the absence of alcohol in the Muslim city a great boon unlike the scourge abundant alcohol was in European cities.

One day she attended a ceremony of opium-fuelled whirling dervishes. She was shocked by the sight of such religious and physical exuberance. "I would not advise any person afflicted with weak nerves to witness it, for he certainly could not endure the sight. I could have fancied myself among raving lunatics and men possessed, rather than amidst reasonable beings. It was long before I could recover my composure, and realise the idea that the infatuation of man could attain such a pitch."[34]

Amongst the Europeans she met were some fellow German speakers: two brothers, Karl Theodor (a lithographer) and Baron Friedrich Karl von Buseck, and the landscape painter Hubert Sattler.[35] They were planning to visit the picturesque and historic town of Bursa across the Sea of Marmara to the south. As Pfeiffer had mentioned her interest in visiting Bursa, the gentlemen invited her to accompany them. But there was a catch. The trip involved taking a steamer across to the port city of Gemlik from where it was necessary to ride hard over bad roads in order to reach Bursa before nightfall. It was essential that she be a good rider to accompany them.

But Pfeiffer had never ridden a horse in her life. Yet she was so determined to see Bursa that she concealed this and trusted to her luck that she would manage it. On 13 May the party steamed the thirty miles across to Gemlik where a guide and a group of horses were waiting for them. The Turkish guide certainly looked ready for anything with several pistols and a dagger in his sash and a scimitar at his side.

At last, the moment of truth arrived and Pfeiffer nervously mounted one of the horses. As the little procession set off slowly she was delighted and relieved to find that she could sit atop a horse. But then the speed was increased from a walk to a trot. As she bounced uncomfortably up and down she could not keep her feet in the stirrups and was in danger of falling off. She wished so much that she could ask one of her companions for advice, but she dared not confess her ignorance. Instead she rode at the rear where she hoped no one would notice her struggles to keep from being unhorsed. She clutched the saddle with both hands and held on for dear life. At last the pace was increased to a gallop. This was smoother than the bumping trot and Pfeiffer, her skirts trailing in the wind, was relieved to find she could keep her balance more easily. This plunge into the unknown and untried would become typical for Pfeiffer and she would do the same sort of thing again and again in her travels. And it usually worked.

It's not clear when Pfeiffer revealed to her friends and family back home that Constantinople was not the end of her journey but merely the springboard. Presumably she sent the news home in letters. Perhaps she phrased it as a change of plan now that no one could stop her.

Pfeiffer sought advice from other travellers about the dangers of journeying on to the Holy Land. Many warned her about recent political unrest, robbery, murder and the plague. Unsurprisingly, Pfeiffer was not deterred. Others advised her to make the journey dressed as a man. She decided against this, preferring instead a simple costume of "a kind of blouse and wide Turkish trousers". She made the right decision: "The further I travelled, the more I became persuaded how rightly I had acted in not concealing my sex. Every where I was treated with respect, and kindness and consideration were frequently shown me merely because I was a woman."

Purchasing once again a second-class steamer ticket, Ida Pfeiffer left Constantinople on 17 May 1842 on board the Austrian steamer *Erzherzog Johann*. From this point on she was utterly alone. There was no sympathetic offer of help on board this time and not one other European. "All was strange. The people, the climate, country, language, the manners and customs—all strange."[36]

She was dressed in a very plain gown of grey surge. From under the brim of her huge straw hat, she watched the minarets of Constantinople slowly sink beneath the horizon. And then, to her surprise, she found that there was another European on board after all. He was the sole first-class passenger. In her book she claimed not to know the gentleman. They spoke in French and found that both were headed for Jerusalem. The gentleman offered to assist her if she liked. She gladly accepted.

The man was a dashingly handsome thirty-seven-year-old Englishman named William Henry Bartlett. An artist, well known for his steel engravings, Bartlett was on another of his countless trips abroad to depict the landscapes and monuments of far-flung lands for his London publisher. He found Pfeiffer's "manner, though observant, was remarkably quiet and retiring, and it was only now and then, when excited by conversation, that the kindling of her dark eye betrayed the fund of enthusiasm which formed the preponderating element of her character."[37]

It's hard to understand how the two did not know or recognise each other already since both had been staying at Madame Balbiani's small boarding house. In those days guests all took their meals at a common dining table. Does this silence on both their parts point to something else? Could there have been a secret liaison in

Constantinople? Bartlett, who was married with five children, was travelling alone. His book on this journey only begins from his arrival at Beirut, so completely passing over his stay in Constantinople. Only in another book published years later did he detail the start of this journey and mention the boarding house.[38] An affair certainly seems very unlikely, but we will never know for sure.

Bartlett wrote his book about travelling to Jerusalem in 1844. He made no mention of Pfeiffer until the second edition of 1850, after Pfeiffer had completed three journeys. In the 1850 edition Bartlett referred to her in quite unflattering, almost insulting terms as "a German lady … if that conventional term may be applied to one, who, on account of some religious motive, and with an insurmountable wish to tread the scenes of Biblical story, travelled without any attendant or any protector from the risks of such a journey, but such as chance turned up. She was a quiet enthusiast, who gave no one any trouble, enjoyed everything in silence."[39] In her first book, and presumably to those she met during the first voyage, Pfeiffer claimed that religious fervour was her reason for travelling to the Holy Land. It is hard to know how much of this was true or a smokescreen to make her wanderlust appear more acceptable.

Amongst their stops was Gallipoli, seventy-three years later to be the scene of one of the great campaigns of the First World War. Then they steamed past the great plain where ancient Troy, the stage for Homer's Trojan War, was believed to have once stood. Pfeiffer wished she could have visited the site, and "there to muse on the legends which in my youth had already awakened in me such deep and awe-struck interest, and had first aroused the wish to visit these lands—a desire now partially fulfilled!" On 19 May they arrived at Smyrna, then thought to be the birthplace of Homer. "I found the most beautiful women I had yet seen; and even during my further journey I met with few who equalled, and none who surpassed them."[40] On the 20th the voyage continued. By the 22nd they reached the island of Rhodes, once the site of the famous statue, the Colossus of Rhodes, one of the seven wonders of the ancient world.

On Cyprus Pfeiffer was shown some of the local sights by a "Dr Faaslanc" whom she had met in Constantinople. Already she was becoming a sight herself. "When I re-embarked in the afternoon, Mr Bartlett came with the English consul [James Lilburn], who wished, he said, to make the acquaintance of a lady possessing sufficient courage to undertake so long and perilous a journey by herself. His astonishment increased when he was informed that I was an unpretending native of Vienna."[41]

On 25 May they reached the port city of Beirut. Still small and struggling, the port had been expanding since Ibrahim Pasha of Egypt captured Acre a decade earlier. Pfeiffer could not fully take in the view.

> The objects are too numerous, and the spectator is at a loss whither he should first direct his gaze,—upon the town, with its many ancient towers attached to the houses, giving them the air of knights' castles—upon the numerous country-houses in the shade of luxurious mulberry plantations—upon the beautiful valley between Beyrout and Mount Lebanon—or on the distant mountain-range itself. The towering masses of this magnificent chain, the peculiar colour of its rocks, and its snowclad summits, riveted my attention longer than any thing else.[42]

No sooner had the ship dropped anchor than it was besieged by small boats full of men shouting to sell their wares or act as porters. Pfeiffer was not amused. "The half-naked and excitable Arabs or Fellahs are so ready with offers of service, that it is difficult to keep them off. It almost becomes necessary to threaten these poor people with a stick, as they obstinately refuse to take a gentler hint."[43]

With the help of these hard bargaining porters with their ever pushy demands for backsheesh (gratuities) she finally reached the house of Mr Battista, the keeper of the only hotel. To her horror, Pfeiffer was informed that there were no available rooms. For a moment the terror of her situation almost overcame her. There were no other places to stay, not even a convent. Where could she go, a lone woman alone in a strange country? Mr Battista was so moved by the sight of this stranded lady that he introduced her to his wife and promised to find her a private lodging. Once again her sex was both her curse and her salvation.

To continue their journey, Pfeiffer and Bartlett boarded a sailing ship and waited for enough wind to sail. Pfeiffer was obliged to sleep on sacks of corn. She noted rather bitterly that Mr Bartlett reclined on a soft couch. But he no doubt travelled first class. It mattered little since both were surrounded by fellow passengers snoring noisily. There were no private cabins.

On 27 May 1842 they stopped to explore the ruins of the ancient Roman port city of Caesarea, which is mentioned several times in the Bible. The captain tried hard to dissuade them from disembarking, warning them of the dangers posed by Bedouins and snakes. Possibly he just didn't want to stop. They went anyway and scrambled over the ruins and fallen columns. No snakes were seen but they did meet a few friendly Bedouin. Pfeiffer would have been delighted could she have known that over a century after her visit excavations at the site of the Roman amphitheatre would uncover a stone plaque inscribed with "TIVS PILATUS", the famed Pontius Pilate, the prefect of Judea who sentenced Jesus to be crucified according the Bible. It is the only archaeological evidence that Pilate ever existed.

Later the same day their ship reached the ancient port city of Jaffa. From the water it looked like a fortress of beige stone houses piled on top of each other and coming right down to the harbour. It was warm but the hot summer weather was still weeks away. As there was no inn, Pfeiffer stayed in the home of the Austrian Consul. He and his family wore Arab clothing. They rode out the next day and Pfeiffer's eager eye recorded everything she saw, the local gardens and fig trees, the dress of the local women, the many camels and the landscape of naked sand all around Jaffa.

When it was time to ride on to Jerusalem, Mr Bartlett decided that they would make the entire sixteen-hour ride in one stretch. Pfeiffer was obliged to go along with this. A sixteen-hour drive or flight would exhaust most people, but a sixteen-hour ride over stones and potholes is hard to fathom. They also suffered terribly from the oppressive desert heat and swarms of tiny gnats.

When they reached the base of the mountains there was a well where they watered their horses and refilled their leather water bottles. Pfeiffer could not believe she could "quench my thirst with so disgusting a beverage as the muddy, turbid, and lukewarm water". They picked their winding way up into the rocky mountains where she noted "here and there single olive-trees are seen sprouting from the rocky clefts".[44]

After five hours of very bad roads, Pfeiffer felt dizzy and feared she might soon fall off her horse. She had to dismount and walk beside it. But she was too afraid or too proud to tell Bartlett of her condition. She wasn't going to let anyone think she could not take as much as a man. As she plodded on, suffering in silence, Bartlett too began to feel ill and dismounted. He proposed that they rest a few hours at the next village as they would never make it to Jerusalem before sundown anyway. Pfeiffer felt silently thankful about this change. As she later told her readers: "Thus I accomplished my object without being obliged to confess my weakness."[45]

After resting a few hours, Bartlett wanted to push on during the night. So on they rode. Finally they came over the crest of a hill and before them lay the "holy city" of Jerusalem. The small party reached the Jaffa Gate, walled about like a fortress, at 4.30 a.m. Jerusalem then had a population of about 25,000. The countryside all about it struck the travellers as barren, desolate and sterile. The vastness of the sky was tinged with the red of the emerging dawn. As Pfeiffer looked upon the culmination of her long journey she felt that "the most beauteous morning of my life dawned upon me!"[46]

Pfeiffer stayed at the Nuova Casa, a pilgrim house maintained by Franciscan friars. Once settled she began the conventional sightseeing which had long been established for Christian pilgrims. Foremost among these was the Church of the Holy Sepulchre, supposedly built on the site where Jesus was crucified by the Romans and buried. In fact it was built on the site of an earlier Roman temple. Generations of enterprising businessmen had created sites for virtually every person, event and place mentioned in the New Testament. One could see the house of Pontius Pilate, a stairway that Jesus climbed, the birthplace of John the Baptist, the field where Judas Iscariot hanged himself (or burst asunder, depending on which gospel one reads), the grave of the Virgin Mary, the well where she fetched water and so forth. Of course almost all, probably all, of these holy sites were fakes or misidentifications. Pfeiffer, despite her professed Catholic zeal, was not fooled and described them again and again as "supposedly" the site where this or that biblical event had occurred. For example, she recounted "the spot where the three disciples are said to have slept during the night of their Master's agony. We were shown marks on two rocks, said to have been footsteps of these apostles!" Or there was the "convent of the 'Holy Cross,' a building supposed to stand on the site where the wood was felled for our Saviour's cross!"[47] Her astonishment at these absurd claims is clearly expressed through the exclamation marks.

Two other German travellers arrived at the Nuova Casa, the sort of people who normally made such long journeys – aristocrats, Count von Berchtold and Count Salm-Reifferscheid. Pfeiffer joined her fellow German speakers to make further excursions to Bethlehem and the Dead Sea. Bartlett joined the group when heading to the Dead Sea.

The party rode all day through the desert towards the Dead Sea. Always keeping up with the men, one of them noticed that Pfeiffer "never uttered a murmur during the heat and fatigue of our journey".[48]

That evening they arrived at the Eastern Orthodox monastery of Mar Saba. The walled compound hangs dramatically onto a cliff over a deep ravine. The monastery was supposedly founded by St. Sabbas in 483. One of the lasting legacies of this God and female-fearing saint was that women were not allowed in the monastery. When the party arrived and knocked at the gate, it was opened and the counts, Bartlett and their Arab and Bedouin servants were admitted. But as soon as Pfeiffer was spotted someone shouted, "Shut the gate!" It was slammed in her face.

And so Pfeiffer was left standing alone, shut out not just physically, but socially, from her fellow pilgrims. The thought of spending the night outdoors in this desolate region was, she admitted stoically, "rather disagreeable". At length the gate opened again and a lay brother from the monastery emerged. He pointed at a square stone tower about 500 metres from the monastery. It is known as the Women's Tower. Pfeiffer understood that she was to be lodged there for the night. The lay brother took a ladder from the monastery and walked with Pfeiffer over the dry crunching gravel to the tower. Using the ladder they climbed twenty feet up to a small iron door. Inside, a wooden staircase lead upstairs where there were two small rooms. One was a chapel for prayer and the other was the lodging room for female pilgrims. It contained only a divan. The lay brother then left her, promising to bring food and bedclothes later. He not only locked the door behind him, but took away the ladder. Bemused at all this fuss, Pfeiffer felt like "a captive princess".[49]

Inside the monastery the men were preparing to take their evening meal. Only then did Bartlett look around and notice that Madame Pfeiffer was missing. He was told that women were not permitted inside the walls of the monastery and that Pfeiffer was in the Women's Tower. When the lay brother returned with the ladder and her supper, Bartlett accompanied him to check on Pfeiffer. He found her resting "with her usual expression of calm and fearless tranquillity".[50]

Bartlett thought that "to be left in such a situation might have made many women nervous; and I have indeed heard that certain English ladies refused to comply, and fairly stormed the monks into submission; but our quiet German, after her supper was ended, bid us good night without the smallest discernible sign of tremor." After climbing back down the ladder Bartlett looked around at the bleak stony landscape. "Wild in the extreme was the scene as we stood at the base of the lonely tower, and glanced over the dreary wilderness around."[51]

After her night held captive in the tower, the following day the party rode on to the shores of the Dead Sea. When they arrived, the travellers prepared their breakfast under parasols on the hot sandy shore. Pfeiffer looked out over the expanse of pale green water. She "thought of the past, and saw how the works of proud and mighty nations had vanished away, leaving behind them only a name and a memory".[52]

Next the group rode on to see the river Jordan where, according to the Bible, Jesus was baptised by John the Baptist. Pfeiffer collected several cans of river water to take home with her. Shortly after they returned to Jerusalem, Pfeiffer planned to start her journey home. However, her travelling companions proposed taking a circuitous route, by way of Nablus, Nazareth, Tiberias, Galilee and Canaan. Pfeiffer was eager to see more. So they all set out on 11 June 1842. The travel was extremely rough and fatiguing.

They finally arrived at the port city of Acre on the Mediterranean. The white stone town was dominated by a large domed mosque with an imposing minaret. Its walls still bore the holes from canon balls from the war ten years earlier. Here they stayed in another small house for pilgrims. The following day the party of travellers went to see the residence of the pasha. His highness received his guests graciously and had them served with refreshments.

The ladies of the pasha's harem heard that a European woman was amongst the visitors. Excited by such an unusual event, they sent Pfeiffer an invitation to visit them. She gladly accepted, especially as it promised the possibility of "gratifying my curiosity". Pfeiffer was led to a room of moderate size in another part of the house. The male interpreter had to wait outside. Inside this room were several women reclining on cushions. The oldest was "rather elderly" and the youngest about eighteen. "I did not see any signs of particular beauty, unless the stoutness of figure so prevalent here is considered in that light." Pfeiffer herself was the object of fascination: "First they took my straw hat and put it upon their heads; then they felt the stuff of my travelling robe; but they seemed most of all astonished at my short hair, the sight of which seemed to impress these poor ignorant women with the idea that nature had denied long hair to the Europeans." In fact, in a gesture of coldly rational utility, Pfeiffer tells us: "I had cut my hair quite close, because I was seldom sure of having time and opportunity during my long journey to dress and plait it properly."[53]

After returning to Beirut, Pfeiffer found an impromptu lodging with a French school teacher named Pauline Kandis. This accommodation turned out to be "the most uncomfortable of any I had yet occupied during my entire journey". But one of the few consolations a traveller can get from a bad experience is the opportunity to complain about it later. And Pfeiffer did.

> From eight o'clock in the morning until seven at night four or five girls, who did any thing rather than study, were continually in the room. The whole day long there was such a noise of shouting, screaming, and jumping about, that I could not hear the sound of my own voice. Moreover, the higher regions of this hall of audience contained eight pigeons' nests; and the old birds, which were so tame that they not only took the food from our plates, but stole it out of our very mouths, fluttered continually about the room, so that we were obliged to look very attentively at every chair on which we intended to sit down. On the floor a cock was continually fighting with his three wives; and a motherly hen, with a brood of eleven hopeful ducks, cackled merrily between. … During the night the heat and the stench were almost insupportable; and immediately after midnight the cock always began to crow, as if he earned his living by the noise he made. … My friends must pardon me for describing my cares so minutely, but I only do so to warn all those who would wish to undertake a journey like mine, without being either very rich, very high-born, or very hardy, that they had much better remain at home.

Pfeiffer applied to see the Austrian Consul of Beirut but he did not receive her when she called. She believed this was because she was "neither rich nor high-born". He finally saw her after her second attempt. But as for her appeal for assistance he merely shook his head and said "he was very sorry for me—it was really extremely unfortunate".[54]

During a journey into Lebanon, Pfeiffer became herself a tourist attraction.

It is, of course, seldom that a European woman is seen in these regions, and thus I seemed to be quite a spectacle to the inhabitants; at every place where we halted many women and children would gather round me, busily feeling my dress, putting on my straw hat, and looking at me from all sides, while they endeavoured to converse with me by signs.

On her return to Beirut on 10 July 1842 Pfeiffer had just missed the monthly English boat to Alexandria. There was no choice but to stay again in the menagerie of Pauline Kandis's school room. "Never shall I forget what I had to endure in Beyrout. When I could no longer bear the state of things at night in the Noah's ark of my good Pauline, I used to creep through the window on to a terrace, and sleep there; but was obliged each time to retire to my room before daybreak lest I should be discovered."[55]

On 28 July 1842 Pfeiffer sailed on a small Greek brig for Alexandria. She was incredibly relieved to leave Beirut behind her. But, as she reflected later, it was out of the frying pan, into the fire. For ten days and eleven nights she endured a miserably crowded boat. Not only was there no privacy but the people around her would lie down and sleep on her mat if it was vacant for a moment and otherwise use her things without asking. "One day I cleaned my teeth with a toothbrush; one of the Greek sailors, noticing what I was about, came towards me, and when I laid the brush down for an instant, took it up. I thought he only wished to examine it; but no, he did exactly as I had done, and after cleaning his teeth returned me my brush, expressing himself entirely satisfied with it."[56] One hopes she had a spare.

From Alexandria, Pfeiffer went on to bustling, chaotic Cairo. But first she had to settle her bill with the ship's captain. She owed him three and a half dollars. She gave him four and awaited her change. He did not give it to her. The captain explained that he would divide it up as a tip for the crew. Pfeiffer seriously doubted this. Acting quickly, she snatched one of the coins from his hand and put it in her pocket. She told him she would not give it back until she was given her change. "He shouted and stormed, and kept on asking for the money. I took no heed of him, but continued quietly packing up my things. Seeing, at length, that nothing was to be done with me, he gave me back my half-dollar; whereupon we parted good friends."

As soon as Pfeiffer stepped ashore a man rushed forward to transport her baggage. He put her trunk on the back of an ass. Pfeiffer handed him a piastre, a coin worth about one and three-quarters pence. The man returned the coin and demanded four piastre instead. Pfeiffer refused. The man "shouted and blustered … but I remained deaf, and rode forward towards the custom-house. Then he came down to three piastres, then to two, and finally said he would be content with one, which I threw to him."[57] As her confidence grew, feisty Pfeiffer was becoming a force to be reckoned with.

She called at the Austrian consulate and discovered that Herbert Sattler, the artist, had arrived in Cairo shortly before by the more expensive commercial steamer. She called on him briefly. His painting of the pyramids of Giza with its almost Daliesque colours must record almost the identical view that Pfeiffer experienced shortly thereafter.

Pfeiffer continued on alone to Giza to see the pyramids. With the help of local guides she climbed the massive and difficult blocks of Cheops, the great pyramid. It's base was still entombed in a skirt of desert sand, concealing its true height. Reaching the summit she looked all the way around. "For a long time I stood lost in thought, and could hardly realise the fact that I was really one of the favoured few who are happy enough to be able to contemplate the most stupendous and imperishable monument ever erected by human hands." The guides then took her into the interior down slippery narrow shafts. She was not overly moved, "for a woman like myself, brought hither only by an insatiable desire to travel, and capable of judging of the beauties of nature and art only by her own simple feelings, it was enough to have ascended the pyramid of Cheops, and to have seen something of its interior."[58] The melancholy head of the Sphinx nearby was impressive even though mostly buried in the windblown desert sands.

Once back in Cairo, Pfeiffer had a week for further sightseeing before her steamer arrived. There followed a characteristically Pfeifferian reaction. "The more I saw, the more my curiosity became excited, and I felt irresistibly impelled to proceed." She had tried almost every means of travel so far, but she had never ridden a camel. So she hired two camels and a driver to take her and a servant on the desert crossing to Suez. Although this was twenty-seven years before the Suez Canal would open, an overland route was already long established for crossing the narrow strip of land to the Red Sea. For this forty-mile excursion the only provisions she took with her were some bread, dates, hard-boiled eggs and a piece of roast meat. Water was kept in leather bags slung on the camels which became progressively more unpleasant with each passing day. Pfeiffer found riding a camel not unpleasant though eventually the swaying back and forth became rather tiresome. Mile after mile she teetered through desert, featureless except for the occasional shrub or desiccated bodies of dead camels laying by the wayside. At one point during the heat of the day, she could make out the Red Sea ahead. Pfeiffer pointed it out to her servant but he replied that it was only a mirage. She could not believe it, it looked so real. But all day the supposed sea got no closer. As she had little time, they rode all through the night. There were small rest houses along the way, five hours' ride apart. These had been built by an enterprising English hotelier from Cairo. Pfeiffer concluded that these could only be afforded by the very rich because they cost 100 piastres per night. Her entire camel excursion cost 250. So she slept on the ground in front of the rest houses with the camel drivers and poorer travellers.

The town of Suez itself was not much of a sight and she had to hurry back to catch her steamer. The first night of the journey back they shared an encampment with Bedouin, a people Pfeiffer was very taken with. Almost back at Cairo, Pfeiffer had been wearily travelling for four days, riding usually more than twelve hours a day. She wanted to rest and so ordered her servant to stop the camels so that she could sleep for a few hours. But the "rascals" refused to obey. They said the road was too dangerous there to halt. Pfeiffer thought this was just a ruse in order to get home more quickly. She had made careful enquiries in Cairo before setting out and been told that the route was quite safe. Despite telling them that she knew it was safe, they still refused to comply. Pfeiffer then became angry. She insisted that she had hired both camels and men and was therefore in charge. She threatened the servant that he could go on with the driver, but that she would stay where she was and would later bring him to justice with the consul in Cairo.

The servant stopped her camel and he and the driver kept walking, leaving her behind and alone. Pfeiffer suspected they meant to frighten her into following. But, if that was the idea, as she put it "he was vastly mistaken". She remained steadfastly in the same spot. Occasionally the servant would look back but Pfeiffer just motioned to him to keep going. At last the servant broke down.

When he saw how fearless and determined I was, he turned back, came to me, made my camel kneel down, and after helping me to alight, prepared me a resting-place on a heap of sand, where I slept delightfully for five hours; then I ordered my things to be packed up, mounted my camel, and continued my journey. My conduct astonished my followers to such a degree, that they afterwards asked me every few hours if I wished to rest. On our arrival at Cairo the camel-driver had not even the heart to make the customary demand for backsheesh, and my servant begged pardon for his conduct, and hoped that I would not mention the difference we had had to the consul.[59]

This desert crossing was later depicted in a fine woodcut for her book of travels. In it she is seen writing in her journal in her hurried and slanting handwriting.

When Pfeiffer returned to Cairo she found that her little purse had been stolen from her pocket. She had only taken a small amount of money with her so the loss was not great – but she had also lost the key to her trunk. A local locksmith was able to open the trunk and make a new key. After she paid for it she noticed that there was a weak spot in the middle and the key would certainly soon break. In an impulsive flash, she grabbed one of the man's tools and declared he could only have it back when he made her a new key. The locksmith declined and Pfeiffer refused to return the tool. Obstinate to a fault, she stood her ground until the bewildered locksmith resignedly made her a new key. And if obstinacy didn't work, she could threaten real force.

Pfeiffer was becoming ever more adept at handling cheats. Shortly before she boarded an Arabian vessel bound for Alexandria, her donkey driver tried to pass her counterfeit coins. "This attempt disgusted me so much that I could not refrain from brandishing my whip at him in a very threatening manner, although I was alone among a number of his class. My gesture had the desired effect; the driver instantly retreated, and I remained victor."[60]

On 7 September 1842 Pfeiffer boarded the French steam-packet *Eurotas*, "a beautiful large vessel of 160-horse power" for the voyage to Malta. (A "packet" steamer was one designed to carry post office mail packets as well as passengers and freight on a regular, scheduled service.) From Malta she made her way to Sicily and then to the Italian mainland where she visited Palermo and Naples. Here she saw the famed ancient Roman ruins at Pozzuoli and Pompeii and climbed the volcano Mount Vesuvius, the source of the destruction of the ancient towns.

Home

Pfeiffer stayed for two weeks sightseeing in Rome where her stature as a female European pilgrim to Jerusalem obtained her an audience with the elderly Pope Gregory XVI near the Sistine Chapel. For a supposedly pious Catholic, her account of meeting the pontiff seems less enthusiastic than her description of the view across the hills of Lebanon.

Pfeiffer wrote more about touring the moving remains of ancient Rome which, even in decayed fragments and ruins could still boast of its immeasurably vast superiority to the present city. Since the Renaissance it was becoming possible to see the present age as a world of barbarians still scuttling over the ruins of the greater civilisation that had preceded it. The most striking of the remains is the amphitheatre of Flavius, or Colosseum as it is now known, and the forest of toppled marble of the Forum.

The best-preserved building, and to this day one of the finest buildings in the world, is the Pantheon, built between 113–125 CE as a temple to all the gods. Its magnificent concrete dome was the largest in the world for over 1,300 years. "The interior is almost in its pristine condition," Pfeiffer reported. "The Rotunda has no windows, but receives air and light through a circular opening in the cupola."[61] It's elegant marble exterior, the original bronze ceiling of the portico and bronze roof tiles had all survived into modern times but were looted and destroyed by the Christian barbarian rulers of modern Rome. It is often through such acts as these that aged great structures become ruins.

In the end Pfeiffer threw up her hands, unable to record all of the works of art and architecture to be seen in Rome – let alone the 108 fountains, but the magnificently ebullient Trevi Fountain deserved special mention as "foremost among them in size and beauty". Pfeiffer continued homewards while taking in the historic cities of Siena, Florence, Bologna, Ferrara and finally returned home to Vienna after nine months away.

At home she found her friends and family all well. What surprise and perhaps reproaches she experienced we don't know. Vienna was prospering. The new sound of Johann Strauss II was becoming all the rage and for many remains to this day the sound of Vienna.

Pfeiffer had many stories to tell. "During my journey I had seen much and endured many hardships; I had found very few things as I had imagined them to be."[62] She had done something truly extraordinary. News of and interest in her exploits rippled outwards from her friends and family through successive social circles of Vienna. One of those who heard about her adventure was the publisher and bookseller Jakob Dirnböck. He is best remembered in Austria today as the composer of the idyllic homeland hymn, the *Dachsteinlied*. Dirnböck knew Anton Halm, the pianist who had taught the precociously talented Oscar Pfeiffer, and so Dirnböck heard news of Pfeiffer's travels even before she returned. With a sharp eye for a potential bestseller, Dirnböck asked if he could read her journal which was doing the rounds of friends and family. She only agreed "with some timidity". Dirnböck was instantly smitten with her account. "Seldom has a book so irresistibly attracted me, or so completely fixed my attention from beginning to end," he wrote.[63] He tried to convince Pfeiffer to allow him to publish it as a book. One could almost describe Dirnböck as the man who "discovered" Ida Pfeiffer.

For her part, Pfeiffer was very reluctant for her journal to be published. This was not what she had intended. Only after a great deal of persuasion did she agree. In return Pfeiffer received 700 guilders, fifty copies of the book and six presentation copies in special bindings.[64] To put this in perspective, a first-class steamer ticket to Constantinople cost 120 guilders, and second-class was 85.

The book was published, discreetly anonymously, in 1844 as *Journey of a Viennese Lady to the Holy Land*. It was printed in lovely gothic script with dated entries, which gives the appearance of an authentic travel journal. It was an instant success and went through three editions by 1846, and was translated into Czech in 1846 and English in 1852. Periodicals such as Vienna's *Sonntagsblaetter* began to report on this unusual lady. This book, just as much as the journey itself, would change everything for Madame Pfeiffer. The road ahead was open.

CHAPTER 3

IN SEARCH OF ARCADIA
(1845)

Of the gladdest moments in human life, methinks, is the
departure upon a distant journey into unknown lands.
Shaking off with one mighty effort the fetters of Habit, the
leaden weight of Routine, the cloak of many Cares and the
slavery of Home, man feels once more happy. The blood
flows with the fast circulation of childhood ... the glorious
face of nature gladdens the soul.

Sir Richard Burton, 1856[65]

Safely back home in Vienna, Ida Pfeiffer could not resist the
insatiable temptation to travel once more. The profits from her
book were enough to finance another journey – and certainly one
of her sort of budget travel. She feared many would think that
her "love of adventure" was not becoming of the fairer sex. And
she was well aware that people would say that "this woman only
undertakes these journeys to attract attention".[66] But she would go
nevertheless. After all, she said, "I had found by experience, that a
woman of an energetic mind can find her way through the world
as well as a man, and that good people are to be met with every
where."[67] This time her destination would be the North Atlantic
island of Iceland.

Iceland might not strike a modern reader as the next most desirable destination after the landscapes and historic sites of the Middle East but it was exactly the sort of place to attract Pfeiffer. Iceland had a reputation as both impossibly remote and as a land of dramatic natural wonders. Situated midway between Europe and North America, Iceland sits on several global crossroads. It lies at the juncture between the North Atlantic and the Arctic oceans. And today we know it also straddles the mid-Atlantic ridge, the boundary between two of the earth's great tectonic plates. This particular point in the mid-Atlantic ridge floats above a mantle plume that wells up from deep within the earth's interior causing great seismic and volcanic activity on the island far above. All of this makes Iceland a unique mixture of tundra, lakes, mountains, glaciers, geysers, volcanoes and dried lava fields. As Pfeiffer explained, she hoped to find in Iceland "nature in a garb such as she wears nowhere else. I feel so completely happy ... when I contemplate sublime natural phenomena, that in my eyes no degree of toil or difficulty is too great a price at which to purchase such perfect enjoyment."[68] Remoteness and wildness were hallmarks of the romantic sensibility, and so was a solitary embrace of nature. Johann von Goethe's fictional Werther (1774) was likewise obsessed with his solitary appreciation of nature (not to mention his unrequited love for the attached Lotte). And the people of Iceland were part of her imagined romantic island world. "I therefore expected to find Iceland a real Arcadia in regard to its inhabitants, and rejoiced at the anticipation of seeing such an Idyllic life realised."[69]

Although she had no formal education, Pfeiffer spoke French and Italian in addition to her native German. These languages were useful during her trip to the Holy Land. In preparation for her next journey she studied English and Danish. She also learned how to collect, catalogue and preserve natural history specimens to sell to museums, then a burgeoning trade that around the same time would make good livings for naturalists such as Hugh Low, Thomas Lobb, Alfred Russel Wallace and Henry Walter Bates.[70] She also learned the basics of taking daguerreotypes, the early photographic process introduced by the French inventor Louis Daguerre in 1839. These were two congenial and interesting ways to generate more revenue from her travels, in addition to publishing another book.

Pfeiffer's Nordic adventure began on 10 April 1845. Travelling first by river steamers from Vienna to Prague, Dresden and Leipzig she continued by rail to Magdeburg. Another steamer took her to the great German port of Hamburg. She stayed a week with family before moving on via Kiel where she boarded the 180-horsepower steamer *Christian VIII* which was, alas, "a vessel dirtier and more uncomfortable than any with which I had become acquainted in my maritime excursions".[71] On 27 April she arrived in the Danish capital of Copenhagen. Pfeiffer stayed for a week with German merchants who were, of course, her kind of people. She would often resort to this sort of social connection in her travels. A week was long enough for a gentleman of her acquaintance to assist by introducing her to a wealthy businessman named Knudson. Only a few ships visited Iceland each year so there were not many opportunities to travel there or to return. There was no tourist transport of any kind. Knudson was about to sail for Iceland and gave Pfeiffer a free passage aboard his ship, the brig *Johann*. This was a great gift and certainly the result of the fact that Pfeiffer was a woman and the unprecedented novelty of a lone female tourist or traveller.

On 4 May 1845 she boarded the *Johann*. The ship's company consisted only of Knudson, a merchant named Brüge, the captain, the mate, six or seven sailors and Madame Pfeiffer. As always she was the odd "man" out. "The anchor was weighed, and the sails, unfolding themselves like giant wings, wafted us gently out of the harbour of Copenhagen." But the smooth sailing was not to last. Once the little brig reached the open sea almost gale force winds threw the ship about violently. No one could walk upright amidst the powerful pitching and rolling. Lying in her minuscule wooden bunk, Pfeiffer became horribly seasick. For more than a week she endured exhausting nausea, retching and vomiting. She became so weak that she could barely sit up. The sailors at length tried traditional recipes such as "hot-water gruel with wine and sugar" which she could barely bring herself to swallow. Even worse were "small pieces of raw bacon highly peppered" and a mouthful of rum.[72] At length taking food seemed to help and she gradually began to regain some strength.

After a voyage of eleven days they reached Hafnarfjörður, (Harbour Fjord), on the southwest coast of Iceland and the following day Pfeiffer stepped ashore eager to begin her new adventure. It didn't take long to examine the spot. The settlement consisted of only three wooden houses and numerous peasant cottages of lava rock with turf roofs looking more like Hobbit holes than houses. There was no firewood on the island. The rich had it imported but the poor were obliged to burn turf mixed with fish guts. Perhaps understandably, Pfeiffer found the smell of these dwellings unbearable. This was not a promising first impression. But it did not stop her from entering people's homes and inspecting their rooms and furnishings with a discerning eye.

Pfeiffer set off on horseback for the capital, Reykjavík, a few miles away. Her horse was led by an indomitable old Viking woman who seemed as strong as an ox. Pfeiffer was surprised by her first views of Iceland. "I could see over an area of at least thirty or forty miles, and yet could not descry a tree or a shrub, a bit of meadowland or a friendly village. Every thing seemed dead. A few cottages lay scattered here and there." When Reykjavík came into view she was taken aback to find that it was "a mere village" with only about 500 inhabitants. "Through the kind forethought of Herr Knudson, a neat little room had been prepared for me in one of his houses occupied by the family of the worthy baker Bernhöft, and truly I could not have been better received any where."[73] Her kind host, a German by birth, and his family would take her for walks and help her search for flowers, insects and shells to collect as specimens.

But the specimens of the local high society were not so pleasant. As too often happens in provincial places, Pfeiffer found that "nothing was more disagreeable to me than a certain air of dignity assumed by the ladies here". Despite her letters of introduction and her calls on several of the local elites, she received no return visits or invitations to any of the parties during her weeks in Reykjavík. "It appears I had scarcely arrived at Reykjavik before diligent inquiries were set on foot as to whether I was *rich*."[74] Finding that she was not, none of the local elites deigned to trouble or sully themselves with this foreign oddity.

Pfeiffer then set out to see the sights of Iceland. This proved more difficult than she had expected. "Altogether I found the travelling in this country attended with far more hardship than in the East." Horses could not be rented but only bought, and then at the end of a journey no one wished to buy them. "The worst hardship of all, however, is the being obliged to halt to rest the horses in a meadow during the rain. The long skirts suck up the water from the damp grass, and the wearer has often literally not a dry stitch in all her garments." With no inns or hotels in the tiny villages she was obliged to either sleep in the local churches or in peasant cottages. "I found the cottages of the peasants every where alike squalid and filthy."[75] Their dark, cramped and ill ventilated bedrooms were "without exception the most disgusting holes that can be imagined", certainly not Hobbit holes after all.[76] "Throughout my stay in Iceland, nothing annoyed me more than the slowness and unconcern displayed by the inhabitants in all their undertakings." They were, in short, an "indolent race".[77]

Pfeiffer was unaware that a cooling of the climate had recently made Iceland far less habitable than it had been. The ensuing hardships led to widespread emigration. It has been estimated that fully 15,000 out of its original 70,000 inhabitants left the island as a result.

Pfeiffer visited the geothermal area of Krýsuvík and stayed in a tiny wooden chapel only twenty-two feet long by ten broad. It too was filthy. And then the local people came and stared at her and would not leave until she was forced to ask them to go away. In the night there was a terrible storm: "my thermometer inside the church showing only two degrees above zero".[78]

Pfeiffer set out to witness an eruption of the famous "great geyser". It was the largest on the island and the one that has given its name to geysers in general. The word geyser comes from an old Icelandic word meaning "to gush". A local man volunteered to lead her horse to the spot. Pfeiffer doubted whether the man, teetering from drunkenness, would get her there intact. She bivouacked alone near the largest geyser in order to see one of the random eruptions. Eventually, after waiting patiently for two days, she witnessed an eruption as fountains of water were ejected 60–80 metres into the air with a thunderous roar. "The water spouted upwards with indescribable force and bulk," Pfeiffer recalled. It was a "magnificent and overpowering sight" and far exceeded her expectations.

At the end of June she visited Gullfoss (Golden Falls) the magnificent two-tiered waterfall on the river Hvítá. The glacier-fed river is so charged with glacial till that it looks like milk pouring over one broad fall and then another deeper one.

Pfeiffer proceeded on to climb the volcano Mount Hekla which towers 1,400 metres above the surrounding tundra. The name of the mountain, meaning a hooded cloak, was possibly derived from its frequent covering of clouds. Someone told her that no visitor had climbed it since the French naturalist Paul Gaimard had visited nine years before. The ascent was extremely difficult with rocky paths and chasms covered over with snow. Pfeiffer and her guide had sticks to probe for a safe path ahead. Near the summit she had to dismount and continue on foot. "We had to climb steep masses of lava, sharp and pointed, which covered the whole side of the mountain. I do not know how often I fell and cut my hands on the jagged points of the lava. It was a fearful journey!" When she reached the summit she looked about her.

> I could see far into the uninhabited country, the picture of a petrified creation, dead and motionless, and yet magnificent,—a picture which once seen can never again fade from the memory, and which alone amply compensates for all the previous troubles and dangers. A whole world of glaciers, lava-mountains, snow and ice-fields, rivers and lakes, into which no human foot has ever ventured to penetrate.[79]

The volcano had lain in desolate repose for eighty years. Five weeks after Pfeiffer's visit it erupted again.

After returning to Reykjavík, Pfeiffer was forced to wait "four very long weeks … in the most wretched accommodation" before a ship could take her back to Denmark. There was more than enough time to reflect on her experiences. She had come to Iceland expecting to find an unspoiled landscape of wonders, a place where nature reigned in all its romantic glory and the people lived in Arcadian harmony with the world. But it was not just the climate that was icy. Instead, she found the "Icelanders are second to no nation in uncleanliness" and, of course, laziness.[80] More than that, the Icelanders were, she thought, snobby, rude and ugly. Almost the only positive thing she had to say about them was that they did not steal.

At last on 29 July 1845 a small old sloop, the somewhat ironically named *Haabet* (Hope), was to sail for Copenhagen. Pfeiffer did not record if any Icelanders came to the quayside to wave her good riddance. There was clearly little love lost on either side. Then for twenty days she endured being tossed by the sea in a tiny, stinking cabin with only miserable food at mealtimes. When they reached prosperous Copenhagen she declared to her journal, it "so beautiful and grand, as if I had seen nothing so beautiful in my whole life".[81]

But Pfeiffer had no intention of heading immediately homewards. Instead she took a small steamer north to Gothenburg, Sweden. From there she proceeded further north to the port of Christiania (now Oslo) in Norway. She was delighted with the tidy port city with its canals and public buildings. Just as impressive was the novel (to her at least) Scandinavian practice of street signs giving the names of the roads. Her visit coincided with the Storthing, the national parliament of Norway. Pfeiffer attended the meetings daily for an hour though she could understand little of the Norwegian language.

Ever restless, Pfeiffer "could not resist the temptation of a journey to the wildly romantic regions" of Telemark. She was told that "it would be a difficult undertaking for a female, alone and almost entirely ignorant of the language, to make her way through the peasantry. But I found no one to accompany me, and was determined to go; so I trusted to fate, and went alone."[82] This last sentence could stand as Pfeiffer's epitaph.

She rented a small two-wheeled carriage called a carriole. Like her riding adventure in Bursa, she had never driven a cart before. In her homeland it was quite improper for a lady to drive a carriage. Had she tried this at home she would have been stared at with disapproval, and had never attempted it. But in a foreign country she was undaunted. She took the reins and off she went. And like the first time she rode a horse, she soon got the hang of it.

Pfeiffer was delighted with her tour. "I never saw such peculiarly beautiful scenery," she noted as she drove through green valleys dotted with "beautiful country-houses" and sometimes views of the mountain-girdled fiords and the sea beyond.[83] Having made a loop of 100 miles through the territory she returned to Christiania and on 30 August left for Gothenburg.

She took another trip through the picturesque Göta Canal to the port of Stockholm. While there she was honoured with an introduction to Queen Joséphine of Sweden who had heard of the travels of the remarkable Madame Pfeiffer. From Stockholm Pfeiffer travelled to Uppsala to see the iron mine of Dannemora which had been in operation for hundreds of years.

At last it was time to start back towards home. Pfeiffer returned via the German ports of Travemünde and Hamburg before visiting Berlin on her way back to Vienna. In one of the coaches before she reached home she was engaged in conversation by fellow passengers who had read her book. They were fascinated to meet her. Her fame was growing.

Pfeiffer arrived back in Vienna on 4 October 1845, shortly before her forty-eighth birthday, after a journey of six months.

> I had suffered many hardships; but my love of travelling would not have been abated, nor would my courage have failed me, had they been ten times greater. I had been amply compensated for all. I had seen things which never occur in our common life, and had met with people as they are rarely met with—in their natural state. And I brought back with me the recollections of my travels, which will always remain, and which will afford me renewed pleasure for years.[84]

Newspapers all over Germany updated their readers on "the famous traveller, Frau Ida Pfeiffer" who had returned and was currently "spending time in Graz, where she is busy following her first interesting travel book with a second. Frau Ida Pfeiffer plans, after such a toilsome travelling life, to spend the rest of her years in Vienna, the city of her birth, in the circle of her family."[85] This latter report could not have been more wrong.

Pfeiffer's travel journal was published the following year in two volumes as *Journey to the Scandinavian North and the Island of Iceland* (1846). It was dedicated to her sons Alfred and Oscar. This time the title page prominently bore her name, and identified her as the authoress of *Journey of a Viennese Lady to the Holy Land*. (Likewise the 1846 third edition of the first book bore her name.) Readers of the influential and pioneering German literary magazine *Morgenblatt für gebildete Leser* (Morning Paper for Educated Readers) were promptly informed that "a Nordic travelogue by the strange and tireless tourist Ida Pfeiffer is even now gracing the bookshops".[86] Two English translations appeared in Britain and the USA in 1852.

Despite its less ambitious scope than her first book, it was still a treasure trove of interesting observations and topics. Few other books could combine such a story with Tycho Brahe's chair, boiling pits of volcanic mud, spending the night in an Icelandic peasant cottage, Norwegian beer carts, Swedish waterfalls and cab fares in Berlin. At the end she appended a brief list of the plants and insects she had collected. It was a very modest beginning for the collections she would eventually accumulate. These specimens were sold to the Royal Museum in Vienna, many of which still survive. Presumably the daguerreotype equipment proved too unwieldy and she never took it again. Two of her daguerreotypes of houses in Reykjavík survive and may be the first photographic images of Iceland.[87]

The Leipzig literary magazine *Blätter für literarische Unterhaltung* (Leaves for Literary Entertainment) analysed this anomalous person for its readers. "Mrs Ida Pfeiffer is no normal woman ... She is distinguished by an ineradicable wanderlust deep within her, through which she takes on an almost masculine character, she is unusual through her courage, deliberateness and perseverance." Indeed, the magazine editor felt, "Ida Pfeiffer is educated like other tourists are, but not learned, and this deficiency is her most lovable side".[88]

The British literary journal the *Athenaeum* reviewed the book in May 1851, sympathetic to Pfeiffer's travels and the hardships she endured. Similarly the *Spectator* introduced its readers to her in April 1852 as "the German lady who is rather celebrated for making a journey round the world without any particular object beyond a love of travelling".[89] The *Dublin Review* had a very different perspective. In a harsh and damning review it criticised the presumption of this "second-rate traveller" for not speaking Icelandic and not actually knowing anything about Iceland while complaining too much about being snubbed by the local elites.[90]

Even more damning were the remarks by the American travel writer Pliny Miles who wrote with unusual contempt and scurrility in his 1854 book on his own visit to Iceland. "Madame Pfeiffer, in her snarling, ill-tempered journal, complains greatly of the idle curiosity of the people in crowding about and looking at her. From what I heard of her, she was so haughty that the simple and hospitable Icelanders could not approach her near enough to show her any attentions." No doubt copies of Pfeiffer's book were by then known in Iceland and had probably caused a great deal of gossip, offence, and closing of ranks. (An Icelandic translation appeared only c. 1945.) Miles continued his tirade:

> I can inform the old Austrian dame—that Madame Trollope, the conceited Ida Pfeiffer—that all the Iceland clergymen I met were as hospitable ... This is the woman that runs all over the world,

and writes books about what she sees, and much that she does not see; and because the governor of Iceland would not be bored by her shallow Highness, then she pens all manner of false and libellous stories ... The best comment that can be made on her book is, that she describes her journey to Mt. Hekla, and *ascent to the summit*, when the people here on the ground told me she never put her foot on the mountain at all![91]

No doubt the fact that her popular book was a competitor to his own helped incite such intemperate remarks. Not much has changed there.

CHAPTER 4

AROUND THE WORLD
IN 900 DAYS
(1846–1848)

"Once the travel bug bites there is no known antidote."
Michael Palin

Almost as soon as Ida Pfeiffer had returned home after her Nordic journey, she left her native Vienna again for a short trip to Trieste. Perhaps this was just to visit her aunt, Constantia von Reyer. Or perhaps Pfeiffer was keen to avoid her newfound fame at home.[92] At the same time, maybe she also felt all too keenly the restrictions and constraints of home society after the innumerable, almost indefinable freedoms of being amongst total strangers in foreign lands where one could dress as one liked and go where one liked and behave with more freedom. She was not long in plotting a new voyage and after only nine months, was ready to travel again. But this time it would be on a far, far grander scale. She applied for a passport from the Austrian government to travel to England, Asia, Africa and Australia.[93]

On the first of May 1846 Pfeiffer once again left Vienna on a great voyage. It was to be nothing less than a circumnavigation of the entire globe. She would head first for tropical Brazil and then westwards from there and take whatever opportunities arose along the way. Brazil had long been well known to her as the land explored by her hero, Alexander von Humboldt.

The first stop after leaving home was Prague where she had the good fortune to run into Count Friedrich von Berchtold with whom she had travelled in the Holy Land. The grave and earnest looking von Berchtold, now sixty-five, was a physician interested in botany and natural history. He published a technical treatise on the botany of Bohemia (1836–1842) and wrote on a host of other subjects. When he heard Pfeiffer was headed for Brazil he proposed accompanying her. Pfeiffer promised to wait for him in Hamburg where the transatlantic ships embarked.

On the steamer from Prague to Dresden, Pfeiffer had a second fortuitous meeting. She became acquainted with the widow of the naturalist Johann Mikan who had been part of the Austrian Brazil Expedition that began in 1817 after the marriage of the Austrian princess Maria Leopoldine with Crown Prince Dom Pedro of Portugal, the founder and first ruler of the Empire of Brazil. Frau Mikan had accompanied her husband into the Brazilian interior and was able to give Pfeiffer helpful tips and advice.

Pfeiffer arrived in Hamburg on 12 May but she was forced to wait, chomping at the bit, for her travelling companion as ships daily departed onto the boundless oceans. Count von Berchtold finally arrived in the middle of June. No doubt dropping everything to head off for Brazil took a little time. Pfeiffer hated delays, and hated to be kept waiting. But she was more than happy to travel with her friend and to enjoy the advantages of a male companion.

They took passages on the Danish brig *Caroline*, under Captain Bock. This was Pfeiffer's usual sort of budget travel. Transatlantic passenger crossings were by this time made in modern, fast and comfortable steamships. Sailing ships were smaller, far less comfortable, with poorer food and were much, much slower. But they were consequently much cheaper. What von Berchtold thought of this went unrecorded. But at his age, he may have been most accustomed to the traditional maritime technology anyway.

The *Caroline* sailed southwest, through the English Channel and past the white cliffs of Dover, close enough to see Dover Castle clearly. Once out in the Atlantic the ship was sometimes becalmed for agonizingly long spells, sometimes as much as two weeks, forced to wait helplessly and frustratingly for the winds to return.

The modern traveller sits, not always comfortably or congenially to be sure, in sealed metal machines – isolated from the environment. In the 1840s, travellers were still in intimate contact with the environment through which they travelled. They saw many things that are now quite unimaginable. Stuck out in the middle of the sea where few today have ever been, they saw flying fish, bonitos, dolphins, Portuguese men-of-war, and at night there were spectacular displays of bioluminescence as microscopic sea creatures in their billions created breathtaking light displays unlike anything outside of computer graphics today. To pass the time Pfeiffer made a wooden needle and then wove a net from string. She caught a jellyfish which she examined in a bowl of water and then hung from the stern to dry. Some of the tentacles reached the water twelve feet below.

On 29 August, at 10 p.m. they "crossed the line". Crossing the equator had long been an occasion for celebration and ceremonies on board ships, especially in the Royal Navy. Even the gentleman naturalist Charles Darwin could not avoid a ceremonial dunking when HMS *Beagle* crossed the line in 1832. On board the *Caroline*, however, the passengers were content to shake hands and congratulate each other. Someone had brought some champagne and so they toasted the new hemisphere. "The corks sprang gaily in the air, and with a joyful 'huzza', the health of the new hemisphere was drunk."[94]

As the ship plodded its way westward the weather was gradually becoming warmer. Although they had not yet sighted land, on 13 September the helmsman came to Pfeiffer and encouraged her to hang her head over the rail of the ship and smell the air. "I breathed a most beautiful perfume of flowers," she recalled. The smell of the land had preceded the sight of it. But this was undetectable on deck or inside the cabin. Later in the day she was fascinated to behold "the sea itself was covered with innumerable dead butterflies and moths, which had been carried out to sea by the storm. Two pretty little birds, quite exhausted by their long flight, were resting upon one of the yards." Only when seeing such vast numbers of living things constantly blown out to sea and lost every year, can one understand how oceanic islands are gradually, and naturally, colonised by new species.

On 16 September, after two and half months at sea and sailing about 14,000 kilometres, they could just make out the famous sentinel mountains flanking Rio de Janeiro. At 2 p.m. they entered the harbour crowded with ships from many nations and overlooked by the two great granite peaks.

Modern air passengers who grumble about security inspections and baggage handling delays would be apoplectic at what happened next. First the ship's papers had to be checked under the shadows of a guarding warship. Then the passengers had to "appear before an officer, who took from us our passports and sealed letters". All letters were opened and read by a censor. Then the passengers were checked by a doctor "who inspected us to see that we had not brought the plague or yellow fever; and lastly, before another officer, who took possession of different packets and boxes, and assigned us the spot to anchor in."[95] By this time it was so late that they had to stay another night on board the ship and could only land the next day.

The following morning Pfeiffer and her fellow passengers had to take their baggage to the customs house "where all effects are strictly examined, and a heavy duty levied upon merchandise, books, etc., etc". No unopened letters were allowed into the country. This is an enormous shift from attitudes to privacy and personal "data" today.

If the officers opened any of Pfeiffer's letters they could not have read them anyway because she wrote in the *Kurrent* or old German script which is illegible to anyone who has not learned it. The captain warned his passengers, "In no part of the world were the Custom-house officers so strict, and the penalties so heavy."[96] As the character Captain Kewley quipped in 1857 in Matthew Kneale's novel *English Passengers* (2000) "truly, there's no thoroughness like Customs' thoroughness".

Rio de Janeiro was the capital of the Empire of Brazil since its independence from Portugal in 1822. Pfeiffer found that it was architecturally a very European-looking city though not very impressive or beautiful. The public buildings and churches struck her as nothing special. The natural history museum was mostly empty although "the collection of birds, which is the most complete of all, is really fine". She found the humid tropical climate "very weakening". The mosquitoes, ants, bugs, and sand fleas were another source of annoyance.

The populace struck her as far worse. She was horrified at her first sight of the poor blacks, many of them slaves, that made up most of the population. Never shy to give her opinion about what was beautiful or ugly, she described them in terms that would now be considered distastefully racist. But in time her eye grew accustomed to seeing the Brazilians and soon she found many were fine-looking people after all. Then she saw that many blacks were skilled craftsmen. Yet the wealthy, fair-skinned inhabitants told

Pfeiffer that "they can only be looked upon as a link between the monkey tribe and the human race". And this was many years before Darwin's *Origin of Species* appeared in 1859. Misunderstanding Darwin, some still mistakenly think that he believed that some races are closer to monkeys or apes.

Pfeiffer thought they were "somewhat behind the whites in intellectual culture; but I believe that this is not because they are deficient in understanding, but because their education is totally neglected". After all, no schools had been made for them and they received no education or assistance. As for the institution of slavery, which was still widespread in Brazil, to her surprise Pfeiffer thought it was perhaps not as bad as was commonly portrayed in Europe. Anti-slavery feeling in Europe had been very widespread for decades. In Britain, Parliament passed the Slave Trade Act of 1807 which outlawed the slave trade in British controlled territories. Slavery itself was outlawed in a further act in 1833. Britain essentially bribed Spain to abolish the slave trade in her New World colonies in 1820. Slavery was finally abolished in Brazil only in 1888.

Never content to stay in one spot, Pfeiffer and von Berchtold visited nearby waterfalls and botanic gardens. She heard much praise of Petropolis, a German colony not far inland. The road there was rumoured to pass through beautiful country and virgin forests. On the 26th they sailed on a barque for Porto da Estrela on the north side of Guanabara Bay. From there they decided to make the journey inland on foot to better see and enjoy the lush forest and so von Berchtold could botanise to his heart's content. Pfeiffer was "greatly amused" to see hummingbirds for the first time. (These live only in the Americas.) "Nothing can be more graceful and delicate than these little creatures," she penned in her journal.

Further treasures were to be seen every inch of the way. "We gathered a rich harvest of flowers, plants, and insects, and loitered along, enchanted with the magnificent woods and not less beautiful views, which stretched over hill and dale, towards the sea and its bays, and even as far as the capital itself."[97] They were so engrossed with the seething vibrancy of tropical splendour all about them that for some time they did not notice or pay any attention to a black man who was coming along the road behind them.

When they reached a rather lonely spot in the road, the man suddenly sprang forward brandishing a long knife in one hand and a lasso in the other. The two Austrians concluded that the man meant to rob and murder them. They were unarmed except for their parasols although Pfeiffer had a small clasp knife. She instantly took it out of her pocket and opened it "fully determined to sell my life as dearly as possible". As the attacker came at them, they tried beating him back with their parasols but these didn't last long. The robber grabbed Pfeiffer's parasol and as they struggled, it broke. She was left only with a piece of the handle with two silk tassels hanging helplessly from it. In the scuffle, the man had dropped his knife. With incredible presence of mind, Pfeiffer fought back.

> I instantly made a dash [for his knife], and thought I had got it, when he, more quick than I, thrust me away with his feet and hands, and once more obtained possession of it. He waved it furiously over my head, and dealt me two wounds, a thrust and a deep gash, both in the upper part of the left arm; I thought I was lost, and despair alone gave me the courage to use my own knife. I made a thrust at his breast; this he warded off, and I only succeeded in wounding him severely in the hand.

The Count jumped in and grabbed the robber from behind allowing Pfeiffer time to get up off the ground. Enraged the robber slashed at the Count and cut his hand terribly. All of this had taken just a few seconds. Then the clop of approaching horses came from down the road. Hearing this, the robber ran off into the forest. Two

European horsemen came around the corner and seeing Pfeiffer and the Count bleeding from wounds, instantly understood the situation. Just then two black men came along the road on foot from the other direction and all four set off together into the forest after the assailant.

They soon captured, bound, and dragged the robber back to the road. He refused to walk so they beat him severely. Pfeiffer thought his head would be smashed. The prisoner was taken to the nearest house where the Austrians had their wounds cleaned and dressed. What became of the attacker went unrecorded. Pfeiffer carried the "deep and ghastly" scars of this encounter between the elbow and shoulder for the rest of her life.[98] She preserved the broken handle of her parasol for the rest of her days.[99]

About a week later the two Austrians set off for another trip into the interior with the aim of seeing a tribe of Indians still living in the forest by hunting and gathering. Travelling first by ship and then up the Rio Macacu, they proceeded overland and by 6 October reached the small town of Neufreiburg (Nova Friburgo) about 100 kilometres inland. Here they met a German naturalist named Carl Heinrich Bescke and his wife Elizabeth. Pfeiffer, the amateur naturalist, was impressed to find that Frau Bescke was "almost as scientific" as her husband. "We enjoyed many an hour in their entertaining society," Pfeiffer recalled, "and were shown many interesting collections of quadrupeds, birds, serpents, insects, etc.; the collection of these last, indeed, was more rich and remarkable than that in the Museum of Rio Janeiro. Herr Beske [*sic*] has always a great many orders from Europe to send over various objects of natural history."[100] Indeed the *Entomologische Zeitung* (Entomological Newspaper) from Stetten, Austria, carried notices of the varied types of high-quality bird and insect specimens that could be purchased from him.[101]

Unfortunately von Berchtold's wounded hand became infected and he could not continue the journey into the interior. It seemed that Pfeiffer would not be able to see the natives she had come so far to see. The intrepid traveller was not to be vexed on this account. Characteristically, she decided to go on alone. "I procured a good double-barrelled pistol and set out undaunted upon my trip." With the help of a guide she headed on and on into the interior. They passed areas where the Brazilian forest was being burned and cleared to grow crops. A scene still all too familiar today. Further on they came upon a particularly beautiful and unspoiled spot that seemed untouched by the hand of man. Pfeiffer took in this ultra-romantic scene.

> I was so happy, that I felt richly recompensed for all the fatigue of my journey. One thought only obscured this beautiful picture; and that was, that weak man should dare to enter the lists with the giant nature of the place, and make it bend before his will. How soon, perhaps, may this profound and holy tranquillity be disturbed by the blows of some daring settler's axe, to make room for the wants of men![102]

When they stopped at the occasional fazenda (farm or plantation) the "Pfeiffer effect" struck all who saw her.

> Great astonishment was manifested in every venda [shop] and fazenda at seeing a lady arrive accompanied only by a single servant. The first question was, whether I was not afraid thus to traverse the woods alone; and my guide was invariably taken on one side, and questioned as to [why] I travelled. As he was in the habit of seeing me collect flowers and insects, he supposed me to be a naturalist, and replied that my journey had a scientific object.[103]

She spoke only a few words of Portuguese but with her considerable powers of signing with her hands and knowledge of other languages she managed surprisingly well although many of the things she thought she was told were no doubt complete misunderstandings.

At these remote fazendas she again saw many slaves. Although she declared, "I am certainly very much opposed to slavery, and should greet its abolition with the greatest delight, but, despite this, I again affirm that the negro slave enjoys, under the protection of the law, a better lot than the free fellah of Egypt, or many peasants in Europe, who still groan under the right of [feudal] soccage."[104]

They continued heading northwest, crossing rivers including the Paraíba do Sul, until 11 October when Pfeiffer was guided from the last Brazilian fazenda into the virgin forest by a black woman and a Purí Indian to find a native village. After a further eight hours walking, a village of the Purí people appeared in the forest. It was not what she had expected. "I beheld a picture of the greatest misery and want: I had often met with a great deal of wretchedness in my travels, but never so much as I saw here!"[105]

Crowded round by lofty trees was a clearing with five palm-thatched houses, each eighteen feet long and twelve broad. As was her usual practice, Pfeiffer visited or, perhaps one should say, inspected the houses. Small fires smouldered inside where roots or bananas were being roasted. Their meagre possessions struck Pfeiffer as poverty. She was probably unaware that the Purí were traditionally a nomadic people. She noted that "the long bows and arrows, which constitute their only weapons, were leaning in the background against the wall". She found the people themselves quite ugly. They were short or rather "stunted" and she did not find their facial features at all attractive. "Most of them, both men and women, were tattooed with a reddish or blue colour, though only round the mouth, in the form of a moustache."[106] Afterwards these amiable forest dwellers took their eccentric visitor with them into the forest to hunt. Pfeiffer admired the skill with which they used bow and arrow. They shot a monkey from a tree and even shot a parrot on the wing.

By this time the day was fading, there was no way she could make the long trek back to the fazenda. The Purí invited her to stay the night and Pfeiffer gladly accepted. She spread her cloak on the ground and put a log at the head of it for a pillow.

Meanwhile the Purí were roasting the monkey and parrots they had killed. They pulled some banana leaves off nearby trees to use as plates and served Pfeiffer roast monkey, parrot and maize. After such a long day she was very hungry. She knew that hunger and a long day's march makes food taste better, but all the same she found monkey "superlatively delicious".

After this Pfeiffer asked the Purí to perform some of their dances, which they did. Their stamping and swaying around the fire moved her and some dances frightened her. At length it was time for sleep. But as the campfire died down and Pfeiffer lay on her cloak in the midst of the forest, she could not help thinking of the snakes and other wild animals that might be all around in the impenetrable darkness of the forest. This kept her awake until she realised that the Purí slept here every day of their lives. If it were safe enough for them, it must be safe enough for her. And indeed it was. These kind people were almost out of time. With the gradual destruction of their forests and the persecution of outsiders, their numbers dwindled. By the end of the nineteenth century the Purí were regarded as extinct.

On 18 October 1846, shortly after her forty-ninth birthday, Pfeiffer and von Berchtold returned safely to Rio de Janeiro. She probably sent back her natural history collections to the Royal Museum in Vienna. One gem in her collection was a brilliantly multi-coloured bird, the paradise tanager which was later mentioned in a scientific publication.

Pfeiffer alone would carry on beyond Brazil. She was obliged to pay a hefty £25 for a place on a fine English barque called the

John Renwick under Captain Bell. Count von Berchtold and other friends saw her off as the ship weighed anchor on 9 December 1846. There were only nine passengers on board, all Europeans. The ship stopped at Santos to unload 200 tonnes of coal and take on 6,000 sacks of sugar. This meant they were forced to wait three weary weeks. Annoyed, Pfeiffer used the time to visit São Paulo, the largest inland town of the Brazils, about forty miles from the port.

On 2 January 1847 they set off again. In the night they saw a slave ship in the distance, secretly unloading its ghastly illegal cargo. Although Brazil, following several European powers, had abolished the importation of slaves in 1831 and British Royal Navy ships patrolled the Atlantic and the Brazilian coast, some smugglers still got through.

By the 9th they were off the Rio Grande. It looked as though a storm were brewing and Captain Bell constantly consulted his barometer and issued orders to the crew. Just after 8 p.m. the storm struck.

> Flash after flash of lightning darted across the horizon from every side, and lighted the sailors in their work; the agitated waves being illuminated with the most dazzling brilliancy. The majestic rolling of the thunder drowned the captain's voice, and the white foaming billows broke with such terrific force over the deck, that it appeared as if they would carry everything with them into the depths of the ocean.

Far from cowering away from the danger, Pfeiffer had herself lashed Odysseus-like to the ship near the stern "and let the tremendous waves break over me, in order to absorb, as it were, as much of the spectacle before me as possible".[107] At least this is what she reported in her book.

Another storm descended on them on the night of the 20th and the winds tore at the ship so violently that the mainmast was badly damaged. Captain Bell decided that they needed to put in to the nearest port for a new one. In the meantime the mast was made fast with cables, chains and wooden props. Too late they found they were so far south that they would either have to turn back or continue round the Cape. They skirted the tangled puzzle of frozen islands at Tierra del Fuego so closely that they could distinguish every individual bush along the shore.

The ship then entered some of the roughest seas on the planet where the Atlantic and Pacific oceans collide. It proved impossible to sail around the bad weather so they just had to push through it. At one point the top of a mast broke off and sailors had to climb aloft to make repairs despite the weather. The ship was being tossed about so roughly that the poor passengers were unable to sit at table to eat. Instead they had to crouch on the floor of the cabin bracing themselves while holding a plate in their hands. One day as they rolled and bucked, the steward stumbled and dumped the hot contents of the coffee pot onto Pfeiffer. Ever stoical, she remarked only: "Luckily, only a small portion fell upon my hands, so that the accident was not a very serious one."[108]

At last they left the rough seas behind them and sailed north up the west coast of South America. On 2 March 1847 the crew furled the sails and dropped anchor at Valparaiso, the chief port of Chile. When HMS *Beagle* arrived there in July 1834, Darwin described the view in his diary: "the town is built on the very foot of [a] range of hills, which are 1600 feet high, & tolerably steep; the surface is worn into numberless little ravines, which exposes a singularly bright red soil between patches of light green grass & low shrubs".[109] As in Rio, Pfeiffer was not very impressed with the local people. She thought the lower classes "remarkably ugly" and with "such a peculiarly repulsive cast of countenance, that any physiognomist would straightway pronounce them to be robbers or pickpockets at the least".[110]

Pfeiffer made arrangements to sail on the next ship bound for China. Again there were annoying delays and the ship she found did not sail when she was told. But she did have time to pay a visit to a resident merchant and the Frankfurt Consul, Philipp Bayerbach. This was the same man who told Darwin in 1834 about seeing a nearby volcanic eruption at night from the sea. Darwin incorporated the testimony into a scientific paper in 1840.[111] Bayerbach introduced her to some local families and one of these showed her a remarkable collection of mussel shells and insects. Pfeiffer made her usual excursions to the surrounding areas, examining the homes and cultural practices of the local people and collecting specimens.

Pfeiffer fell ill with what she described as a bout of "English cholera" just when the "polite and kind" Dutch Captain van Wyck Jurriaanse, sent word that it was time to sail. "I did not, however, wish to miss the opportunity of visiting China, knowing how rarely it occurred, nor was I desirous of losing the two hundred dollars (£40) already paid for my passage, and I therefore went on board, trusting in my good luck, which had never forsaken me on my travels."

The Dutch barque *Loopuyt* left Valparaiso on 18 March. After a few days Pfeiffer recovered from her illness. This time she was convinced that saltwater baths had done the trick. The ship was remarkably clean and tidy and the drinking water always fresh. As for the sailors "I was far from finding seamen so rough and uncivil as travellers often represent them to be. Their manners are certainly not the most polished in the world, neither are they extraordinarily attentive or delicate, but their hearts and dispositions are mostly good."[112]

After thirty-nine days' sailing across the featureless and boundless blue expanse of the Pacific, they reached Papeete, the principal port of Tahiti. Even before the anchor was dropped the ship was surrounded by a half dozen native outriggers whose occupants lithely clambered up on the deck to offer fruit and shellfish for sale.

A verdant pyramid in the middle of the Pacific, surrounded by a ring of coral reef enclosing a crystal clear turquoise lagoon, Tahiti had long been painted as a tropical paradise by western writers. But the days of the supposedly happy-go-lucky natives and carefree bare-breasted nubile girls were gone. The successive visits of western ships from Captain Cook, the mutinous HMS *Bounty* and the culture-extinguishing Christian missionaries had eroded and forbidden their innocent Eden. Since 1842 Tahiti and its dependencies had been a French protectorate and there were several French men-of-war lying at anchor when the Loopuyt arrived with supplies for the garrison.

On shore there were no hotels and virtually every possible accommodation was already taken up by French officers and soldiers. The only spot Pfeiffer could procure was "a small piece of ground, which I found at a carpenter's, whose room was already inhabited by four different individuals. I was shown a place behind the door, exactly six feet long and four broad. There was no flooring but the earth itself; the walls were composed of wicker work; a bed was quite out of the question, and yet for this accommodation I was obliged to pay one florin and thirty kreutzers a-week (about 7s)."[113]

She was somewhat more impressed with the appearance of the Tahitians than other peoples she had seen. Like Darwin before her, she thought the men were handsomer than the women.

> The women, both old and young, adorn themselves with garlands of leaves and flowers, which they make in the most artistic and elegant manner … Both sexes wear flowers in their ears, which have such large holes bored in them that the stalk can very easily be drawn through. … All the natives are tattooed, generally from the hips half down the legs, and frequently this mode of ornamenting

themselves is extended to the hands, feet, or other parts of the body. The designs resemble arabesques; they are regular and artistic in their composition, and executed with much taste.[114]

What shocked Pfeiffer most of all was the sexual promiscuousness of the women. Pfeiffer was too delicate to go into too much detail and casual relationships did not bother her as much as what amounted to (in her view) informal, and consensual, prostitution. She saw and heard about many instances of Frenchmen giving gifts to their paramours until the latter lost interest.

In stark contrast to her bitter time in Iceland, here she was invited to join some high society. At dinners given by the French governor, she was able to meet the Tahitian Queen Pomare and the royal family. The queen autographed Pfeiffer's journal for her. The queen, Pfeiffer noted, was "36 years of age, tall and stout, but tolerably well preserved". A decade earlier the queen had toured HMS *Beagle* and Darwin described her unsympathetically as "a large awkward woman without any beauty, grace or dignity".[115]

On 4 May Pfeiffer joined a group, including a French officer and his Tahitian mistress, in a boat to sail to Papara on the southern side of the island. Pfeiffer was amazed by the glimpses of the kaleidoscopically beautiful coral reefs she could see under their boat. At some point Pfeiffer collected five species of red sea algae which were later purchased by the Museum Godeffroy in Hamburg.[116] At Papara she found "a lively old man nearly ninety years of age, who remembered perfectly the second landing of the celebrated circumnavigator of the globe, Captain Cook".[117] Presumably this was Cook's final voyage on HMS *Resolution* which reached Tahiti in 1778 when he returned his Tahitian guide, Omai, from the first voyage. It must have particularly interested Pfeiffer to meet someone who had seen one of her girlhood heroes.

Taking a single Tahitian guide, Pfeiffer trekked inland to see a beautiful lake, Vaihiria. "I was very suitably clothed for the purpose," she wrote, "having got strong men's shoes, without any stockings, trousers, and a blouse, which I had fastened up as high as my hips."[118] Once she had surveyed the view over the lake, her guide made an impromptu raft and with gestures, invited her to step aboard. Warily, as she could not swim, she clambered onto it. The guide, swimming behind, pushed her gently across the lake and back so that she could enjoy the view. On their walk back they were obliged to spend the night in the forest. The guide simply plucked some local plantains, made a fire by rapidly turning a sharpened stick, and roasted their dinner.

On the morning of 17 May 1847 Pfeiffer and the *Loopuyt* left Tahiti, heading west. Pfeiffer did not enjoy the long, monotonous journey across the Pacific. "Very frequently I used to start up from my desk, thinking that I was in some diminutive room ashore; and my mistake was the more natural, as we had three horses, a dog, several pigs, hens, geese, and a canary bird on board, all respectively neighing, barking, grunting, cackling, and singing, as if they were in a farm-yard."[119] Before the advent of refrigeration it was necessary to keep animals alive until they were needed. Likewise chickens supplied eggs and cows could provide milk on larger ships. The floating farmyard passed Saipan and later Luzon.

Finally, on 9 July they anchored in Macao Roads on the coast of the Middle Kingdom, the Celestial Empire, China. There were a few other European ships and several large Chinese junks and many smaller boats to be seen anchored in the area. The trading town, with its population of 20,000, had belonged to Portugal since 1557. Pfeiffer thought that "the most remarkable objects are the palace of the Portuguese governor, the Catholic monastery of Guia [*sic*], the fortifications, and a few fine houses which lie scattered about the hills in picturesque disorder".[120]

Her visit, in the aftermath of the First Opium War, came at an uneasy time of transition. Pfeiffer was in no two minds about the British use of military firepower to force the Chinese Empire to accept hugely profitable drug imports. Under the Treaty of Nanking, five ports were to be open to foreign merchants to discharge their endless cargos of opium.

"What shall we say to the war declared by the English against the Emperor of China," Pfeiffer would later ask her readers indignantly, "who was doing his best to guard his subjects from this poison, by prohibiting the importation of opium?" Was it not in every way a contradiction of the Christian principles so arrogantly puffed by Europeans? "How can we ask uncivilised nations to respect our religion, when we let them see that it does not restrain us from the most unprincipled and shameful grasping, and that a sufficient amount of profit will reconcile us to any proceeding however flagitious?"[121]

Today the story is usually told in similarly superficial terms of good vs. evil. Julia Lovell's book, *The Opium War* (2011) provides a refreshingly complex and myth busting version with the benefit of revealing what the Chinese officials and participants did and wrote about the events at the time.

Unsurprisingly, given the recent conflict at the time of Pfeiffer's arrival, Europeans were still very unpopular in many areas. In Canton (Guangzhou) there were acts of violence and vandalism against them and their property almost daily. Although she was in a European enclave in Macao, almost the entire population was Chinese. "Europeans, both men and women, can circulate freely, without being exposed to a shower of stones, as is frequently the case in other Chinese towns," she reported. Pfeiffer walked all over the town, exploring, observing and taking in all she could of the country that for centuries had been one of the least accessible to

Europeans. She saw groups of men sitting outside playing mahjong, which she mistook for dominoes.

Her naïveté is startling. "Nothing surprised and amused me more than the manner in which the Chinese eat," she declared. "They have two little sticks, with which they very skilfully convey their victuals into their mouths."[122] This innocent discovery of chopsticks may strike us as amusing but it is yet another clue as to how uniformed Pfeiffer was as a traveller. Chopsticks had been known about in Europe for centuries. But Pfeiffer, with her shoot-from-the-hip manner of travelling from country to country had done very little research about the peoples and places she visited. Even a year before she had had no idea she would ever visit China. She seldom mentioned what other authors had said about the same locations, which gives little information about any research she may have done. One of the few books she cited was Eberhard Zimmermann's popular *Handbook of Travel* (1802–1813). Yet she frequently criticised travel writers in general for exaggerating or repeating hearsay; but it is difficult to know who she had in mind since her own books are little more than her actual travel diary.

Although she had only paid for a passage to Macao, Captain van Wyck Jurriaanse kindly offered to take her as his guest over to Hong Kong. Once they arrived there, as an additional kindness, he allowed Pfeiffer to live on board the ship, thus saving her the expense of accommodation. Pfeiffer would later tell her readers: "The English obtained Hong-Kong from the Chinese at the conclusion of the [Opium] war in 1842, and founded the port of Victoria, which contains at present a large number of palace-like houses built of stone."[123] There were about 200–300 resident Europeans.

In mid July Pfeiffer was ready to head to Canton on the mainland. She decided to take a passage on a small Chinese junk. A local European merchant named William Pustan tried to dissuade her.

Europeans did not travel on these local boats, he told her, only the Chinese did. But the steamer was too expensive and the junk much cheaper. And Pfeiffer was probably tempted by the idea of the unconventionality and novelty of sailing alone on an exotic craft. Nevertheless, she checked and loaded her pistols in readiness. In fact the Chinese aboard the junk turned out to be very friendly and entirely harmless. Pfeiffer observed with surprise how they were constantly "drinking tea, without sugar, from little saucers. I, too, had this celestial drink offered to me on all sides. Every Chinese, rich or poor, drinks neither pure water nor spirituous liquors, but invariably indulges in weak tea with no sugar." She shared a cabin with two Chinese women.

> They soon remarked that I had no stool for my head. They offered me one of theirs, and would not be satisfied until I accepted it. It is a Chinese custom to use, instead of pillows, little stools of bamboo or strong pasteboard. They are not stuffed, but are rounded at the top, and are about eight inches high, and from one to three feet long. They are far more comfortable than would at first be imagined.[124]

The port of Canton was bustling with junks, as well as "Chinese men-of-war, flat, broad, and long, and mounting twenty or thirty cannons ... the mandarins' boats, with their painted sides, doors, and windows, their carved galleries, and pretty little silk flags, giving them the appearance of the most charming houses; but what delighted me most was the flower-boats, with their upper galleries ornamented with flowers, garlands, and arabesques." Pfeiffer had a letter of introduction to a European gentleman named Arthur Agassiz, a relative of the eminent Swizz-born American naturalist Louis Agassiz. A Chinese man was instructed to take her from the junk to the house of Mr Agassiz. But the sight of a European woman walking like this through the crowded streets of Canton was more than bizarre and unprecedented, it was an outrageous provocation. As she weaved in and out of the crowded streets and past food stalls of steaming rice and buns "both old and young turned back to look after me, and they hooted and pointed at me with their fingers; the people ran out of the booths, and gradually formed a crowd at my heels".

When Pfeiffer arrived, and hearing how she had come there, Mr Agassiz was astonished. He could "hardly credit that I had met with no difficulties or injury. From him I learned what risks I, as a woman, had run in traversing the streets of Canton with no escort but a Chinese guide. Such a thing had never occurred before, and Mr Agassiz assured me that I might esteem myself as exceedingly fortunate in not having been insulted by the people in the grossest manner, or even stoned."[125]

Despite the risk of stoning, and the sweltering July heat, Pfeiffer could not sit still. She convinced the merchant and Prussian consul, Richard von Carlowitz, to accompany her about the area. They toured shops and temples, villages and a tea factory. Pfeiffer was particularly grateful to von Carlowitz because by going with her, he was "exposing himself to many dangers on my account, and bearing patiently the insults of the populace, who followed at our heels, and loudly expressed their indignation at the boldness of the European woman in thus appearing in public. Through his assistance, I saw more than any [European] woman ever yet saw in China."[126]

They visited the ornate Buddhist Temple of Honan (the Hoi Tong Monastery) on the other side of the river. Pfeiffer later described it for her readers:

This temple is surrounded by numerous out-buildings, and a large garden enclosed with a high wall. You first enter a large fore-court, at the extremity of which a colossal gateway leads into the inner courts. Under the archway of this portico are two War Gods, each eighteen feet high, in menacing attitudes, and with horribly distorted features. They are placed there to prevent evil spirits from entering. A second similar portico, under which are the four Celestial Kings, leads into the inmost court, where the principal temple is situated. The interior of the temple is 100 feet in length, and 100 feet in breadth. The flat roof, from which hang a number of glass chandeliers, lamps, artificial flowers, and silk ribbons, is supported upon several rows of wooden pillars, while the multitude of statues, altars, flower-pots, censers, candelabra, candlesticks, and other ornaments, involuntarily suggest to the mind of the spectator the decoration of a Roman Catholic church. At the right and left altars were the priests, whose garments and gesticulations also resembled those of the Roman Catholics.

In another side temple, a monk handed Pfeiffer and von Carlowitz some joss sticks to light and place before the altar in an urn of sand. Out of politeness they were about to do so when an American missionary, who accompanied them, tore the sticks from their hands "and indignantly returned them to the priest [monk], saying, that what we were about to do was an act of idolatry. The priest [monk] took the matter very seriously, and, instantly closing the doors, called his companions, who hurried in from all sides, and abused us in the most violent and vociferous fashion, pressing closer every instant. It was with the greatest difficulty that we succeeded in fighting our way to the door, and thus making our escape." In this case the only idolatrous zealot was surely the American missionary.

Today Pfeiffer comes across as refreshingly modern in her cultural relativism, often able to see her own culture as different from others in details but not in kind. After her book was published, one overly sensitive English Catholic took great offence at Pfeiffer's remarks in this respect (quoted above) as if her intention was to "make the Catholic devotion appear as idolatrous and empty as that of the Chinese". This "poison" in her writings was likely to be "lapped up together" with the interesting stories of her travels like poison hidden in a sumptuous dish. Such opinions as hers were dangerous because to "laugh down the Catholic faith" was "Satanic and detestable to the last degree".[127]

Pfeiffer saw and heard much of the usual European stereotypes about the Chinese in Canton. For example, they are, she wrote "not too particular in their food; they eat dogs, cats, mice, and rats, the intestines of birds, and the blood of every animal, and I was even assured that caterpillars and worms formed part of their diet. Their principal dish, however, is rice."[128] The Chinese were said at the time to be cruel, dishonest and cowardly. But she had to confess that she did not know much about this enigmatic people. "With regard to the social manners and customs of the Chinese, I am only able to mention a few, as it is exceedingly difficult, and, in fact, almost impossible, for a foreigner to become acquainted with them. I endeavoured to see as much as I could, and mixed on every possible opportunity among the people, afterwards writing down a true account of what I had seen."[129] Pfeiffer was obviously no authority on China and much that she recorded was mistaken or based on her misunderstandings. But her impressions of what it was like to walk through Chinese streets and villages in the 1840s remain important snapshots of a vanished world.

And despite the prejudices and stereotypes her own culture had about the Chinese, her first-hand experiences led her to reject these. "I never believed that I should really behold the Chinese" to be the exact opposite of the way they are represented "in Europe".[130]

One of the more startling practices of the Chinese witnessed by Pfeiffer were the bound feet of some girls and women. She did not mention these observations in her book but in a letter to her sister Marie she described what she saw.

There were many girls and woman with the crippled feet, it was amazing to see them walking on these tiny feet. The four toes are bent under to the sole, so that the foot is pressed together ... The shoes of such ladies are certainly not over 4 Zohl [approximately 10 centimetres] long. Through extraordinary application I was able to see one of these artificially formed feet in its naked condition. It looked so disgusting, that any other lady than me would have certainly been sick, even I felt very close to being so.[131]

Pfeiffer returned to Hong Kong on another junk on 20 August. Her next destination was Singapore. If only she could have, she would have taken a Chinese junk there. But this was not possible. Instead there was the state-of-the-art monthly British mail steamer of the Peninsular and Oriental Steam Navigation Co., known universally as the P&O. The company was established in 1837, as the Peninsular Steam Navigation Company, to carry the mail across to the Iberian Peninsula. In 1840 the company was awarded government mail contracts and a Royal Charter to carry the mails to the Far East. "Oriental" was therefore added to the company's name. By 1842 a regular mail service reached India "overland", that is, the land crossing from Alexandria to Suez. By 1845 the service was running monthly between Hong Kong and Bombay via Singapore.

The P&O steamers carried mostly first-class passengers. The ticket prices were, for Pfeiffer at least, "exorbitant", analogous to a first-class vs. an economy airline ticket today. Pfeiffer therefore asked for a third-class ticket at the P&O offices. The reaction of the ticket clerk astonished Pfeiffer. Third-class passengers "were not respectable" she was told, and there are no cabins so they are "obliged to sleep upon deck". Considering all that Pfeiffer had experienced and endured in her travels, this would have been nothing unusual. But the P&O office would not hear of it. Pfeiffer was therefore obliged to pay £23 8s ($117) for a second-class ticket. She would later grumble to her German readers "this certainly gave me a very curious idea of English liberty".[132]

On 25 August 1847 Pfeiffer boarded the brand new P&O paddle steamer *Pekin* under Captain Tronson. The ship was 214 feet long with a 430-horsepower engine, a crew of 136 and space for 70 first-class and 22 second-class passengers. This was the first British steamer she had sailed on so she was "curious to learn how second-class passengers were treated". She was not impressed. Her diary records many examples of shabby treatment. For example, "the provisions were execrable; the remnants of the first [class] cabin were sent to us poor wretches". At least in her diary, and as she knew, in her eventual book, she could take revenge. "I have made many voyages on board steam-ships," she wrote, "and always paid second fare, never did I pay so high a price for such wretched and detestable treatment. In all my life I was never so cheated."[133]

After a voyage south of ten days, the *Pekin* dropped anchor at the tropical island of Singapore amidst a vast international crowd of other ships large and small. The small island of Singapore had been purchased by the East India Company more than twenty years before to establish a free trading port. Since that time it had been dramatically transformed from a small fishing village and Chinese plantations into one of the busiest and wealthiest ports in Asia. It has remained such ever since.

The town next to the harbour was overlooked by a small hill known as Government Hill (now Fort Canning) where the governor's bungalow and a signalling flagstaff were located. The town already boasted many beautiful public buildings as well as hotels, temples, mosques and countless shops and houses. The population had already grown from a few hundred in 1819 to 55,000 of which 40,000 were Chinese, 10,000 Malay and about 150 European. Outside the town were many of the houses owned by wealthy Europeans, often built on small hills surrounded by tidy gardens. Around and beyond these Pfeiffer noted were "plantations of the most precious spices, the elegant areca and feathered palms, with their slim stems shooting up to a height of a hundred feet, and spreading out into the thick feather-like tuft of fresh green, by which they are distinguished from every other kind of palms, and, lastly, the jungle in the back-ground, compose a most beautiful landscape." She also noted approvingly that "the whole island is intersected with excellent roads" which was high praise coming from someone with such lofty standards.[134]

The names of arriving or departing first-class P&O passengers were printed in the newspapers. *The Singapore Free Press* must have assumed that the Austrian lady who disembarked with two other passengers was travelling first class. Respectable people didn't travel any other way. So they reported the arrival of "Mrs Pfeiffer" from Hong Kong.[135]

She had brought letters of introduction to the German shipping agents Behn, Meyer & Co. So she walked through the sweltering tropical humidity a few blocks to their offices on Malacca Street. Theodor Behn and Valentin Meyer had established their trading company seven years before. They traded in virtually everything from coconut oil, camphor and pepper to casks of claret and even pianos. The company still exists in Singapore today. Frau Behn was the first German lady Pfeiffer had met since Brazil. The two immediately hit it off. In fact Frau Behn "would not hear of my lodging in an hotel; I was immediately installed as a member of her own amiable family" in their comfortable bungalow on Mount Sophia, not far from Government Hill.[136]

Apart from the incessant heat and inescapable humidity, life was very pleasant in Singapore. There was very little crime and the infrastructure was good. "Twice a week," Pfeiffer noted, "a very fine military band used to play on the esplanade close to the sea, and the whole world of fashionables would either walk or drive to the place to hear the music." But Pfeiffer had little interest in watching something she was familiar with. She preferred to "visit the plantations of nutmegs and cloves, and refresh myself with their balsamic fragrance".[137]

Herr Behn and Herr Meyer took Pfeiffer on a hunting excursion into what little forest the Chinese planters and woodcutters had not yet cleared in the interior of the island. The hunting party hoped, rather optimistically, to bag a tiger or at least a wild boar. They were first paddled up the narrow Kallang River. It was here that Pfeiffer first encountered the vibrant exuberance of a tropical Southeast Asian forest. Occasional fallen branches blocked their way. Pfeiffer felt that "the natural beauty of the scene was so great, however, that these occasional obstructions, so far from diminishing, actually heightened the charm of the whole. The forest was full of the most luxuriant underwood, creepers, palms, and fern plants; the latter, in many instances sixteen feet high, proved a no less effectual screen against the burning rays of the sun than did the palms and other trees."[138] Long-tailed macaques scampered in the trees overhead and kept keen lookout on the humans below. It was the first time Pfeiffer had seen wild monkeys.

The party left their boats and trekked on through the countless pepper and gambier plantations that Chinese settlers had planted across most of the interior. No tigers or wild boar were spotted but there was a large green snake in a tree. In her diary Pfeiffer melodramatically described the shooting of this snake as a dangerous battle against a fork-tongued devil. After the gentlemen killed it with gunfire, one of their Malay assistants dragged it out of the tree with a makeshift noose made from grass. After skinning it, they gave the snake to some Chinese plantation workers. Later that afternoon, returning to the spot from their hunting trip, Pfeiffer could not resist checking to see if the Chinese were eating the snake. She rushed up to one of their houses. Sensing the men wished to hide their repast, "I entered very quickly and gave them some money to be allowed to taste it. I found the flesh particularly tender and delicate, even more tender than that of a chicken."[139]

After a month Pfeiffer was ready to press on around the world. Given the available transportation options at the moment, her next destination was India. Grumbling to herself, she was obliged to buy another second-class ticket for the P&O steamer *Braganza*, under Captain Potts, which sailed on 8 October 1847 (not the 7th as she wrote in her book). Built in 1836, the *Braganza* was one of the company's older steamers. Like most steam ships, it smelled of "tar, coals, steam, and oil". Sailing ships were at least less malodorous. Pfeiffer observed that "the crew was composed of seventy-nine persons, comprising Chinese, Malays, Cingalese, Bengalese, Hindostanese, and Europeans". *The Singapore Free Press* was not fooled this time, it did not list her name amongst departing first-class passengers.

The following day the *Braganza* called in at the island of Penang further up the Malay Peninsula. Penang had been purchased by the East India Company from the Sultan of Kedah in 1786. With five hours to kill, Pfeiffer went ashore and paid to have herself carted about the town and a little into the country in a palanquin. "All that I could see resembled what I had already seen at Singapore," she wrote.[140] With nothing novel to see, her interest was not excited.

The *Braganza* steamed on across the Bay of Bengal to Ceylon (Sri Lanka) on 17 October. Pfeiffer spent ten days sightseeing in Colombo and Candy. On one occasion she almost had her luggage stolen by a dodgy guide but a passing English officer saved the day. On the 27th she boarded the P&O steamer *Bentinck*, named after the former Governor-General of India, Lord William Bentinck.

The *Bentinck* touched at Madras before arriving at Calcutta, the capital of Bengal and British India, on 4 November 1847. Here Pfeiffer had letters of introduction to a German merchant family by the name of Heilgers. The firm of F. W. Heilgers still exists in Kolkata today. Pfeiffer could not help raising an eyebrow at the luxury in which the Europeans in Calcutta lived with grand houses and vast numbers of servants. Here for once she was welcomed into the highest social circles. Resentfully, she remembered how the Austrian minister at Rio de Janeiro had treated her so condescendingly the year before. But a prophet has no honour in his own country, and so it follows not by his own countrymen elsewhere. Or looked at another way, a lone person from very far away is a valuable social commodity, unless from your own country.

Never content living in a European bubble abroad, Pfeiffer did her best to meet Indian people. Introductions were soon arranged for her. She paid a visit to a wealthy Indian family and learned a great deal about their domestic life, beliefs, and so forth. Pfeiffer was shocked to hear that the eldest daughter, who was nine, was to be married off in just six weeks.

Pfeiffer also toured the usual sights such as the Governor's Palace, Bishop's College, a mosque, the English Cathedral, the Botanical Garden and the museum. A guide took her to see the infamous "Black Hole of Calcutta", where British prisoners were held in suffocating conditions and many died in 1756 after the fort was captured by the Bengali army. We will hear an alternative version of this later.

After more than five weeks in Calcutta, Pfeiffer took the steamer *General Macleod* up the Ganges to the holy city of Benares. She travelled second class of course. Eighteen days later, on 28 December, she reached Benares. In strong contrast to Calcutta, here she found almost no Europeans. This was a far more "Indian" city. "At sunrise, a spectacle is to be seen at the river which has not its counterpart in the world," she wrote.[141] Perhaps 50,000 Hindus performed their purifications in the sacred river Ganges. After being presented to the Rajah, Pratap Singh Bhosle, she travelled further up the Ganges in the company of another traveller, a Mr Law who suddenly appears unexplained in her account, to Allahabad and Agra. This may have been Mr Charles E. Law, later Lord Ellenborough, who came out to India in 1844. At Agra Pfeiffer visited that "magnificent treasure of Agra, and, indeed, of all India—the famous Taj Mahal". They then travelled by road to Delhi.

There she and Mr Law toured the city, markets and monuments. Pfeiffer marvelled at the exquisite workmanship of the gold jewellery on offer, as good as any in the world she thought. They toured the imperial palace, which she noted was "considered one of the finest buildings in Asia". They also visited ornate mosques and the ruins of ancient buildings. A particular highlight was visiting and climbing the 379 steps of the spiral staircase of the Qutub Minar, the tallest brick minaret in the world at 73 metres (239.5 feet) tall.

On 30 January 1848 Pfeiffer left Delhi without a European companion by bullock cart heading south on an ambitious attempt to cross northern India to Bombay. Her journey was arranged by the Austrian scholar, Dr Aloys Sprenger, who sent one of his most trusted servants to accompany her. Nevertheless it was a frightening prospect. This part of her journey was outside British territory, often far from any Europeans and she did not speak the local languages.

Along the way she saw many poppy plantations. The opium mass produced here was destined for China in exchange for the tea that was then so valuable in Britain and Europe. On 11 February she reached Kota on the left bank of the broad Chambal River, the chief city of a princely state of Rajpootana. There she was assisted by the British resident, Captain Burdon, and a surgeon, Dr Rolland. Hearing of the arrival of such a unique traveller, the Rajah, Ram-Singh, graciously sent Pfeiffer baskets of fruit and his own elephant so that she could be given a tour about the thriving town with its many colourful temples and mosques.

Perhaps somewhat unusually, Pfeiffer was invited to witness the first surgical operation in the region to use ether. It was the first substance, apart from unreliable alcohol or opium, capable of rendering a patient unconscious during surgery. Ether had only been publically demonstrated to function as the world's first anaesthesia in the USA in 1845. That a man in an Indian princely state should be given ether in early 1848 demonstrates a remarkably rapid diffusion of a new medical technology.

Pfeiffer described the scene of the experimental use of ether:

A large tumour was to be extracted from the neck of a native. Unfortunately the inhalation did not turn out as was expected: the patient came to again after the first incision, and began shrieking fearfully. I hastily left the room, for I pitied the poor creature too much to bear his cries. The operation indeed was successful, but the man suffered considerable pain.[142]

Having surveyed the landscape and all the sights, Pfeiffer set off south again, first on camels and then riding in a palanquin. As *Blackwood's Edinburgh Magazine* would later comment, "she has a perfect mania for locomotion". She was always on the move, driven ever on and on.[143]

Once again the assistance of those she had met, the Rajah and Dr Rolland, greatly eased her next steps. At one stop she found some tents and servants of Captain Burdon's waiting for her convenience. Fatigued from a long stretch of travel, she immediately went into one of the tents to rest. Without any warning, a maid entered the tent and, to Pfeiffer's confused astonishment, "commenced kneading me about with her hands". Wide-eyed and speechless at this unimaginable over-familiarity, Pfeiffer was about to protest when the maid explained that this treatment, which we would call massage, would be refreshing. "For a quarter of an hour she pressed my body from head to foot vigorously, and it certainly produced a good effect—I found myself much relieved and strengthened."[144]

But not all attentions were welcome. At another stop for the night Pfeiffer was annoyed to find "half of the inhabitants of the town gathered round me, and watched all my motions and doings with the greatest attention". She was tired and very annoyed with being stared at so finally, "I afforded them an opportunity of studying the appearance of an angry European female, as I was very much displeased with my people [servants], and, in spite of my slight knowledge of the language, scolded them heartily."[145]

It was 8 a.m. on 3 March when Pfeiffer reached Ajanta in the princely state of Hyderabad. She had letters of introduction to a British officer, Captain Robert Gill. He was just the man to help. Gill had arrived at Ajanta in 1844 and devoted himself to the study of the famous manmade caves there.

When they met, Captain Gill had to inform Pfeiffer that she had already come too far along the way to visit the Ajanta Caves. No matter, she grabbed a horse and rode back. The thirty or so caves are chiselled along a massive crescent shaped cliff face. "Caves" is a misleading term because they are actually Buddhist temples and monuments cut into the living rock. Dating back to the second century BCE, the magnificent ruins were accidentally rediscovered in 1819 by a British officer on a hunting party. In addition to their breathtaking colonnaded halls adorned with exquisite stone carvings are many superb and almost miraculously well-preserved wall paintings. It was these that Captain Gill was labouring to copy and preserve for posterity. Many of the colourful scenes depict large groups of people, their heads tilted at thoughtful angles and their elliptical eyes accented by black eyeliner. The rich colours of yellow and deep earthy brown are still vivid. Some scenes portray the early life of the Buddha. Others show processions of men mounted on elephants, scenes of courtly life or female figures with characteristically narrow waists and full, rounded, protruding breasts.

When Gill completed a painting he would forward it on to Bombay and thence to London and the overcrowded India Museum. For over twenty years he would continue his painstaking work. Tragically, in 1866 all but a handful of his paintings were destroyed by a fire at the Crystal Palace Exhibition.

Pfeiffer browsed through the galleries for several hours. She was awed by the magnificent spectacle. "It appears incredible that human hands should have been able to execute such masterly and gigantic works," she declared. Tired and hungry at the end of her tour, she was delighted to find that the thoughtful Captain Gill had sent her "a choice tiffin, together with table and chairs, into this wilderness".[146]

She also hoped to see the famous hilltop fortress of Devagiri at Daulatabad 120 kilometres south of Ajanta. The fourteenth-century fortress is perched on a near vertical tower of rock jutting 200 metres above the plain below and accessible only via a narrow tunnel cut through the rock itself. It was never taken by force. In Pfeiffer's day no one was admitted without the permission of the commander of Auranjabad. To save her the trouble, the kindly Captain Gill sent a courier seventy miles to obtain a permission card. Pfeiffer was touched. "I looked upon all these attentions as the more obliging, as they were shown to me—a German woman, without distinction or attractions—by English people." The card would be sent to meet her at her next destination, Ellora.

Pfeiffer travelled in a humble ox cart for two days. One night, at the town of Roja, she even slept on the ground under the eaves of the house of local people. The following morning, 6 March, she mounted a horse to visit the equally renowned caves or rather rock-hewn Buddhist temples of Ellora built during the sixth to the ninth centuries. The temple complex stretches for over a mile and consists of thirty-four cave temples and monasteries.

Before she could commence her tour she encountered a group of European gentlemen who were setting out on elephants for a tiger hunt. They invited her along. Of course she could not resist this unexpected adventure. Taking her place in a howdah perched on top of one of the elephants, they marched slowly and silently swaying on. The gentlemen were armed with guns of course, but they gave Pfeiffer a large knife "to defend myself with, in case the animal should spring too high and reach the side of the howdah". In the end the party did bag two tigers. Like the snake fight in Singapore, her account of the half-hour battle with tigers is hard to believe. She admits that she was frightened but as usual, concealed her fears, "I kept myself so calm, that none of the gentlemen had any suspicion of what was going on in my mind."[147]

Pfeiffer visited the Ellora caves or temple complex the following day and they quite understandably took her breath away, even if, like almost all tourists then and now, she did not really understand what she was seeing. Size, symmetry and ornate craftsmanship can impress all on their own. It's the same with tourists in a European cathedral who admire the size and intricacy of the construction but who have no knowledge of the symbolic meanings of the design or iconography. Pfeiffer wrote that the largest temple at Ellora, Kailasanatha, "is the most wonderful of all those which are hewn out of the rock. It surpasses, in magnitude and finish, the best specimens of Indian architecture; it is, indeed, affirmed to have claims to precedence over the marvellous buildings of the ancient Egyptians."[148] Indeed, the Kailasanatha temple is the largest monolithic structure carved from solid stone in the world. Scrambling around the ruins with only a native guide, Pfeiffer was the polar opposite of the timid, if fictional, Miss Quested in E. M. Forster's novel *A Passage to India* (1924). Such an unsinkable character as Pfeiffer could never have faltered in the Marabar Caves.

After climbing to the top of the fortress of Daulatabad, Pfeiffer continued her journey westwards, meeting friendly hosts and guides and seeing as much of the local sights and people as she could. At last she reached Bombay by the middle of March. She could reflect with pride and satisfaction that in seven weeks "I had safely completed the long and tedious journey" across India from Delhi to Bombay. And she made certain to acknowledge her debts in the ensuing book:

> I was especially indebted to the English officials, who afforded me both advice and assistance; their humanity, their cordial friendliness I shall ever remember. I again offer them my most sincere and warmest thanks; and the greatest compliment which I can pay them is the wish that my own countrymen, the Austrian consuls and ambassadors, resembled them![149]

At Bombay Pfeiffer was hosted by the Hamburg consul, Hermann Wattenbach. In addition to seeing the usual sights she succeeded in being introduced to some wealthy Parsee families and was able to visit their homes. Pfeiffer's squinting eyes also carefully studied the dress, lifestyle and public funerals of Hindus with great interest. The local newspaper, *The British Indian Gentleman,* announced that currently in Bombay was "a courageous lady who is the most travelled of her sex in the entire world. ... We don't know the motives of her journey, whether female curiosity or not — but this heroism deserves the admiration of all men, and might as well excite the envy of her sex."[150]

And then came some surprising news from Europe. The greatest political upheaval for a generation had occurred. Pfeiffer learned with astonishment of the so-called February Revolution in Paris in which King Louis Philippe I abdicated and a liberal opposition came to power that promised universal male suffrage and relief for the unemployed. Like a match to a powder keg, the Paris revolution's effects or inspiration would explode outward, influencing at least fifty nations – resulting in the revolutions of 1848.

Ida of Arabia

But Europe was still a very long way away. Pfeiffer still had half the globe to traverse and new lands and peoples to explore. On 23 April 1848 she left Bombay on a small 40-horsepower steamer, the *Sir Charles Forbes*, under Captain Lichfield, which was crammed with 124 passengers. Only two were European. Pfeiffer's opinion of the comfort of English steamers was certainly not improved by the experience of spending the entire journey on deck amidst a crowd of other passengers packed so close that she was afraid of being stepped on when she lay down to rest or sleep. Three passengers died of smallpox during the voyage.

The survivors arrived at Basra, Assyria, then part of the Ottoman Empire (now Iraq), at the head of the Persian Gulf, on 12 May. There was no hotel and the man to whom Pfeiffer had brought a letter of introduction declined to help her. Fortunately, Captain Lichfield let her stay on the ship. A few days later Captain Johns of the British military steamer *Nitocris*, agreed to take her on to Baghdad as his guest, that is, for free. For all her brazen courage, Pfeiffer obviously benefited from being a European woman since she so often received special treatment as in this case, free accommodation followed by a free ticket. Surely no local woman would have received such assistance, nor indeed a European man.

Once in Baghdad, Pfeiffer procured an izar, the local female costume, which she described as "a large linen wrapper ... a small fez, and a kerchief, which, wound round the fez, forms a little turban" but she would not wear the "thick, stiff mask, made of horse-hair, which covers the face ... I pitied the poor women greatly, who were often obliged to carry a child, or some other load, or perhaps even to wash linen in the river ... In my Oriental dress I could walk about without any covering on my face, perfectly uninterrupted."[151]

She explored the city but found its single-storey mud brick houses with their backs to the street uninteresting. The bazaars and "miserable" coffee stalls were no more impressive than the mediocre public buildings. Only after she had climbed "with great difficulty" the dome of the Haydar Khana Mosque could she properly survey Baghdad and the view impressed her. She described what she saw:

> It is impossible to form any idea of an Oriental town by passing through the narrow and uniform streets, no matter how often, as these are all alike ... But, from above, I looked down over the whole town, with its innumerable houses, many of which are situated in pretty gardens. I saw thousands and thousands of terraces spread at my feet, and before all, the beautiful river, rolling on through dark orchards and palm groves, to the town, which extends along its banks for five miles.

She toured several houses and described their layout and even which rooms were occupied at different times of day because of the heat. And at night, she reported, "people sleep on the terraces under mosquito nets, which surround the whole bed."[152] She was allowed to visit the harem of the pasha but found the women so excited to see her and chatty that she was soon exhausted. Pfeiffer thought none of them beauties but was very impressed with the local custom of shaping the eyebrows into a gentle curve which, together with mascara, increased the brightness of the eye to such an extent that "no young man could glance at with impunity". This visit and one to a public bath for women shocked Pfeiffer's feelings as she felt that the young women were exposed to too much indecent conversation of the older women. Shocking, too, was the familiarity with which the servants sat and drank coffee and smoked with their mistresses after a meal.

After thoroughly acquainting herself with Baghdad, Pfeiffer made two excursions away from it on horseback. She visited the ruins of the ancient city of Ctesiphon on the eastern bank of the Tigris where the still impressive high-arched palace, the Taq Kasra, still remains. Ctesiphon fell into decay after the Battle of Ctesiphon in 363 CE between the forces of Roman Emperor Julian and Shapur II of the Sassanian Empire. After inspecting the ruins, Pfeiffer, accompanied by an interpreter, decided to walk over to some tents along the river. All of a sudden, she was approached by a servant who pointed to a very pretty tent and explained that a prince was staying there and had extended an invitation to Pfeiffer to visit.

She gladly accepted and was politely received. Pfeiffer thought the young prince was very handsome. Her spelling of his name is nonsensical, but he was apparently Prince Emam Qoli Mirza, son of a famous Persian Prince of the Qajar Dynasty. Through the interpreter she learned that he lived in Baghdad but was staying by the river for a time to escape the heat. The prince sat on a low divan while his companions reclined on carpets. Pfeiffer was much flattered when the prince asked her to sit on the divan beside him.

The ensuing conversation became ever more friendly and animated and as the prince learned about Pfeiffer's travels his astonishment was unbounded. A beautifully ornamented hookah was placed before them. Out of politeness for her host, Pfeiffer took a few puffs from it. Then tea and coffee were served and afterwards the prince invited her to dinner. This was a sumptuous affair and Pfeiffer observed every detail of how her hosts ate with the right hand from certain dishes and so forth. After dinner the prince, despite being a Muslim, served wine. When the prince learned that Pfeiffer planned to visit Persia next, he immediately wrote her a letter of introduction to his mother, who was at court there. But, he asked her with a smile, could Pfeiffer please say nothing about the wine?

Pfeiffer was allowed to visit the prince's wife, secluded nearby in a small ruined mosque. The interpreter was not allowed to enter. Pfeiffer thought the young woman was as beautiful as an angel. But she could only look at the angel since they did not know a word of each other's languages.

Two days later, Pfeiffer set out from Baghdad for the ruins of Babylon. Days of riding through the desert saw the thermometer reaching 134°F (56°C) with a hot wind constantly blowing sand into her face. The ruins consisted mostly of huge piles of fallen and broken brick, many as large as hills. She stayed with a wealthy Arab who provided her with a secluded terrace as a bedroom and sent up a sumptuous meal. From her eyrie Pfeiffer watched the local woman in their small courtyards below making bread and doing other chores. At supper time the men, women and children seated themselves on straw mats, but, to Pfeiffer's disbelief, rather than eat, the women fanned their husbands while they ate.

On 1 June 1848 Pfeiffer proceeded to the ruins of Birs Nimrud (or Borsippa). It looked like a hill with a ruined tower on top, in the middle of featureless desert. It was in fact the remains of a once gigantic ziggurat.

On the return journey to Baghdad, Pfeiffer was accompanied

by a local soldier for protection. Still riding long after midnight, a sound was heard and the small group halted in fear. Pfeiffer was told to keep still while the soldier crawled off over the sand to reconnoitre. Despite the danger, Pfeiffer began to nod off. Soon the soldier reappeared in high spirits. There was no danger of robbers, it was a sheikh with his retinue on their way to Baghdad. Pfeiffer's little troupe galloped after to join them. The sheikh greeted Pfeiffer with a gesture to his forehead and breast. The following morning she arrived safely in Baghdad.

Pfeiffer's visits to these archaeological sites were facilitated by the British resident, Major Henry Creswicke Rawlinson. Because of his pioneering work in transcribing and deciphering ancient cuneiform inscriptions he is now known as the father of Assyriology.

He told Pfeiffer that there had been a revolution in Austria. Pfeiffer was incredulous. "My comfortable, peace-loving Austrians, and an overthrow of the government!" Rawlinson had to show Pfeiffer the newspaper before she would believe it. "No news had astonished me so much in my whole life,"[153] she recalled. Inspired by the news of the February Revolution in Paris, uprisings in Vienna led to the resignation of the conservative State Chancellor and Foreign Minister, Prince von Metternich. In short order he fled the country. The detested state censorship was repealed. A provisional constitutional national assembly was planned according to democratic principles. Pfeiffer was pleased with the peaceful intentions and enlightened liberal goals of the revolution of 1848 as it came to be known.

Pfeiffer wished to travel next to Mosul, 420 kilometres to the north near the head of the Tigris river. Mosul is near the site of the famous battle of Gaugamela where Alexander the Great defeated the much larger Persian army of Darius III in 331 BCE.

The cheapest way to get there was via caravan. She was advised not to go alone and at least take a servant, but Pfeiffer thought she could not afford one and was at any rate confident she could manage. Her contacts helped her to join a caravan of twelve Arabs and twenty-six animals which was about to leave. Pfeiffer procured a mule for herself. After the usual frustrating delays, the caravan sauntered forth across the desert on the 17th. It was a breathtakingly bold, even foolhardy step. Pfeiffer herself seems to have realised this, at least eventually. As she later wrote:

> In this way I entered upon a fourteen days' journey through deserts and steppes, a journey full of difficulties and dangers, without any convenience, shelter, or protection. I travelled like the poorest Arab, and was obliged, like him, to be content to bear the most burning sun, with no food but bread and water, or, at the most, a handful of dates, or some cucumbers, and with the hot ground for a bed.[154]

At one of the stops along the way, she stayed in the house of her guide and his father, the owner of the caravan. Once again Pfeiffer was mobbed by local women who were fascinated to see the unprecedented sight of a European female. But Pfeiffer was not amused,

> all the women of the place flocked round me to stare at the stranger. They first commenced examining my clothes, then wanted to take the turban off my head, and were at last so troublesome, that it was only by force that I could get any rest. I seized one of them sharply by the arm, and turned her out of the door so quickly, that she was overcome before she knew what I was going to do. I signified to the others that I would serve them the same. Perhaps they thought me stronger than I was, for they retired immediately.

After eight days of eating only bread and cucumbers, Pfeiffer was delighted to see a cauldron of mutton put on the fire by the mother of the family. But when Pfeiffer saw how the meal was being prepared her appetite vanished. The mother put several handfuls of grain and onions into a pan of water. About half an hour later she mixed it all together with her dirty hands. Occasionally she took a mouthful, chewed it and then spit it back into the bowl. Later she took a dirty rag and strained away the juice and poured the rest over the mutton in the pot. Pfeiffer resolved that there was no way she would eat this.

Yet, despite the blow to her appetite, "when it was ready it gave out such an agreeable odour, and my hunger was so great, that I broke my resolution, and remembered how many times I had eaten of food the preparation of which was not a whit cleaner. What was so bad in the present instance was that I had seen the whole process."[155] Nevertheless, she found it delicious and nourishing.

In the end she made the journey successfully, surviving two attempted robberies. At Mosul she was assisted by the British Vice-Consul, Hormuzd Rassam. Unlike other such residents, Rassam was a native Assyrian, born to a Christian family in Mosul. Still only twenty-two years old, Rassam would become a pioneering archaeologist of the region. His most important discovery would come just five years later – the cuneiform clay tablets that record the oldest written narrative poem in the world, the *Epic of Gilgamesh*.

In the story, Gilgamesh undertakes a long and perilous journey to discover the secret of eternal life. It is a tale not without parallel in Pfeiffer's own life, for an epic journey if not immortality. The tablets also recounted a myth of a flood sent by the gods, written 1,000 years before the biblical story of Noah. This discovery, together with the ever more sophisticated biblical scholarship in Germany and elsewhere, would eventually reveal historical explanations for the traditional Judeo-Christian stories.

Rassam arranged for Pfeiffer to be able to tour the town and its environs and the ruins of Nineveh. There she took away "my greatest treasure, a small relief" of a human head. In earlier centuries it was of course entirely normal to carry away souvenirs from ancient sites. When we visit ancient ruins today it is important to remember that they have suffered not just from fire, earthquakes, war and time, but the plunder of centuries of visitors and local residents. Hence what we see today tends to be the solid fragments that were simply too big to be carried off or knocked over.

On 8 July 1848 Pfeiffer set out with another caravan. Rather than ride side-saddle, she rode astride as other women in the region did. A western contemporary observed that she rode with "her small trunk being slung on one side of the animal, and her scanty bed on the other".[156] This time she was told she could hope to meet no more Europeans. She took a letter from Rassam to help. For once she had to admit, "I started on this journey with some feelings of anxiety, and scarcely dared to hope for a fortunate termination. On that account I sent my papers and manuscripts from here to Europe, so that in case I was robbed or murdered my diary would at least come into the hands of my sons."[157]

The journey was long and toilsome and at some of the villages where they halted, Pfeiffer had to endure the usual intrusive attention of people who were amazed to see a European woman. Sometimes it was too much.

> To be continually stared at in this way was one of the greatest inconveniences of my journey. Sometimes I quite lost my patience, when the women and children pressed round me, handling my clothes and head. Although quite alone among them, I gave them several slight blows with my riding-whip. This always had the desired effect; the people either went away altogether or drew back in a ring.[158]

In a later stage of her journey Pfeiffer was stuck in the little town of Sauj Bulak where she stayed with a local Christian family. She bore a letter to a Persian merchant who proved helpful and wise. But she could not rest, she needed to move on. "I daily entreated the Persian merchant to help me to go on further, even if the journey should be attended with some danger. He shook his head and explained to me, that there was no caravan going, and that if I travelled alone I might expect either to be shot or beheaded." Such a warning would give most people more than a little pause.

Pfeiffer bore this forced intermission for as long as she could – five days. At last she entreated the merchant to hire her a horse and a guide to take her to Urmia where there were some Christian missionaries. At length the merchant brought her a "wild-looking" Kurdish man who would be her guide. He was to take Pfeiffer to Urmia on a journey of three days. Feeling apprehensive the evening before starting out, Pfeiffer confessed: "I put my pistols in proper order, and made up my mind not to sell my life cheaply."[159]

She almost needed them. While crossing the wild Kurdish mountains one evening, a caravanner pointed to the tassel hanging from her Turkish fez. He indicated with gestures that he fancied it and that she should give it to him. She shook her head. The man then drew his finger across his neck in a threatening manner to say "give me the tassel as you value your head". Pfeiffer somehow "talked" her way out with gestures.[160] One wonders why she didn't chose to brandish her pistols? Perhaps that would have been her measure of last resort.

Several times during the next few days, her Kurdish guide would halt to encamp when Pfeiffer could see no need. At one place they stopped almost the entire day, apparently waiting for a caravan to come along. She was growing desperate at the apparent lethargy of her guide. He would not obey her. At last she snapped.

> It was now necessary that I should make a strenuous effort to show the fellow that I would not be treated like a child, and remain here as long as he thought fit. Unfortunately I could not scold him in

words, but I picked up the mantle and threw it at his feet, and explained to him that I would keep the remainder of the fare if he did not bring me to Oromia to-morrow on the third day. I then turned my back to him (one of the greatest slights), seated myself on the ground, and, resting my head in my hands, gave myself up to the most melancholy reflections.

She wept. Although he only wanted to rest his tired horses, the obstinate guide's heart, according to his own account, "was irresistibly subdued".

Finally, on the evening of 30 July 1848 Pfeiffer arrived in Urmia, in what is now West Azerbaijan, Iran. The Kurdish guide took her to the house of the missionaries. One of the house servants asked her who she was and what she wanted. Not understanding the language, Pfeiffer simply pointed upstairs. The servant ran up the stairs to find the American missionary, the Rev. Dr Austin Wright. The thirty-eight-year-old had been in Urmia for eight years and spoke all of the local languages fluently. The servant burst in on him and exclaimed that there was a woman in the street "who knew no language, and was entirely unattended, except by a Koordish muleteer".[161] Wright was more than astonished, he was incredulous.

Still waiting below, Pfeiffer asked another servant who stood staring at her for a glass of water, in English. Dumbfounded, the servant bolted upstairs like one possessed. He rushed to Dr Wright to announce that the woman in the street spoke English! Wright could not believe there could be "a lady in European costume, speaking English, in the street, at night, and unattended, in this remote, barbarous land, where the appearance of a European man is a thing of very rare occurrence". And yet it was true.

Dr Wright welcomed her warmly. He later recalled that although "she had rode ... from 1 o'clock, A. M., till eight o'clock, P. M., at the wearisome rate of a caravan, over a very dry, hot, dusty region, a distance of near sixty miles, still, on her arrival, she seemed little tired—was buoyant and cheerful as a lark."

Dr Wright and his family were delighted to host this unexpected visitor at their large and luxurious country house perched on a hill six miles from the town. During their conversations over the next day Wright and his family eagerly listened to Madame Pfeiffer's whole story. They were amazed and delighted with this quiet, simple-looking lady who had travelled all alone to the Holy Land, Iceland, Brazil, China, India, almost around the entire world.

Pfeiffer recounted the knife attack in Brazil and pointed to the scar between her left shoulder and elbow. As for the attacker, she boasted that she had "cut off three of his fingers". This was an outrageous exaggeration. Using a pen knife as she did, one would need a cutting board and a good bit of sawing to sever a finger. She joked that she had a male companion (von Berchtold) but, "finding that she was obliged to protect him instead of his protecting her, she left him and proceeded entirely alone".

And how much did it cost to travel so far her enthralled listeners asked? Her entire world journey thus far had cost about $1,000 she said. In addition to travelling, she was making large collections of insects and flowers and was clearly driven, her hosts could tell, simply by "a passion for travel" – wanderlust.

A report of this extraordinary encounter, written by Wright's colleague, the Rev. Justin Perkins, was later published in the *New York Observer*. To stimulate his readers' curiosity he asked rhetorically "who, then, is Madamme Pfeiffer? She is a German lady, fifty-one years old, of great intelligence, and most perfect accomplishments, and, to appearance, thoroughly sane on every subject unless it be her style of travelling, which is at least somewhat peculiar." Somewhat indeed. This report was widely reprinted in other American newspapers and was yet another way in which Pfeiffer's international fame increased.

The helpful Dr Wright found a "courageous and trusty guide" to accompany Pfeiffer on the next leg of her journey, crossing mountains and skirting the salt lake, Urmia. When she reached Tabriz, the capital of Azerbaijan, on 4 August 1848, Pfeiffer was taken to a man who spoke English, Dr Robert Cassolani, "a courteous, intelligent old gentleman".[162] Cassolani was from Malta and worked as head of the lazaretto and was physician to the Vicegerent. He too was utterly astonished. "How did you come here, alone? Have you been robbed?" he asked in astonishment. Pfeiffer explained her story but "he appeared scarcely to believe me. He thought it bordered upon the fabulous that a woman should have succeeded, without any knowledge of the language, in penetrating through such countries and such people."[163]

It was "the fast month" of Ramadan but as always Pfeiffer saw whatever she could. Through the assistance of Dr Cassolani she was able to meet many local families and visit their homes. She was even presented to the Vicegerent, Bahman Mirza, and allowed privately to meet the young princess. Which one would be hard to determine since Bahman Mirza would eventually have sixteen wives and thirty daughters.

Pfeiffer's successful traverse of the deserts from Baghdad would strike many readers of her travels and the hundreds of newspapers around the world that reported on her exploits as one of her greatest feats. It also seemed to be one of the most dangerous situations she had ever been in. She could so easily have been robbed, raped or killed. In a newspaper interview in America she would later pay homage to the Muslim people who had kindly aided her, while at the same time taking yet another stab at the wrong sort of Christians she had so often encountered. "She paid a warm tribute to the followers of Mahomet, their noble hospitality and truth. Travelling among them; that is, the Turks, Arabs, &c., she said: 'I was apparently poor, but the women treated me like a mother; the men with honor and honesty; but in the same circumstances and conditions among Christians, quite different—quite different!'"[164]

Pfeiffer next hoped to travel north to Nakhchivan, Armenia. This didn't seem possible as she knew, because, owing to the recent "political disturbances in Europe, the Russian government, like the Chinese, had strictly prohibited the entrance of any foreigners". However, Mr Stevens, the British consul "promised to make use of all his power with the Russian consul, Mr. Anitschow, in my favour". And it worked. "I was indebted to this, together with my sex and age, for being made an exception. I received from the Russian consul not only the permission, but also several kind letters of introduction to people at Natschivan, Erivan, and Tiflis."[165] (Now Nakhchivan, Yerevan and Tbilisi.) Perhaps Russia held an extra attraction because her hero, von Humboldt, had travelled there.

And so Pfeiffer set out on horseback on 11 August 1848 for Nakhchivan, 180 kilometres to the north. She arrived there on the 13th. When she reached the custom house she was in for an unpleasant experience. First, the inspector told her to go inside. To Pfeiffer's surprise, the inspector's wife and sister followed her. "I was much astonished at this politeness, but found, however, too soon that other reasons had induced them to come." The two ladies each pulled up a chair so that they could get a better view of the opening of Pfeiffer's portmanteau by the inspector. As soon as it was opened, "three pair of hands were thrust in". All of her private things were taken out, opened, inspected, and tossed about very recklessly out of pure nosiness.

Poor Madame Pfeiffer. How she burned with indignation at this insult, and she could not help noticing "that the inspector's wife had some difficulty in parting with" some of the things when it was time to return them to the bag. When they came to her box containing the brick souvenir, a man took an axe to break it open. To this Pfeiffer finally objected. At this moment a German lady came in and Pfeiffer was able to explain that she did not object to the box being opened, but wished they would open it carefully. "I could not help laughing at the foolish faces which both the women and the customs' officer made when they saw the fragments of brick from Babylon and the somewhat damaged Ninevite head. They could not at all comprehend why I should carry such objects with me." A small stone from Babylon with cuneiform writing, which Pfeiffer took to be a seal, was among these objects.[166]

Pfeiffer spent a few days in Nakhchivan, during which she viewed the supposed grave of the biblical Noah. The small stone monument was surrounded by a low wall. "Many pilgrims come here," she wrote. "Mahomedans as well as Christians; and both sects entertain the remarkable belief, that if they press a stone into the wall while thinking of something at the same time, and the stone remains sticking to the wall, that their thoughts are either true or will come to pass, and the reverse when the stone does not adhere."[167] In fact, Pfeiffer could clearly see that the mortar was always rather moist and if a stone was pushed into it the right way, it would stick.

The Noah grave legend didn't fool Pfeiffer. It's hardly surprising given her sceptical attitude to the scores of apocryphal holy sites that had been eagerly, and not disinterestedly, pointed out to her in Palestine. There are in fact several purported graves of Noah. Belief in the Nakhchivan grave is particularly recent. The Armenians converted to Christianity in the year 301 CE and Armenian literature dates back to the fifth century, but the Noah grave stories only emerged many, many centuries later as pious Christians explained local features according to their holy book.

Having seen enough, Pfeiffer joined a caravan of Tartars heading for Tbilisi on the evening of 17 August. Four days later she was swept up in one last unexpected adventure. When her caravan was encamped, Pfeiffer took a stroll about fifty paces back to the post road. It was about 8 o'clock in the evening. She heard the sound of post horses approaching. A carriage containing a Russian and a Cossack rattled by. Thinking nothing of it, Pfeiffer turned to go back to the caravan. In an instant the carriage skidded to a halt and the Cossack jumped out and seized Pfeiffer by the arms and started to drag her to the carriage. In vain she pointed to the caravan and shouted that she belonged to it. The Cossack immediately put his hand over her mouth and threw her into the carriage while the Russian held her down firmly. The driver then cracked his whip and the carriage bolted on.

When out of earshot of the caravan they uncovered her mouth and asked who she was and where she was from. Pfeiffer understood enough Russian to reply, but they did not believe her. They demanded her passport. She told them that it remained in her portmanteau at the encampment. Her captors took her to the post house where she was held at gunpoint in a cold cell with no food or water. She was not even allowed to stand up or pace about. In the morning her bag was brought and she was able to show her papers. Since she had the proper documents, they released her. Far from apologizing, her overzealous captors just pointed at her and laughed. As before, there was some slight possibility of revenge when she could write about these injustices in her book, though the offending officials probably never heard of it again.

Her freedom restored, Pfeiffer rejoined her caravan and by 24 August 1848 had reached Yerevan, the capital of Armenia. There she had a letter to a Dr Müller, a German, who helped her to get through the incredibly overly complicated bureaucratic mess of a certificate of permission to travel on the Russian post network. With this finally obtained she set off in a post carriage on the 26th. It was an exceedingly uncomfortable vehicle, drawn by three horses abreast and open above and, incredibly, with no seats. Bouncing around in the back, Pfeiffer found that "it requires some care to avoid being thrown out".[168]

The delays, incompetence, and lethargy she experienced on the Russian postal route nearly drove her mad. "Officers, as well as servants, are frequently found at all hours of the day sleeping or drunk." But when an official or officer arrived at a post station, everyone looked busy or could be seen "cringing round the watering-place for fear of flogging". Sometimes she would arrive at a post station to find that all the fresh horses had been taken by an officer and his friends returning from a hunt. Exasperated, Pfeiffer wished she could deal with them as they deserved. "I should have best liked to have spoken to these people with a stick. No idea can be formed of their stupidity, coarseness, and want of feeling."[169]

On 29 August, covered in mud thrown up by the wheels of the carriage, she reached Tbilisi, the capital of Georgia, with letters to the chancellor-director and the governor. When she met them she was quick to give them a piece of her mind about the post system and the treatment she had endured.

My free expression of opinion, perhaps, did not suit them. I made no scruple of speaking my mind ... I, moreover, related my imprisonment, with a few comments; and, what crowned all, I said that I had intended to have gone on from here across the Caucasus to Moscow and Petersburgh, but that I had been completely deterred from doing so by my short experience of travelling in the country, and would take the shortest road to get beyond the frontier as soon as possible. If I had been a man and had spoken so, I should probably have been treated with a temporary residence in Siberia.

Always curious, always eager to see as much of a place as she could, she managed to visit some Greek and Armenian families before moving on.

After Tbilisi, the halting and inefficient stages on the post road continued. After many stops, halts, delays, cheating landlords and boat journeys, she at last reached Redut Kale (Kulevi), a Russian fort on the east coast of the Black Sea. From here she took the 140-horsepower steamer *Maladetz* across the Black Sea. She went on to Kerch, on the Kerch Peninsula in the east of the Crimea and changed steamer. The next stop was Sevastopol on the 29th where she admired the "strong and beautiful fortress" which would be the scene of such bloodshed, suffering and devastation six years later during the Crimean War. Another intrepid lady, Florence Nightingale, would make her own name there as the Victorian heroine of modern nursing.

On 30 September Pfeiffer reached Odessa on the northwest side of the Black Sea. The climate was now so cold that the vegetation had died back to its dull wintery state. It was a great relief to reach this final stop in the Russian Empire. But there would be yet more frustration.

> On leaving the Russian dominions I had as much trouble with the passport regulations as on entering. The passport which was obtained on entering must be changed for another for which two silver roubles are paid. Besides this, the traveller's name has to be three times printed in the newspaper, so that if he has debts, his creditors may know of his departure. With these delays it takes at least eight days, frequently, however, two or three weeks to get away; it is not, however, necessary to wait for these forms, if the traveller provides security.[170]

With this last wrangle with the many-headed hydra of Russian red tape, Pfeiffer was free at last. Boarding the Russian steamer *Odessa* on 3 October, she headed for Constantinople. But she had one last Russian insult to enjoy. As the night was very mild, she left the stifling cabin below and went up on deck and began to sleep in the fresh air, wrapped in her mantle. "One of the sailors came, and giving me a kick with his foot, told me to leave the place. I thanked him quietly for the delicate way in which he expressed himself, and requesting him to leave me at peace, continued to sleep."[171] One wonders if she was quite so temperate at the time.

In Constantinople Pfeiffer found that her friendly boarding-house keeper, Madame Balbiani, had moved away so she stayed briefly in a hotel. She left Constantinople on the evening of 7 October 1848 on the French steamer *Scamander*. By the 22nd she had reached Athens. The climate was now hot and sunny and the countryside seemed parched and thirsty. Pfeiffer had planned to stay in Athens for eight days to see the famous monuments and ruins of classical antiquity.

But almost as soon as she arrived she heard the news from Vienna – yet another revolution. The October Crisis had broken out. The newspapers reported street violence and attacks on Austrian troops in her beloved Vienna. She felt compelled to return home to her family as soon as possible. Before she could leave there was just enough time to visit the Acropolis and to ponder the partially tumbled marble columns of the incomparable Parthenon whose "ruins excite the astonishment of the world".

The Parthenon had stood remarkably intact until 1687 when it was blown up in a catastrophic explosion. The Ottoman Turks were using the building as a gunpowder magazine while under siege by the Venetian army. A Venetian mortar shell struck the building and detonated the gunpowder. The terrible explosion and the massive looting that followed in subsequent days and years produced the appearance of the ruin as it is today. Such are the whips and scorns of time which turn proud monuments of one age into neglected old buildings in another. Like antiques, only those that manage to pass through a long period of being the worthless old junk of yesteryear, can emerge into a time when they are instead valued as precious traces of a time long gone.

On 24 October 1848 Pfeiffer left Athens on the small 70-horsepower steamer *Baron Kübeck*. She would have fully sympathised with the annoyance to modern tourists of having to change train or plane: "nothing is more unpleasant in travelling than changing the conveyance".[172] After just a few more changes she finally arrived at Trieste on the 30th and hastened on by express coach to Vienna the following day.

When she finally returned home after more than two years away, Pfeiffer was relieved to find all of her family and friends were unharmed. Her circumnavigation of the globe was an astonishing achievement. Even Austria's navy would not manage to go all the way around the world until the SMS *Novara* expedition in 1859. Newspapers excitedly reported that the famous traveller Ida Pfeiffer had just returned home after surviving incredible adventures.

Pfeiffer was not the first woman to make it around the world. That distinction belongs to a young French woman named Jeanne Baret. She secretly joined the French naval expedition under Louis de Bougainville between 1766–1769. Although women were totally forbidden on navy ships, Baret was disguised as a young man and employed as the assistant of her secret partner, Philibert Commerson. (In Paris she had been his housekeeper.) As naturalist to the expedition, Commerson was given the captain's cabin on one of the expedition's two ships. This included its own toilet facilities which meant that Baret could avoid the head shared by the rest of the crew.

After visiting South America, the expedition landed at Tahiti where the Tahitians instantly and loudly recognised Baret as a woman and the secret was out. Commerson and Baret left the expedition at the island of Mauritius. Commerson died there in 1773. Baret then ran a tavern before eventually marrying a non-commissioned officer in the French Army with whom she eventually returned to France and thus completed the first ever circumnavigation of the globe by a woman. Bougainville's published journal first revealed Baret's extraordinary story.[173] What Pfeiffer achieved was to be the first woman to circle the globe by herself, rather than as a passenger on navy ships.

For Pfeiffer back home again it was time to begin the by now familiar process of turning her travel diary into a book. The diaries and papers covering her journey through Hindustan to Mosul, which she had sent home in case she died, took more than a year and a half to arrive and this delayed the completion of her book.

A Woman's Journey Round the World was published in 1850 in three volumes. For the first time, the book was also published simultaneously in London. Her first two voyages had made her famous in Vienna and Austria and other parts of German-speaking Europe. But her unprecedented and unbelievable journey around the world was orders of magnitude greater – and it impressed accordingly. Quite simply, the world voyage led to world fame.

What other book by a lone lady traveller could offer vivid first-hand descriptions of Brazilian vegetation, the gold mines and customs of the lower classes of Valparaiso as well as Chinese funerals and the Lantern festival in Singapore? Indeed no other could describe an elephant hunt in Ceylon, Hindu religious festivals, houses of the dead or Muslim and European marriage customs in India or the manner and dress of Bedouin tribes.

The following year, two independent English translations of *A Woman's Journey* appeared in Britain. A third illustrated edition followed in 1852 and further editions followed in subsequent years. One of the translations was also published in America. A Dutch translation was published in 1852 and French translations appeared from 1858. A Russian translation was published in Moscow in 1867. In the wake of the book's success, Pfeiffer's previous books were also translated and published in English that year. The intense interest in Pfeiffer's world journey is also reflected in the many reviews of *A Woman's Journey* that appeared from the *Magazin für die Literatur des Auslandes* in Leipzig to *Le Constitutionnel* in Paris. But the English reviews seemed to outnumber all the rest including the *Athenaeum, Westminster Review, Literary Gazette, Foreign Quarterly Review, Household Words, Blackwood's Edinburgh Magazine, Sharpe's London Magazine* and the *Eclectic Review.*

The *Athenaeum* called her journey "the boldest adventure of its kind" and the *Foreign Quarterly Review* declared it "an exploit which, all things considered, we may regard as unparalleled".[174] The *Economist* opined that "as a lesson of courage and forbearance, of active exertion and passive submission to slight and unavoidable evils, Madame Pfeiffer's book is of great value".[175]

Another British review pointed out the bold and dramatic fact that this Viennese lady had now seen more of the world than any woman who had ever lived. Surely a superlative of which Pfeiffer must have been very proud. One German literary magazine called her "one of the strangest characters not only of our times, but in all of history".[176] Indeed the *Foreign Quarterly Review* expressed sincere sympathy and admiration for what everybody knows but few articulate: "Every one who ventures to depart in any way from the beaten path in which the world expects him to travel, must, in most cases, make up his mind to have some unworthy motive attributed to him, and this is especially true with respect to women."[177]

The American writer Henry David Thoreau in his bucolic treatise on living a more natural life, *Walden* (1854), quoted her: "When Madam Pfeiffer, in her adventurous travels round the world, from east to west, had got so near home as Asiatic Russia, she says that she felt the necessity of wearing other than a travelling dress, when she went to meet the authorities, for she 'was now in a civilized country, where ... people are judged of by their clothes.'"[178]

The widowed English journalist and translator Jane Sinnett added a brief preface to her highly abridged edition of *A Woman's Journey*, remarking "we have often heard of late years of a certain, probably fabulous, creature, supposed to exist in the latitude of Berlin, and elsewhere, and denominated an 'emancipated woman:' nothing can be less like Madame Pfeiffer; yet truly she has emancipated herself in earnest—not from the fashions of gowns and petticoats, but from indolence, and vanity, and fear."[179] Even Charles Darwin's family wanted a copy. In her pocket diary for 1851, Darwin's wife Emma made a note, "Lady's voyage round world". She had seen a publisher's advertisement for the Sinnet translation and jotted a brief note to remember to order a copy.[180]

Pfeiffer was exceptional but she need not be seen as undermining conventions of femininity nor the predominant role of men in society. Indeed, she was certainly no proto-feminist. In short, she needn't be seen as off-putting or a threat. In fact she could be seen, by the sympathetic at least, as an inspiring example of individual self-improvement.

A London biographical dictionary of "Eminent Living Characters" quoted from a private letter from Pfeiffer to an unnamed friend. The editor of the dictionary wanted to correct "any erroneous idea of her womanly character which might have arisen from these details of more than feminine achievements". Her letter reads:

> I smile when I think of the many who, knowing me only through my travels, fancy that my character, manners, even my figure and

movements, are more like those of a man than a woman. How falsely do they judge me! But you, who know me, know that those who expect to find me six feet high, with a bold, imposing gait, and a dagger and pistol in my belt, discover in me the very reverse; and that in every-day life I am plainer, quieter, and more reserved than thousands of my own sex who have never left the seclusion of their native villages.[181]

But Pfeiffer's criticisms of what she saw and experienced often met with resentment. For example, in an otherwise very long and favourable review, Singapore's *Straits Times* took offence at her bashing of the P&O steamers. These were the pride of Singapore as well as its ultra-modern connection to the world.[182] An otherwise sympathetic writer in the *Calcutta Review* pointed out that Pfeiffer's description of the "Black Hole of Calcutta" and its monument were entirely erroneous. These are obvious symptoms of the well-known phenomena that those who know an area or topic don't like an interloper's description. The same writer found many other errors and no value in her portrayals of places so well known in India. Whereas the *Foreign Quarterly Review*, brimming with jingoistic loathing of the Russian Empire, highly approved of her criticisms of the evil empire in the east. Such sentiments would continue simmering until they boiled over in the Crimean War in 1853.

The weekly *Eliza Cook's Journal* was delighted with Pfeiffer's book and the intrepid exploits of this remarkable authoress. But surely, the review concluded, after such an extraordinary adventure "we should think [Pfeiffer] will not again trust her life to the accidents and dangers of foreign travel".[183] Wrong again.

CHAPTER 5

THE WORLD IS NOT ENOUGH (1851–1855)

"It was not long before I felt an irresistible longing to travel again about the world and to visit distant cities and islands."
Sindbad the Sailor[184]

Shortly before Pfeiffer returned home from her first world journey she wrote from Tbilisi to her sister Marie. The idea of returning to Vienna, she said, was like a schoolboy returning to the yoke of the schoolroom after the holidays.[185] Pfeiffer could not sit still at home for long. She made frequent short trips from Vienna to visit friends and relatives. More importantly, she devoted herself to a programme of preparation for another great voyage.

To fund another expedition, Pfeiffer carefully poured over columns of figures and lists of her natural history collections and the anticipated earnings from her new book. The Royal Museum of Vienna had purchased many of her specimens for 300 guilders. Pfeiffer reckoned that the travel costs of the last journey had been 2,914 guilders.[186] She asked P. Ferdinand Breunig, the custodian of the natural history collection of the Schotten Gymnasium, a private Catholic school, if they would like to purchase specimens from her collections.[187]

Once her specimens were sold and her book advance was cashed, she had made far less of a profit than she had hoped. Foreign translations were, at the time, very often pirated and so little or no income could be expected from them. There was not enough to begin another tour.

Another source of funding was needed to kick-start the next voyage. She pressed her contacts at the museum, such as the director of collections, Carl von Schreibers, and Josef von Arneth, for help. They appealed to the government on her behalf for funding on the grounds that she had proven herself enormously skilled at procuring many rare and valuable specimens for the collection from far-flung parts of the globe that the museum had no other way of sampling. Her collections included archaeological, ethnographic, zoological, botanical and mineralogical objects of great rarity. The application was successful and Ida Pfeiffer was awarded 1,500 guilders (£100) to facilitate her future travels for "scientific purposes".

Now a government-funded amateur collector, Pfeiffer began to visit more museums to find out what they needed and valued and to further her education on how to collect and prepare different kinds of specimens. Insects like beetles needed to be dried and pinned onto cork boards. Butterflies needed to have their wings laid flat and dried in position. More substantial things like reptiles or fish need to be preserved in spirits. Animals such as birds or mammals were skinned. Once scraped clean, a preservative such as arsenic soap was applied and the skin left to dry. Plants had to be pressed and certain parts included, preferably a flower for flowering plants, for example. Labels had to be written to indicate where they were collected. All specimens had to be carefully packed in order to survive shipment back to Europe.

At the same time Pfeiffer began plotting where to travel next. She had so enjoyed her time in Singapore that she was tempted to return there. From there she could make large and profitable collections and no doubt catch a ship to even more remote Australia.

And so on 18 March 1851, Pfeiffer set off with only a humble portmanteau on her next great voyage. She was throwing off the yoke of the constraints of home yet again. To be free and underway again she could have "hurrahed and rejoiced beyond all measure" like a schoolboy once the bell finally tolls, as Heinrich Heine expressed in *Die Harzreise* (The Harz Journey, 1826).

Pfeiffer's first stop was Prague, presumably to visit her old travelling companion, the botanist Count von Berchtold, before proceeding to Berlin where she was received like a celebrity. Journalists interviewed her and noted down everything for the entertainment of their curious readers from her adventures, her unpretending appearance, to her Viennese accent. For one head-spinning week she was wined and dined by giants of the social and scientific worlds.

Amongst these was one of her greatest heroes, the grand old man of European science, Alexander von Humboldt. Between 1799 and 1804 he had explored and investigated the Cape Verde islands, Venezuela, Brazil, Mexico and Cuba. His subsequent scientific publications were extremely popular and influential. He inspired generations of scientific travellers. Charles Darwin thought Humboldt was "the greatest scientific traveller who ever lived".[188] Many historians of science think that his work generated a new holistic way of studying nature which has been dubbed Humboldtian science. This combined precise measurement and observation with the sensitivity and aesthetic appreciation of romantic nature. Hence it was possible to study the natural world, to seek to understand it's complex workings, while at the same time teetering on the edge of perceiving the sublime. Humboldt's work even inspired romantic painters such as Caspar David Friedrich with his *Wanderer above the Sea of Fog* (1818). This solitary figure gazing out over the rugged landscape below and beyond the peak where he stands could almost be Humboldt himself, viewing the beautiful and unobtainable peak of Mount Chimborazo in the Andes. It is no stretch of the imagination to picture Pfeiffer standing in the same painting, surveying a wild landscape and appreciating its substance and sublime effect.

For decades Humboldt had been perhaps the most famous man of science in the world. He was showered with honours and his company much sought after by King Frederick William IV of Prussia. The great poet and polymath Johann Wolfgang von Goethe claimed that he learned more in an hour's conversation with Humboldt than eight days of reading books. Humboldt was now, aged eighty-four with white wispy hair, one of the most famous men in Europe tout court. And yet this great man was so excited when he met Ida Pfeiffer that he kept enthusiastically repeating, "You have done the unthinkable!"[189]

Pfeiffer was also welcomed by the directors and professors of the Berlin museums and university. Particularly important for Pfeiffer's career was the geographer Carl Ritter. Now in his early seventies, Ritter was Professor of Geography at the University of Berlin. His great work, eventually all nineteen volumes of it, was entitled *Geography in Relation to Nature and the History of Mankind* (1816–1859). He compiled and catalogued the many ways in which the natural environment shaped human societies. After she left, Ritter and Pfeiffer would continue to correspond. She was now, more than ever before, plugged into the scientific community in Europe and recognised as a contributor to the progress of knowledge.

From Hamburg Pfeiffer took a steamer to London where she arrived on 10 April 1851. As her steamer entered the harbour of "the metropolis of the world", as she called it, in the early morning light, she surveyed the novel scene with the eyes of an artist.

> The forest of masts, which from a distance appeared quite impenetrable, gradually unfolded itself to our view as we advanced; and the countless vessels of all sizes, from the largest East Indiaman to the tiniest yacht,—some lying at anchor, some unfurling their sails, and setting off on their voyages in various directions, or being taken in tow by little smoking bustling steamers,—all this afforded certainly a grand and stirring sight.[190]

Even so, few could have appreciated the scene from the same perspective as Madame Pfeiffer. Who else could be so blasé about one of the busiest harbours in the world because it was not so colourful as Canton, Bombay or Singapore?

Nevertheless, the Victorian metropolis did manage to impress. "The feverish rush of life through the thronged streets of London can hardly be imagined by any one who has not witnessed it," she wrote.[191] But London's public transportation system left something to be desired. (This observation will no doubt shock modern Londoners.) She tried to take one of the city's 3,000 omnibuses. These large two-horse carriages seated twenty-one passengers – twelve inside and nine on rooftop benches. These forgotten conveyances are the origin of our word "bus". Like the word, the function of the modern bus and even many of the routes they ply are derived directly from the Victorian omnibus. To Pfeiffer's dismay, however, she found that "a considerable amount of study is required to determine which is the right one to get into".[192] The signs and maps had so much detail that it was not easy for a visitor to navigate.

As she sat in a swaying omnibus, while the rain drizzled outside, she looked around with her discerning eagle eye – dirty shoes had tracked in the mud and dung-covered filth of the streets; closed umbrellas dripped puddles on the floor. Mischievously she compared this to the stereotypical comfort of which the English liked to boast. Was it all a conceited sham? Some of the natives certainly agreed. One writer to *The Times* complained that London omnibuses were inferior to those on the continent and were, "inconvenient, unwholesome, and indecent".[193]

Once established in her lodgings, Pfeiffer had similar reflections. After a very wet March, April was at least seeing the advance of spring, but it was still quite chilly. How could the English endure always being cold indoors she wondered in disbelief? She found the English open coal fireplace a strangely compromised technology. It was pleasant to look at and gave a room a cosy look, but only the person sitting directly in front of the little glowing pile was actually warm, whereas everywhere else in the room one was cold. Pfeiffer had never shivered at home so much. In Germany one used a tile stove. The fire is enclosed behind a small door and a large brick and usually tile covered structure absorbed and radiated the heat efficiently and evenly for a long time. The English fire, on the other hand, was pretty and comforting, but dissipated and lost most of its heat up the chimney. "But," she concluded, "the English are so immoderately fond of the sight of a fire, that rather than not see it they will often patiently endure the not feeling it."[194]

Pfeiffer also thought that England was a particularly expensive place to live from the expenses of transport, cabs, which then cost eight pence a mile, and opera seats were priced so that only the wealthy could afford them. The lot of English women also struck her as less than ideal.

> The life of the women of the middle rank seemed to me particularly monotonous. They are mostly alone all day, and when their husbands return in the evening from their business, they are generally too tired for conversation, and do not much like to be disturbed by visitors; but sit down in an arm-chair by the fire, take a newspaper, and now and then, I believe, fall asleep.[195]

And then of course there were the notorious details of Victorian social life. "In no country in the world, Persia and China excepted," she complained, "can one so easily offend against the laws of etiquette as in England. If at dinner you should take your fork in your right instead of your left hand,—if you should cut your meat into small pieces all at once, instead of cutting off each piece as you require it,—or in a hundred other little matters vary from the modes established here, you must be content to resign at once all pretension to good breeding."[196]

Press reports were making her name known and Pfeiffer enjoyed the attention of social notables eager to meet her. In one of her surviving letters, Pfeiffer wrote one sentence in English about this time which gives a clue as to the extent of her fluency in English. She wrote to a friend that in London many well-to-do ladies greeted her warmly saying, "I am very pride to shake hands with you."[197]

Pfeiffer was struck by another apparent irony in the English. This country boasted of being constitutional and free as opposed to strictly monarchical countries like Austria. And yet, she quipped in not so gentle irony, in England the aristocracy is "regarded with more profound—perhaps I should say servile—awe than in our land of absolutism". Indeed, it was clear that "there is scarcely a country in the world where people would do so much to gain admittance into stiff, cold, lordly circles, whose chief care is to exclude them".[198]

In a private letter, Pfeiffer would reveal her true feelings about London, even more so than she would in her published book:

> No city was so annoying as London. The appalling distances, the endless bustle of people, the stiff demeanour of the higher classes, and above all the nasty weather, the bleak air reeking of coal smoke, the ice cold rooms ... and the tea time gossip were so revolting to me that I blessed the minute that saw me leave this world city.[199]

125

In addition to visits to Woolwich, Kew, Windsor, Chiswick and Greenwich, Pfeiffer toured the usual tourist sites of the capital such the great pile of St. Paul's Cathedral – the most conspicuous edifice of the metropolis as one guidebook called it.[200] Sir Christopher Wren's great dome was still by far the tallest structure in the city. Pfeiffer then climbed the narrow corkscrew steps to the top of the Monument (to the great fire of 1666) to gain a view over the sprawl of London. The neo-Gothic Palace of Westminster or Houses of Parliament were still under construction and the Commons would not occupy its chamber until the following year. The now iconic tower housing Big Ben was barely two stories tall and would not be completed until 1859.

Pfeiffer also toured the notorious Bedlam, the massive Bethlem Hospital for the Insane at St. George's Fields. By this time things had come a long way from the days of Samuel Pepys who recorded in his diary in the late 17th century, "Stept into Bedlam, where I saw several poor, miserable creatures in chains; one of them mad with making verses."

Then there was the neoclassical East India House, on Leadenhall Street, the administrative centre of the company that was at that time proudly referred to as "the most opulent and extensive in the world".[201] In addition to governing much of India, with its own army, and its massive trade empire, the building housed an extremely rich Oriental Museum. This is where Captain Gill's paintings of the Ajanta caves were destined to be kept. She also inspected the paintings at the National Gallery at Trafalgar Square.

But Pfeiffer's favourite was surely the British Museum. It was "a magnificent building, and for the treasures with which its halls are filled, certainly the grandest in the world".[202] At that time it already housed the great library but its famous, and now sadly disused domed reading room would not commence construction for another three years. Polite visitors filed thoughtfully past Egyptian antiquities, the "Elgin Marbles" as well as miles of natural history specimens in the mineralogical, geological and zoological galleries.

It was at the British Museum that Pfeiffer met George Robert Waterhouse, Keeper of Mineralogy and Geology. The top of his head was quite bald but he made up for it by growing enormous outreaching sideburns that made him look a bit like a stuffed lion. A man of great ability, his 1846 book on marsupials was the only one for which Charles Darwin ever wrote a review. Pfeiffer recalled, "Mr. Waterhouse ... devoted many hours to me, and instructed me in the mode of making collections."[203]

Perhaps through Waterhouse, Pfeiffer became acquainted with the natural history auctioneer and agent Samuel Stevens whose showroom was near the museum at 24 Bloomsbury Street. She contracted to sell some of her specimens through him. He performed the same role for other travelling collectors such as Frederick Strange in Australia or Alfred Russel Wallace and Henry Walter Bates who were then diligently collecting bird and insect specimens in the Amazon basin and shipping them to Stevens to be sold to museums and collectors.

A scientific tourist could also not miss the Hunterian Museum at the Royal College of Surgeons, on the south side of Lincoln's Inn Fields. Its museum was divided into two sections, a physiological and a pathological. Its long lofty hall had an elephant skeleton at one end and the other had the skeletons of two extinct South American giants: a *Mylodon* and a *Glyptodon*. Both of these discoveries were credited to Charles Darwin during the voyage of the *Beagle* in the 1830s. Visitors were particularly keen to see the skeleton of Charles Byrne, "the Irish giant" who stood eight feet tall, erected on a tall plinth towering above the display cases. And by his side was the diminutive Caroline Crachami, "the Sicilian dwarf" whose skeleton stood 20 inches tall.

Pfeiffer had the good fortune to meet the conservator, the enigmatically brilliant savant Professor Richard Owen. He showed her about the hall, pointing out specimens of particular interest. Owen has had the misfortune to go down in history as the villain in the story of Charles Darwin. This is unfortunate; although Owen was a man of breathtaking ego, arrogance and animosity, he had brilliance, ability and accomplishments to match. Nor was he the creationist foil to Darwin the evolutionist. Perhaps Owen's most obvious legacy today (apart from the Natural History Museum in London) is the name he coined for another group of creatures that had recently been discovered. He called them "terrible lizards" – dinosaurs.

And finally there were the Zoological Gardens in Regent's Park, now the London Zoo, where Pfeiffer bought an admission ticket for 1s. The collection was replete with an excellent ensemble of exotic animals including monkeys, lions, tigers, leopards, giraffes and a new hippopotamus sent from Egypt. Some of the buildings were no less impressive for the time, especially the heated giraffe house, designed by Decimus Burton, allowing animals from warm climates to survive Britain's dreary winters, at least for a time. The building still houses giraffes today.

One other person Pfeiffer sought out for advice was an unmarried twenty-nine-year-old German geographer named Augustus Petermann. As a young man he had assisted Humboldt with the maps for his publications, before moving to Edinburgh in 1845 to work on commercial atlases. After two years Petermann moved down to London where he continued his work and became a regular contributor to the *Athenaeum*. He would eventually become one of the foremost geographers in the world. Although sometimes dismissed as an armchair geographer, Petermann was a master of diplomacy and lobbying. He helped countless young explorers to find support for their expeditions. He would do his best to advance Pfeiffer's interests too. He would publish several reports on her progress and hint at her need for financial assistance in the *Athenaeum*.

He was also a particular expert on Africa. This may be why Pfeiffer sought him out. Looking down his nose through his tiny silver spectacles, Petermann told her what, for him at any rate, was exciting news; there was a great lake in Southern Africa called Ngami that had recently been discovered by the famous missionary explorer David Livingstone. This intelligence, Petermann later reported "made her determine on stopping at the Cape, and trying to proceed thence, if possible, northwards into the equatorial regions of the African Continent".[204]

The Great Exhibition

Pfeiffer's visit to London coincided with one of the greatest spectacles of the entire nineteenth century – the opening of the Great Exhibition in Hyde Park on 1 May 1851. Charles Buschek, Austrian commissioner for the Exhibition, gave her a ticket to the opening and a further five visiting tickets. Thus amongst the crowd of the great and the good gathered to witness the solemn opening of the exhibition by Queen Victoria and Prince Albert was Madame Pfeiffer.

The exhibition was housed in the Crystal Palace – by far the largest iron and glass structure the world had ever seen. This great building, designed by Joseph Paxton, was 1,851 feet (about 564 metres) long and 454 feet (about 138 metres) wide. The vast space it enclosed dwarfed the full-grown trees it was built around. It contained exhibits from Britain, the empire and forty-four other countries – totalling over 100,000 objects of machinery, manufacturers and fine arts, displayed along more than ten miles of exhibition space. Wonders of Victorian high tech were elegantly presented with everything from hydraulic presses, steam printing presses, steam locomotives, talking telegraphs, printing telegraphs, steam turbines, scientific air pumps, microscopes and cameras to marble statues, gold watches, sumptuous tapestries, ornate laces and embroidery.

Equally impressive, if not exactly on public display, were the "retiring rooms" – the first major installation of public flushing toilets in the world. During the exhibition over 800,000 visitors made use of these public conveniences for the price of one penny. This purportedly gave rise to the euphemism still used today of "spending a penny".

Bartlett

There was to be one last meeting before Pfeiffer departed on her next great adventure. Her travelling companion from the journey to Jerusalem, William Henry Bartlett, saw in the newspaper that the celebrated traveller Madame Pfeiffer was then in London. Here was the "German lady" that he had once mocked in his book on the Holy Land. But now almost a decade later she was world famous and everyone was talking about her exploits. He wrote a letter asking to see her. Just a week before her departure, they arranged to meet at the counting house of her unnamed host in Crutched Friars, near Tower Hill.

Bartlett wrote a detailed account of the meeting for *Sharpe's London Magazine* and included the same text in the next edition of a book of his travels. Considering how dismissive he had been when he first mentioned her in his book on Jerusalem, the lengthy and personal details given make a striking contrast. Perhaps he just wanted to spice up his book with details of the famous traveller. Or perhaps he was just genuinely surprised that the unpretending and unremarkable German lady he had met on the way to Jerusalem in 1842 was the same Madame Pfeiffer that everyone was talking about. He told the story almost as if he had been granted an audience with royalty.

> I pushed my way through the multifarious obstructions of our crowded streets to the place of rendezvous, I could not help speculating as to what changes had been wrought by the interval of time and incidents of travel that had occurred since our previous meeting.
>
> I reached the house, hurried up two flights of dirty stairs, tapped at the door of an office differing in no respect from the thousand dark and dingy ones in the city. "Come in," was the response; and on entering, in the shadow of the room and looking strangely out of place in the midst of a heap of ledgers and day-books, was, sure enough, the well-remembered face of my old fellow-traveller, who rose and received me with the most lively expression of satisfaction. I, too, was rejoiced to find no change for the worse in the appearance of my friend after so severe an ordeal as a journey round the world.
>
> After exchanging our mutual congratulations, the conversation (which was carried on in French, Madame speaking English but imperfectly) naturally turned upon the subject of her recent journey.

Pfeiffer briefly outlined the itinerary of her world journey which left Bartlett quite astonished. He continued his account:

> Such a narrative of adventure, and from the mouth of a female, might well take away one's breath. I really seemed to be dreaming as I looked upon the frail little body before me, and heard her describe a devious career like this with far less excitement of manner than the mistress of a cockney boarding school would throw into her account of the perils of a journey to Boulogne. ... Far from her taste for travel having been satisfied, it seemed only "to have grown by

what it fed on," and she was already preparing for a second voyage around the globe ... the Professors had given her instructions in the best mode of preserving specimens, and collecting objects of value to science.

Pfeiffer told him that she planned to visit Australia and New Zealand and then go on to Southeast Asia. It is curious that she did not mention Africa.

Bartlett had read an account in a New York newspaper of her visit to the American missionaries in Urmia in 1848. "This account," he told her, "mentioned your being wounded by a robber, stating moreover that you had valiantly defended yourself, and cut off one or two of your adversary's fingers with a knife, and that, I suppose, is also an invention of the editor's."

"On the contrary," she replied, "that's strictly true, and I bore away with me a lasting memento of it;" she then extended her arm, enveloped in a muslin sleeve, and invited me to make an examination of it. As I did so, my hand sunk, with a sickening sensation, into a hollow, midway between the elbow and the shoulder, the token of a deep and ghastly wound, which she will carry with her to the grave.

Reminiscences such as these filled up the remainder of our interview. I was disappointed in my hope of seeing this extraordinary woman again before leaving England. Shortly afterward she set sail upon her long and perilous enterprise, at a time of life when most persons are only anxious to repose calmly by the fireside for the remainder of their days.[205]

And yet Pfeiffer would outlive him. Bartlett died of fever on his way home from a trip to the Near East just three years later, a poignant reminder of the very real dangers of foreign travel during the nineteenth century.

On 27 May 1851 Pfeiffer departed on the 300-tonne sailing ship

Allandale, under Captain Brodie, destined for Cape Town, South Africa. Unlike a steamship, a sailing ship did not just proceed in a straight line down the west coast of Africa. Because it was subject to the winds, the ship made a great arc almost as far west as Brazil, adding a further 3,000 miles to the voyage, and then turned back eastwards to the Cape of Good Hope. Throughout her journeys, Pfeiffer kept careful count of the number of miles travelled by land and by sea.

On board the *Allandale* Pfeiffer suffered bad fare and, as so often, bad company. The captain's conversation at table consisted of nothing further than the state of the winds. She would have agreed with the words of Mark Twain's Tom Sawyer, "there ain't no surer way to find out whether you like people or hate them than to travel with them". Pfeiffer was always a martyr to the ill-behaved. But then she could take solace from the thought that her sufferings made good copy.

Her ship arrived on 11 August. Cape Town had been laid out by Dutch settlers in 1652 and enlarged by the British since 1795. It now had a gasworks for lighting, and botanic gardens. The 1842 census showed two-thirds of the population was Christian and another third Muslim; 9,359 were counted as "whites" and 12,481 as "coloured".[206] By 1851 the population had risen to 32,000. Pfeiffer was told that the population was one-third "whites, one-third mulatto, and the remainder negro".[207]

She brought with her a letter of introduction to Maximilian Thalwitzer, the consul for The Hanseatic Cities of Hamburg, Lübeck, and Bremen, and his wife. They graciously hosted the famous traveller at their home. Pfeiffer's fame had reached the Cape and as a consequence she received many social invitations.

Like London, Pfeiffer found living "rather dear" at Cape Town. Fortunately one of her favourite pastimes was quite free, if not always quite safe. She ambled about the environs of the town collecting insects and "objects of natural history".[208] She wrote about her impressions in a letter to Petermann on 20 August.

> The impression which this place made on me, was not an agreeable one. The mountains surrounding the town are bare, the town itself—London being still fresh in my recollection—resembles a village. The houses are of only one story, with terraces instead of roofs. From the deck of the vessel a single tree was visible, standing on a hill. In short, on my arrival I was at once much disappointed, and this disappointment rather increases than otherwise.[209]

One day, just as she was rejoicing at the capture of a little snake, two black women suddenly rushed out of the trees and seized her. The women "overwhelmed me with abuse, spit on the ground before me, in token of their hatred and contempt, and called me a witch and a sorceress, who ought to be put an end to. There is no saying how this scene might have ended—probably in no very agreeable way for me—had not a man fortunately at that moment made his appearance at a distance. I cried to him for help, and thereupon the two women took to flight."[210]

When Pfeiffer returned home, shaken but unharmed, she told Herr Thalwitzer what had happened. He instantly sent for a magistrate. The women were soon captured. At the ensuing inquiry it was determined that the women had intended to drag Pfeiffer into the bush and rob her. One of the women had dropped a long knife at the scene and when this was produced, they were sentenced to four weeks imprisonment "upon rice-water". Pfeiffer thought this punishment was "rather severe, and I begged for some alleviation of it—but in vain. I was told that these women were notorious offenders, and passed more time in prison than out of it."

Pfeiffer sent a box of specimens to Vinzenz Kollar, Keeper of the Royal Museum of Vienna. Kollar, to judge from his portrait, wore a permanent expression of scowling disapproval. But he was nevertheless very supportive of Pfeiffer. She thought some seaweed samples were the best items in the collection.

Her original, and as usual half-cocked and terrifyingly ambitious plan for an expedition into the interior of Africa to reach as far as Lake Ngami, had to be abandoned. Even apart from the inherent difficulties of traversing 1,800 kilometres of foreign lands and peoples, the expense was simply beyond her means. She listed for her readers what would have been required. "You must purchase a long wagon, covered with linen or matting, and five or six pairs of oxen. This wagon must be fitted up like a house, for it is to serve the purpose of a dwelling and of secure nightly quarters; you must engage a driver, an ox-boy, and a servant, and lay in a stock of provisions, and very often of water also, for the journey."[211] Joseph Freeman, of the London Missionary Society, estimated that kitting out for a lengthy journey into the interior would cost £100.[212] Pfeiffer hoped to travel around the entire world on about this amount.

Would Australia prove as impossibly expensive? Emigrants were rushing there from all over the world to chase the recent gold rush. This would mean that prices would be extremely inflated. At any rate, there were no ships heading to Australia anyway. As so often, serendipity suggested the next step in her voyage. A Bremen-registered brig, the *Louisa Frederika*, was then lying in harbour bound for Singapore and at Singapore, she well knew, "you may find ships to all the regions of the earth". Even better, she could travel on her special discount. An English government officer, Thomas Hoare, offered to help. He explained her circumstances to the ship's master, Captain Nienhaber, who kindly charged her only for her board. And even that was only to cost £3. At this rate she would travel at the extraordinary rate of 1,000 miles per pound.

The *Louisa Frederika* set sail to cross the Indian Ocean on 26 August 1851. After forty days sailing, they ran through the Sunda Strait between Sumatra and Java and past the pointed volcanic island of Krakatoa which would erupt with such world-shattering violence thirty-two years later. One night, while the ship lay at anchor, the watch woke the ship's company with the alarm: "Two boats in sight from the land!" Their first thought was pirates. Muskets, pistols, ammunition and sabres were distributed to the crew. The ship's two six-pounders were loaded and ready. But it was a false alarm. The boats never even came near them. In fact, attacks by pirates on European ships in the area were now extremely rare. The British settlement at Singapore, with its armed steamers that could move against the winds, had made the region too risky and unprofitable for pirates.

The *Louisa Frederika* dropped anchor in the bustling and cluttered harbour of Singapore on 16 November 1851. As during her 1847 visit, Pfeiffer was warmly welcomed by the Behn family. *The Singapore Free Press* announced the arrival of the "undaunted and adventurous traveller" whose "remarkable courage and perseverance" were now near legendary.[213] Things had changed since it didn't even bother to list her name as a departing passenger during her last stay.

The port town had continued to grow and prosper exponentially. Pfeiffer heard that "a magnificent lighthouse had been built" from the granite quarries of the small neighbouring island called Ubin.[214] This was the Horsburgh Lighthouse, named after the Scottish hydrographer of the East India Company who surveyed the waters of the area. It had been built precariously on a rocky islet twenty-four miles east in the Malacca Straight. The islet had been known for centuries as Pedra Branca, Portuguese for "white rock", a reference to its whitish appearance from accumulated bird guano. It had been a nesting site of the black-naped tern. The lighthouse continues in operation to this day.

Shortly before Pfeiffer's arrival, a small cottage had been built in the forest far from the town as a holiday retreat. As it happened to be unoccupied, Herr Behn knew that he could give Ida Pfeiffer no greater pleasure than "passing a few days in the midst of the jungle, and enjoying to my heart's content the scenery, and the amusement of searching for insects".[215] He sent with her a boat, to visit nearby islets, and five Malays to help her. The men came every morning and asked if she wanted the boat. If she didn't, they would join in her rambles through the jungle hunting insects and protecting her from tigers.

"These animals have of late increased tremendously," she was told. And the beasts "do not hesitate to break into the plantations and carry off the labourers in broad daylight. In the year 1851, it is stated that no less than the almost incredible number of four hundred persons were destroyed by them." Even these harrowing stories, could not prevent her "finding the greatest delight in roaming from morning till evening in these most beautiful woods". Her Malay companions were armed with muskets and long knives. "We saw traces of tigers every day; we found the marks of their claws imprinted in the sand or soft earth; and one day at noon, one of these unwelcome guests came quite near to our cottage, and fetched himself a dog, which he devoured quite at his leisure only a few hundred steps off."[216]

One night, as she slept alone in the little cottage, her guards staying in a hut far off, she heard a sound outside that frightened her. It did not sound like a tiger, but perhaps a man. There was a government station nearby where convicts were kept for felling timber. Perhaps it was one of them? The doors had no locks. She had a large knife near her bedside but, perhaps remembering her encounter in Brazil, that was a risky and last ditch defence. She cried out in a loud voice, "Who's there?" A man answered that a tiger had been spotted in the area and they were in pursuit. She heard no more that night. The tiger had crept away.

Although Pfeiffer reported to her readers that 400 people a year were killed by tigers in Singapore, she was in fact repeating a myth that virtually every visitor in those years was told. Alfred Russel Wallace would repeat the same dramatic story for his readers in 1869. In fact, the death toll was more like twenty per year.[217] At any rate the richness and diversity of the forest was far too absorbing for Pfeiffer to cower indoors.

> I was busy with the beautiful objects that presented themselves to my observation at every step. Here merry little monkeys were springing from bough to bough, there brightly plumed birds flew suddenly out; plants that seemed to have their roots in the trunks of the trees, twined their flowers and blossoms among the branches or peeped out from the thick foliage; and then again the trees themselves excited my admiration by their size, their height, and their wonderful forms. Never shall I forget the happy days I passed in that Singapore jungle.[218]

Passages like this make it perfectly clear that her natural history collecting was not solely for mercenary purposes but part of a sincere personal interest in living things and the natural world, even if an untutored and self-taught one.

On 30 November 1851 she wrote to Herr Kollar, her museum contact in Vienna. The insect collecting was not as productive as she had hoped. Nevertheless, she was sending back another case of specimens. There was a black and white caterpillar which she found crawling through the rotting leaves on the forest floor. Since she did not find it on the plant it fed on, she was unable to take it home and keep it until it metamorphosed. Unfortunately, she had not taken enough spirits to preserve many specimens that could not be dried. All of her larger collections rotted almost immediately in the hot and humid tropical atmosphere. One of these unpreservable captures was a black and brown snake she found amongst the tree roots along the beach. Seaweed she could dry and pack. She collected a new species of mole cricket (*Gryllotalpa fulvipes*) in the forest. For almost a century, hers was the only specimen ever found.[219]

She also sent a number of fish that ultimately earned her a handsome £25 from the British Museum, according to Wallace. He later wrote to Samuel Stevens, their shared agent, from Singapore saying he could also procure fish in the market but asked, "How did Madame Pfeiffer preserve hers?"[220] He specialised in insects and birds. Carefully packed, Pfeiffer's insects, seaweed, fish, crustaceans and other creatures made their slow way back to Europe by sailing ship around the Cape of Good Hope.

"Oh my dear Herr Kollar," she wrote seeking some sympathy, "you cannot believe how difficult it is to send collections when funds are so extremely limited as with me." She hinted that perhaps some more government funding might be forthcoming. It wasn't. Kollar indeed tried his best. He presented a certificate to appeal for further state funds for Pfeiffer in which he praised her collections of rare and often overlooked animals.[221] Pfeiffer asked Kollar to sell the specimens not needed for the museum's collection. Could he please, turn them "into money because to me every small profit is of great value".[222] The £25 for the fish must have been a rare godsend.

As she feared, the costs of travelling to and exploring Australia sounded prohibitive. Pfeiffer could not go that way. At least it didn't look likely. But she would not give up hope just yet. Then another destination presented itself: Sarawak, a province of the great island of Borneo, just 500 miles to the east. For the past decade it had been ruled by the famous "White Rajah", Sir James Brooke.

Born to British parents in India, Brooke spent time in the

army serving in the first Anglo-Burmese war before resigning his commission due to injury. When his father died in 1833, Brooke inherited a £30,000 fortune. He bought a 142-tonne schooner, *The Royalist*, and sailed for Borneo in 1838. Brooke and his crew helped the Sultan of Brunei to defeat an uprising and in 1842 Brooke was given the hereditary title of Rajah of Sarawak. He established a Singapore-style free trade port there and sought to suppress the rampant piracy in the area. In 1847 Brooke was knighted by Queen Victoria. His life story was the inspiration for Rudyard Kipling's *The Man Who Would be King* (1888) and Joseph Conrad's *Lord Jim* (1900). Communications between Singapore and Sarawak were therefore frequent. One of the ships that regularly plied the seas between the two ports was the *Trident*, a barque of 320 tonnes. Her master, Captain Lyall, offered to take Pfeiffer for an "extremely moderate price".

On 2 December 1851 the *Trident* set sail for Sarawak.[223] It took twelve days to reach the mouth of the Sarawak River, then, with another half day waiting for the tide to rise enough to enter, it could take a further three days to make the twenty-five miles up river to the capital, Kuching. Still stuck on the *Trident* at the mouth of the river, Pfeiffer wrote to her host in Singapore, Herr Behn, on 17 December asking him not to send her suitcase on to Adelaide as she had originally planned. Sarawak and perhaps Java were likely to occupy her longer than she had originally expected.[224]

Sir James was not then in Sarawak so his nephew and heir apparent Captain John Brooke was in charge. Sir James was in England dealing with accusations that he had used excessive force, tantamount to atrocities, in the suppression of piracy along the coast of Borneo in 1849. The political wranglings and accusations dragged on for a further five years before he was exonerated by a Royal Commission in Singapore in 1854.

No sooner had Captain Brooke received news that Ida Pfeiffer was aboard the *Trident* than he sent his own small proa down river to bring her to the town without further delay. When she arrived at the landing place, Captain Brooke was there waiting for her. She presented her letter of introduction but Brooke "was so kind as to assure me that my name was so well known to him that any other introduction was unnecessary".[225]

Pfeiffer was taken to Sir James' bungalow with its encircling verandah surrounded by sweet smelling roses and jasmine. Nearby was a little menagerie with unique native animals such as a honey bear, a proboscis monkey and two large orangutans.

The town of Sarawak, or Kuching, seemed like little more than a large village. There were no roads, and the houses, including that of the rajah, Sir James, were all made of wood with thatched roofs. Pfeiffer provided a brief description.

> The population of Sarawak consists of Malays and Chinese; for the few Dyaks you see form no families; they are mostly either in service, or they have come here on business. The Chinese and Malays inhabit separate quarters of the town, and the former depart in nothing from the habits of life and costume of their native country … The country round Sarawak is very pretty, and rendered prettier by a few European houses that are scattered about on the hills around, where are also a small fort, a neat church and mission house, and a court of justice.[226]

Cities throughout Southeast Asia had populations of Chinese and Malay peoples and, as at Kuching, they usually chose to live next to people who spoke the same language and ate the same foods they did. In recent years it has become fashionable to claim that when Sir Thomas Stamford Raffles proposed a layout for building the town of Singapore, which had different areas demarcated for the Chinese and the Malays, that this was part of a strategy of "divide and rule". This is a fabrication, there was no such strategy and no need for one. Raffles was simply following what seemed at the time a rational scheme. These different peoples always lived in separate areas – they did so all over Southeast Asia. Raffles was merely setting aside parts of the town for the different types of people who lived in and were rapidly migrating to Singapore.

As everywhere Pfeiffer observed and recorded the clothing and other habits of the people. Almost everyone seemed to chew sirih, a stimulant of betel nut, sirih leaf and lime paste which reddens the teeth and leads to very copious spitting, leaving thick red splatters all over the ground. And, with her usual forwardness, she got into the houses of locals such as Malay chiefs to snoop about in order to give her readers Pfeiffer's "house beautiful".

Sir James's secretary, Spenser St. John, later described Pfeiffer as "of middle height, active for her age, with an open countenance and a very pleasant smile".[227] Alfred Russel Wallace visited Sarawak almost exactly three years later. He also stayed in the bungalow of Sir James and was told about the celebrated Madame Pfeiffer. Wallace wrote to his sister, "Capt. Brooke says she was a very nice old lady something like the picture of *Mrs. Harris in 'Punch'*."

This was not a very flattering image. In Charles Dickens' *Martin Chuzzlewit* (1843–1844), Mrs Harris was an imaginary friend of Mrs Gamp, the dissolute, sloppy and usually drunk family nurse. Gamp constantly used the words of the apparently fictitious Mrs Harris to establish her own good reputation. For example: "If it wasn't for the nerve a little sip of liquor gives me," says Mrs Gamp to Mr Pecksniff,

> I never could go through with what I sometimes has to do. "Mrs Harris," I says,… "leave the bottle on the chimley-piece, and don't ask me to take none, but let me put my lips to it when I am so dispoged, and then I will do what I'm engaged to do, according to

the best of my ability." "Mrs Gamp," she says, in answer, "if ever there was a sober creetur to be got at eighteen pence a day for working people, and three and six for gentlefolks—night watching," said Mrs Gamp with emphasis, "being a extra charge—you are that inwallable person."

The satirical magazine *Punch* made frequent use of the ridiculous Mrs Harris to lampoon the conservative stalwart newspaper, *The Standard*. Mrs Harris was an aging, opinionated, gossiping, bossy and clearly ridiculous busybody. The caricature, with an oversized and old-fashioned bonnet, was recognisable to everyone in the 1840s and 1850s.

Wallace also informed his sister that "the insects she got in Borneo were not very good, those from Celebes & the Moluccas were the rare ones for which Mr Stevens got so much money for her. I expect she will set up regular collector now, as it will pay all her expenses & enable her to travel where she likes. I have told Mr Stevens to recommend Madagascar to her."[228] Just as it is possible that Wallace's advice led Pfeiffer to Madagascar, her collecting in the Malay archipelago may have helped Wallace decide to go there on his second expedition. He would later visit many of the same places that Pfeiffer did before him. These included Singapore, Sarawak, Banda, Ambon, Paso, Seram, Wahai, Ternate, Minahassa, Lake Tondano, Makassar, Goa, Maros, Surabaya, Batavia and Sumatra.

To entertain her, Captain Brooke proposed taking Pfeiffer for an excursion into the interior to visit the Dyaks, the contemporary name for indigenous peoples of Borneo. They were traditionally, and notoriously to outsiders, headhunters. Captain Brooke warned Pfeiffer that she "must be a good climber for such an undertaking, as the Dyaks do not like living in plains, but build their huts on the points of rocks, the higher and more inaccessible the better".[229]

Brooke and St. John selected a very fast, long proa for the voyage upriver. "The proa was well decked, brightly lighted, and divided by curtains into various apartments, in one of which a soft couch under a mosquito-net was made ready for me." They stopped at the Chinese village of Siniawan, on the plain at the foot of mount Sirambau. There were two rows of houses with a road down the middle.

Pfeiffer hurried about examining the homes of the Chinese. "I saw here that the Chinese have no more objection to dirt than the Malays; the only difference is that the Malay puts his house upon piles, and lives over the filth, and the Chinese keeps it before his door."

For St. John, "It was quite a pleasure to look at the little Chinese maidens in their prim, neat dresses, and their parents evidently had a pride in their appearance." But to the Chinese, Madame Pfeiffer herself was the great attraction and "a crowd followed her everywhere, and wondered at the eagerness she displayed in the chase of a butterfly, or the capture of an insect". With her eccentric dress and conical hat she was a strange sight to behold.

After breakfast they gathered Dyak porters who had come to meet them and set off inland. The Dyak village was about 1,100 feet up on the sides of a large hill called Mount Serambu. St. John speculated, "I imagine Madame Pfeiffer, in all her travels, had never met worse paths, particularly when we commenced ascending the hill."[230] And indeed she seems to have agreed. In her own book she wrote:

> I had heard much of the bad roads in Borneo, but I was really astonished nevertheless when I saw the path—absolutely perilous to life—that led to the summit. Pools, marshes, brooks, and chasms, were to be crossed by means of two bamboo sticks, or the thin round trunk of a young tree; and to climb up almost perpendicular cliffs, there was no other help than one of these thin stems, in which a

few notches were made for the foot to rest in, to steady you for a moment. At the most dangerous places there was indeed a sort of hand-rail, but of such fragile construction that a fall would have been inevitable had one leaned upon it in earnest; so that I was obliged to keep my eyes constantly fixed upon the path I had to tread, and could not give the smallest attention to the beauty of the surrounding scenery.[231]

At length they reached the Dayak village of Sirambau. The Dyaks lived in enormous longhouses – wooden structures built on stilts ten feet above the ground and sometimes 200 feet in length. Pfeiffer looked wide-eyed at the sea of muddy filth that lay under and around the longhouse. Only pigs and dogs dared venture there. How could people live in such proximity to foul odours and not fall ill, she wondered?

The chief, Mita, took them to their sleeping places. St. John recalled, "they very politely gave Madame Pfeiffer an inner room, and provided her with neat white mats".[232] Pfeiffer looked with horror on a row of thirty-six dried human heads hanging in the longhouse, war trophies of fallen enemies. In the area of Sarawak, Rajah Brooke's government had tried to suppress the taking of heads and this was purportedly no longer practiced.

The Dyaks too did not strike Pfeiffer as very attractive. The men wore their black hair short, and the women grew theirs long. The men wore a very narrow strip of brown bark cloth around the waist and the bare breasted women, a sort of skirt of the same material. The women were sitting about plaiting mats and baskets and the men were carving ornate little boxes for tobacco or sirih and parang (machete) handles. In the evening Captain Brooke gave the Dyaks brandy and asked them to perform some dances around the fire which burned on a bed of rocks sitting on a circle of soil on the wooden floor of the longhouse.

Although not terribly impressed with the dancing or the music of two drums and a gong, Pfeiffer did think that "nowhere have I been so little tormented by impertinent curiosity as among these people".[233] The visitors spent the night in the longhouse and the next morning set off to return to the village of Siniawan. Heavy rain had fallen during the night and the path was very wet and slippery. Pfeiffer could not keep her balance until she took off her shoes and went the rest of the way barefoot. It must have been muddy indeed. Only in the most extreme circumstances would she remove her shoes.

After returning to the proa they visited the open antimony ore mines. Antimony is a bluish-white metal used as an alloy for printers' type, hard pewter, medallions, white metal spoons and many other industrial purposes. The Dyak women used it to give a jet black polish to their teeth. The open pits were manned by armies of Chinese labourers working bare-chested, their long braided queues wrapped around their heads out of the way. After a brief visit to a summer residence and farm of Sir James, the party headed back to Kuching which they reached on Christmas eve.

Into the heart of Borneo

After celebrating Christmas with the small European community in Kuching, Pfeiffer quickly grew restless. She had seen all the major sights in the vicinity, and now wanderlust was driving her on. Her next plan was as breathtakingly ambitious as ever. She would take a boat up the mighty Batang Lupar river, deep inland to the base of the great Klingkang mountain chain that forms the backbone of Borneo, cross the mountains on foot, and then travel by boat again on the rivers that drain the other side of the range down to the sea to arrive at the Dutch settlement of Pontianak on the west coast.

Captain Brooke tried very hard to dissuade Pfeiffer from this harebrained scheme. "He assured me that the interior of the country was full of wild, mostly independent tribes of Dyaks, and that he himself, as a man, would hesitate to attempt such a journey." But her typical reaction was no surprise. "I did not, however, allow myself to be frightened, but remained steady to my resolution."[234] What probably attracted her beyond measure was the fact that no Europeans were known to have ever crossed overland to Pontianak. The only thing that attracted Pfeiffer more than travelling was to see or do what no European had before.

To celebrate the new year, Captain Brooke invited the resident Europeans to dinner at the Rajah's bungalow. As the guests were seated around the table, he raised his glass for the first toast. "The Queen," he said. The others raised their glasses in response, "The Queen." The second toast was to the absent Rajah Brooke. And, as a special honour, the third toast was to Madame Pfeiffer. She, in turn, toasted the gentlemen present. Thus well lubricated they slid merrily into the new year 1852.

After setbacks due to rough seas and bad weather, Pfeiffer finally set out by boat on her great expedition on 11 January 1852. Captain Brooke sent a Malay guide with her. After three days they reached the mouth of the Batang Lupar river and a voyage of sixty-nine hours upriver brought them to the recently completed wood and earth rampart Skrang Fort on the border of Rajah Brooke's territory. The fort, with its thirty native soldiers, was commanded by Alan Lee. He received Pfeiffer with all possible courtesy. Having had word of her arrival, Lee had told the locals of their impending visitor. Consequently people had come flocking from the surrounding area to see the unprecedented sight of a European female explorer. "From morning till night, therefore, I had to present myself to be gazed at; but I must do my visitors, both Malays and Dyaks, the justice to say that they behaved with much modesty and discretion, and their curiosity was not at all troublesome."[235]

The next day Pfeiffer visited an enormous Dyak longhouse. The goods and wares of these people were quite different from the first village she had visited with Captain Brooke. She carefully recorded the myriad differences of costume, jewellery and ornamentation she observed. Then she visited another village and there saw two freshly taken human heads hanging to dry. It was, she thought, "a horrible appearance". Nevertheless, she had to describe it for her readers.

> They were blackened by smoke, the flesh only half dried, the skin unconsumed, lips and ears shrivelled together, the former standing wide apart, so as to display the teeth in all their hideousness. The heads were still covered with hair; and one had even the eyes open, though drawn far back into their sockets. The Dyaks took these heads out of the baskets in which they were hanging, in order to exhibit them to me with great complacency. It was a sight that I shall not easily forget! As they took these heads in their hands to show them to me, they spat in the dead faces; and the boys struck them and spat on the ground, while their usually quiet and peaceful physiognomies assumed an extremely savage expression.[236]

But even as Pfeiffer stood in the midst of the Bornean jungle, confronted with this horrifying spectacle of the most brutal cruelty, she could still see it for what it was, what man does to man, here and everywhere, at one time or another.

> I shuddered, but could not help asking myself whether, after all, we Europeans are not really just as bad or worse than these despised savages? Is not every page of our history filled with horrid deeds of treachery and murder? What shall we say to the religious wars of Germany and France?—to the conquest of America—to the deeds of violence and blood in the middle ages—to the Spanish Inquisition? And even if we come to more modern times, in which

we are outwardly more refined, are we at bottom more mild and merciful to our enemies?

Pfeiffer planned to travel next beyond the territory of Rajah Brooke into that of the independent Dyaks of the interior. Like Captain Brooke, Mr Lee also tried hard to dissuade her. He had heard that the chief of a tribe had recently been killed and that therefore the whole district was at war. Nevertheless, Pfeiffer replied, "I was determined to go as far as I could." Neither Mr Lee, nor Pfeiffer in writing up her experiences, was exaggerating the dangers. Mr Lee was killed in skirmishes with Dyaks the following year.

On 22 January 1852 Pfeiffer set off upriver. Her little party consisted of the Malay guide from Captain Brooke, eight Malay boatmen and Mr Lee's cook who spoke some English and the language of some of the Dyaks. In the afternoon they reached another Dyak village where the people were utterly staggered to see a European female come ashore to visit them. Pfeiffer sat with the near-naked villagers all around her. She took children on her lap and communicated as best she could with hand signals and with help from the cook.

Once she seemed to be an accepted friend, Pfeiffer headed into the forest beside the village to hunt for insects. The entire village followed her to see what on earth she wanted with butterflies and "what was the use of the box in which I preserved them, and which I always carried with me; in short, they contemplated my doings with full as much curiosity as I did theirs". At first they laughed at the sight of her running after butterflies. But once she explained that they were valuable to her, they joined her in collecting. In her eventual book she would cite the Dyaks' sympathetic assistance to score a revenge point for the "ignorant ridicule" she suffered from "so-called civilised European colonies, and even in the United States of America" where she was laughed at for collecting insects.[237]

She stayed with the Dyaks in the longhouse that night. After the fires were extinguished all was dark. Like the night she spent with the Purí Indians in Brazil, Pfeiffer now felt very powerfully how utterly alone she was with these remote people. No help could reach her amongst these headhunters.

The next night she stayed at another village where the men had just returned from war. Near Pfeiffer's sleeping place in the longhouse hung three human heads in various stages of drying. Her sleeping place was so close to the heads that she was very miserable. The wind from the window rattled the skulls together and "the vapour and stench from the fresh head was suffocating, and from time to time driven by the wind right into my face".[238]

The people in this longhouse were very agitated and continued moving about the house long after the fires went out. "Sleep was impossible," Pfeiffer found, "and I got by degrees into a perfect fever of terror ... expecting, I own, every moment to feel the knife at my throat, until at length the morning dawned, and I sank back completely exhausted on my couch." It seems obvious from so many examples that the one thing Ida Pfeiffer feared was the dark.

For Pfeiffer, the travelling thus far was intolerably slow. Her team would not make an early start but leisurely made their breakfast and lay about smoking or chewing sirih. The worst of these was the man sent by Captain Brooke. Pfeiffer suspected that had she been a man he would have done as she asked, instead of often ignoring or even turning his back on her. But in the end they would continue the journey, paddling slowly upstream into the mountains amidst a symphony of bird song and insect calls from the dark forest all around. Through her spectacles of romanticism, Pfeiffer described the experience.

> The scenery of the country we were passing through now became more lovely with every stroke of the oar. The morasses had disappeared, and were succeeded by luxuriant rice-plantations, with

smiling hills in the background. Among the trees there were some glorious specimens,—some with trunks a hundred and forty feet high,—others spreading out their mighty branches, and hanging their leaves down into the water, so as to form deliciously cool leafy bowers. Large hives of the wild bee were often hanging on lofty slender stems with very few branches.[239]

On the 26th the quiet stillness of the surrounding forest was broken by a small canoe frantically paddling downstream towards them with four Dyaks. As the Dyaks went past they screamed at Pfeiffer's boat to turn back. A tribe not far off was coming to make war. Pfeiffer received this news with her usual understatement, it was, she said, "of course a little startling".

She held a short discussion with her men. All but the cook were for turning around and fleeing. But Pfeiffer and the cook overruled them so they pushed on. But first they hoisted the well-known flag of Rajah Brooke's government, a yellow field with a cross of half black and half red, expecting that it would afford some protection.

They paddled warily on. Soon they could hear the sound of a war-song with drums and gongs. They rounded a bend in the river and suddenly were in full view of a hundred Dyaks on the shore with high narrow shields. When the Dyaks spotted the proa they screamed and made threatening gestures. The clever cook kept his wits about him. He hopped out of the boat onto a sandbank in the middle of the river and began to parley with the chief of the Dyaks. Pfeiffer could not understand a word.

Suddenly the Dyaks rushed down the bank and into the river, surging unstoppably towards the boat. Within moments they had surrounded the boat and began to climb in. "Now," Pfeiffer thought, "this is the last moment of my life."[240]

But it soon became clear that the Dyaks were clambering aboard not from aggression, but friendly enthusiasm. "No one who has not been in imminent danger of a terrible death can, I think, form a very clear idea of the feeling of that moment, or of the sudden revulsion when I knew that I was saved."

They joined the group on shore for a meal. The food, however, consisted of small pieces of rice flour apparently cooked in rancid fat. Pfeiffer could barely put the stinking morsels in her mouth but ate as much as she could to please her hosts. After the meal they invited her to come to their longhouse which lay deep in the forest. She agreed and went with them alone, not even the cook, her translator, came along.

Pfeiffer had become adept at communicating without language. The prolific American poet Bayard Taylor, who was himself an experienced traveller and writer, once asked Pfeiffer how she "managed to communicate with the people in Tahiti, in Persia, Circassia, and other countries where she was unacquainted with the language. 'Entirely by signs,' she answered, 'until I have acquired the few words which are necessary to express my wants; and I have never experienced any difficulty in making myself understood.'"[241] After much of this signing, gesticulating and touring the longhouse, Pfeiffer returned to the boat so that she could press onwards, ever onwards.

That evening her boat reached a village of about a dozen houses at the foot of the mountains. Here she said goodbye to the boat and the men. Pfeiffer carried a letter of introduction from Captain Brooke to the Malay rajah of the place. The rajah received her graciously. He even proposed to accompany her on the next stage of her journey.

Alfred Russel Wallace wrote somewhat dismissively about this portion of Pfeiffer's journey in a letter to their shared agent Samuel Stevens, perhaps still thinking of her as the ridiculous busybody, Mrs Harris from *Punch*. Or, perhaps, Wallace was repeating the views of his hosts in Sarawak. He was clearly replying to a letter from Stevens that does not survive. Stevens must have mentioned Pfeiffer's account, and presumably praised her adventurous exploration of the interior of Borneo. Wallace, in reply, sought to cut her accomplishments down to size. "M. Pfeiffers account of the mountains &c in Borneo can not be relied on; by the route she went there are no mountains more than 2–3 thousand feet high, & the men who were sent by Captn Brooke to accompany her into the Dutch territories said that she *never once* got from under the cover of her canoe all the voyage & could therefore see nothing whatever of the country or the people!"[242] These two versions seem impossible to reconcile. According to Pfeiffer, she left Brooke's men at this point in the story. As we shall see, this was only half the journey. And, after all, Pfeiffer did come out on the other side alive.

On the 28th Pfeiffer's great trek through the mountains was to commence. The rajah's men readied their weapons and provisions to accompany her. For this long trek she had prepared a special outfit "consisting of trowsers, a petticoat not reaching below the ankle, and which, on the march, frequently had to be tucked up still higher, a jacket, and a magnificent bamboo hat from Bali, impervious alike to sun and rain. As an additional protection against the heat I also laid immediately on my head a piece of banana leaf."[243]

The procession consisted of Pfeiffer and her servant, the rajah and twelve Dyak and Malay attendants, half of them armed. The trek was hard but not as difficult as she expected. Rather than climb up and over the mountains, their way wound through valleys avoiding steep paths as much as possible. Twice their path actually led up and through the middle of Dyak longhouses. Each time they reached a village it was necessary to seek permission to pass through. After an eighteen hour march they found shelter in another longhouse for the night.

The next day the way became even more difficult as the path through the dense forests was very overgrown and constantly impeded by vines, fallen trees or branches so that they had almost as much clambering as walking. There were also frequent streams and bogs that were crossed on a single bamboo pole laid across. But it was not just the overgrown jungle path that needed attention.

> Whenever the deep silence of the forest was disturbed by any sound, however slight, that seemed at all suspicious, we halted and stood as motionless as if rooted to the spot, not daring to speak, and scarcely to breathe, till some of the men had been sent to reconnoitre, which they did by crawling like serpents, and winding themselves among the trunks and roots of the trees.[244]

After two further days of eight-hour marches of this kind they reached Pangkalan Bunut, a landing place on a small river. Here Pfeiffer bid farewell to the rajah and his company. The next stage of her journey was in a small boat rowed by one man. The narrow stream wound through dark and impenetrable woods. The branches of the trees met overhead creating a green tunnel through which the boat was paddled. The stream eventually opened up onto two lakes with grand views of mountains all around. From the second lake the Kapuas river flowed, heading south.

During this river voyage towards the coast they stopped overnight at the principality of Sintang about halfway to the sea. It was home to Sultan Abdu'l Rashid Muhammad Jamal ud-din and about 1,500 inhabitants. Pfeiffer was received like a visiting queen, canons were fired in her honour, she was, in fact, the first European the sultan had ever seen. By now she knew enough Malay to get by. She was even allowed to visit the sultan's harem. But as usual Pfeiffer decided it concealed no great beauties.

The sultan provided a sampan and boatmen to take her further down the Kapuas to the Dutch settlement of Pontianak. Pfeiffer was sorry to leave the region of the independent Dyaks behind her. She had enjoyed her time among them very much and found them honest and good-natured. The journey down the broad river was very rapid and in three days she reached Pontianak on 6 February 1852. She had crossed through the very heart of Borneo. Petermann would later describe it in the *Athenaeum* as "one of the most extraordinary journeys made by a European in Borneo".[245] Could this be a reason for Captain Brooke and Wallace to think so dismissively of Madame Pfeiffer, because she had penetrated deeper into Borneo than either of them?

In fact, Pfeiffer was not the first European to cross the Klingkang range.[246] In December 1844 a German missionary, Johann Michael Carl Hupe, travelled from the Sultanate of Sambas to Kuching. However, Sambas was much closer than Pontianak and involved only a short overland stretch between the highest navigable rivers on either side of the range. There were various routes across the region used by Malay and Chinese traders. But the route Pfeiffer took was decidedly the most dangerous because it passed through the territories of Dyaks allied with Malay groups opposed to the rule of Rajah Brooke.

As Pfeiffer's sampan approached the town with its large earthen fort, she had mixed feelings about entering a Dutch settlement. She had always heard that the Dutch colonials were cold, unhelpful and only interested in making money. When, however, her letter of introduction was taken up by one of the men, Secretary van Hardenberg personally came down to meet her and was so friendly and polite that her reservations immediately melted away. The place received so few visitors that there were no inns or hotels. The wife of Resident T. J. Willer invited her to be their houseguest.

Pfeiffer's goal now was to visit the famed diamond mines of Landak far upriver and again far inland. Unfortunately a thirty-five-year-old Catholic missionary named Jan Sanders had departed in the government boat that morning. It was too late to catch up with him. Van Hardenberg procured Pfeiffer another boat with rowers, but, like Captain Brooke and Mr Lee before him, tried to dissuade her from such a wild scheme. He wanted to send some servants with her but she had been so annoyed with those sent by Captain Brooke that she preferred to simply go alone. As she commenced her journey anyway, he declared, "If I had not myself witnessed the fact of your setting off on such a journey as this entirely alone, I really would not have believed it."[247]

After two days Pfeiffer was informed that the river ahead was impassable because of a state of war with the Dyaks. Her Chinese host at a village along the way gave her a Chinese guide and a Dyak porter to take her overland instead. That evening she was under the care of a Malay rajah. The Chinese servant, she later discovered, had stolen some money from her travelling bag, "the first time I had been robbed in all my travels". (She was forgetting her purse and keys stolen on the way back to Cairo in 1842.)

The next day was another march through rough forest. At one point Pfeiffer was crossing a marsh on a Dyak bridge, which was little more than a bamboo pole five feet above the surface, when she slipped and fell head over heels into the mud below. Her guides had some trouble extracting her, but she was uninjured. At the next stream she sat down in the current and had water poured over her until the mud was washed out of her trousers and petticoat. She then carried on marching several hours in her wet clothes. Such hardiness and perseverance is rare indeed. Most people would simply give up and turn back.

Day after day Pfeiffer recorded the hazards and hardships and the various villages that she passed through. On the 14th she reckoned they walked twenty miles. Spenser St. John later suggested that, "I have the strongest suspicion that Madame Pfeiffer measured her miles by her fatigue. She talks of twenty miles a day as a common performance of hers; and another visitor to this island beats her, recording walking thirty miles in one day through Bornean forests—an utter impossibility."[248]

However far she went, she certainly did trek many miles through forests, up steep ridges, and stumbled down the other side, going barefoot through marshes and crossing enormous Dyak bridges across steep ravines that made her giddy. Often it would suddenly rain and utterly drench her. There was nothing to do but keep walking and let the subsequent hot tropical sun dry the clothes on her back. At one Dyak village there was no one who spoke Malay so she had to resort to drawing a picture of a small boat with one rower before the inhabitants could understand what she wanted.

At last she arrived at Landak. There Mr Sanders was "not a little astonished to see me arrive thus entirely alone; but still more when he heard of the rough journey I had had to make, and that on foot, in order to avoid the disturbed districts of the Dyaks".[249] Landak was a town of about 1,000 Malays living in a scattering of bamboo houses along the river bank. Pfeiffer observed the method by which earth was washed to separate out the diamonds. Having reached her remote destination and seen the mining, she was happy to leave it just as suddenly.

Having chalked up seeing a remote site, it was time to move on. There is something in this that differentiates a tourist from other sorts of traveller. As Mr Eager says of tourists in E. M. Forster's *A Room with a View* (1908): "their one anxiety [is] to get 'done' and 'through' and go somewhere else". Of course today the tourist not only wants to see this and that sight, but needs to have a photo taken in front of it. But there is little material difference in the activity of going from place to place and once that's done, immediately heading on somewhere else.

On 19 February 1852 Pfeiffer and Mr Sanders set off down the river to return to Pontianak, which they reached on the 22nd. She visited the Chinese quarter of the town and entered some opium dens to investigate.

> The smokers sat or lay upon mats, and had at their side small lamps to light their pipes ... There sits one with hollow cheeks, fixed eyes, trembling in every limb, the very picture of misery, for he has now no more money with which to attain to this enviable condition, and smoke himself into idiocy. ... Those who have once accustomed themselves to this poison cannot live without it; they can neither work nor think until they have inhaled another momentary supply of life from the terrible drug.[250]

In her book she condemned the British and Dutch governments for not only failing to suppress the opium trade but doing all they could to promote and profit by it. Pfeiffer declared that this was a stain on Christianity.

The majority of her time, despite the heat and swamps, was spent collecting insects and reptiles. She later wrote to Carl Ritter in Berlin that she felt that the preservation of natural history specimens was nowhere so difficult as in Borneo because of the extreme humidity. "Today one dries something and in a few days it is mouldy and rotting."[251] One of her finds was a millipede that would eventually make its way to the Berlin Museum where it would be described as a new species in 1881.[252]

One morning while she sat at the breakfast table with Mrs Willer, the sound of screaming and running feet came from the street. They went to see what was the matter and saw a servant of the police running across the street with his sword drawn. People were running in every direction and there was a loud cry "Amok, Amok!" Pfeiffer and Mrs Willer rushed inside and locked all the doors and windows. No European's account of travels in the region would be complete without a "running amok" scare. Wallace described running amok in his *Malay Archipelago* (1869):

> It is the national and therefore the honourable mode of committing suicide ... A Roman fell upon his sword, a Japanese rips up his stomach, and an Englishman blows out his brains with a pistol ... A man thinks himself wronged by society—he is in debt and cannot pay—he is taken for a slave or has gambled away his wife or child into slavery—he sees no way of recovering what he has lost, and becomes desperate. He will not put up with such cruel wrongs, but will be revenged on mankind and die like a hero. He grasps his kris-handle, and the next moment draws out the weapon and stabs a man to the heart. He runs on, with bloody kris in his hand, stabbing at every one he meets. "Amok! Amok!" then resounds through the streets. Spears, krisses, knives and guns are brought out against him. He rushes madly forward, kills all he can—men, women, and children—and dies overwhelmed by numbers amid all the excitement of a battle ... It is a delirious intoxication, a temporary madness that absorbs every thought and every energy.[253]

And yet for Pfeiffer in Pontianak, as for Wallace at Makassar, the amok turned out to be a false alarm.

Having seen all that she wanted to see in Borneo, Pfeiffer felt the urge to press on. She bought a passage on an Arabian ship bound for Batavia, the capital of the Dutch East Indies. A few days before she was due to sail, the Dutch resident, Thomas J. Willer, returned from abroad. Willer, forty-three, had been in the colonial civil service since 1832 and was long stationed in Sumatra. He had written detailed articles on the indigenous Batak peoples of Sumatra and the Alfuros of Seram. He was delighted to meet Madame Pfeiffer and immediately interested himself in helping her.

The master of the Arabian vessel was a "worthless fellow" he said and advised her not to travel with him. Willer insisted that she continue to lodge in his house until a better ship came along. In the meantime Pfeiffer drilled him for information about the Batak and Alfuros. She was mesmerised by the thought of aboriginal islanders that were little known to Europeans.

A few days later a Dutch ship, the *Christiaan Huygens*, arrived and Mr Willer gave her a ticket to Batavia. It was a transport ship carrying 120 soldiers and 46 women. Pfeiffer was scandalised by the behaviour of the thirty Europeans with the Javanese women. She was too delicate to give details so one can only speculate what it was that so shocked her. Perhaps it was just flirting, but probably rather more than that. At any rate Pfeiffer could only thank "God that I had no daughter or young girl with me, for I should have had to keep her locked up in her cabin".[254]

The ship finally got clear and under way on 6 April and sailed eighty miles north up the coast of Borneo where, two days later, they dropped anchor at the roadstead of Sambas. The entrance to the broad estuary was guarded by the little Fort Sort, perched atop a low hill. The commandant of the fort, Captain van Houten, took Pfeiffer as his guest even though the fort only boasted of two rooms. Pfeiffer described the place in her diary.

> I never saw so deplorable a little fort; it contained only a few low huts thatched with leaves, that just served to shelter two officers, the surgeon, and the soldiers. They said it had been erected in the greatest haste, when the Chinese at Mandora revolted and refused any longer to acknowledge the authority of the Dutch or pay their opium taxes. Three regular battles took place in the plain that lies at the foot of the hill Pameburg, on which the fort stands, and 4000 Chinese were defeated by 600 of the Dutch troops. The Chinese thereupon vowed obedience again; but their fidelity, as may be

supposed under these circumstances, is not much to be relied on, and, in fact, further disturbances are expected.[255]

After waiting at the fort for two days, a government boat was sent down from Sambas by the assistant resident Mr R. C. van Prehn. With the aid of this special conveyance, Pfeiffer reached Sambas in the evening. Mr van Prehn's house was already fully occupied with visiting officers so Pfeiffer was taken to the house of "the *Pangerang-rato*, a dignitary who … holds an intermediate rank between a rajah and a sultan".[256]

Every morning Mr van Prehn sent Pfeiffer a small boat with two Malay assistants to take her into the forest. Armed with her butterfly net and collecting box, Pfeiffer rambled about in search of animals. It was a delightful time for her, "neither insect, reptile, nor butterfly escaped our merciless scientific enthusiasm," she recalled. "In the afternoons I had employment enough to get my morning's victims into order."[257]

In Borneo she found what would later be declared a new species of freshwater prawn which was named after her: *Palaemon idea*. One of her scarab beetles was named *Myrina pfeifferi*. She also collected a new species of terrestrial slug, perhaps not the most glamorous of creatures, which was likewise named after her as *Vaginula idea*. In the evenings she could write letters. Among these were some to Petermann in London from which he chose to publish extracts in the *Athenaeum*. Thus even in utterly remote parts of her travels, she kept her supporters and the public informed of her adventures.

On 26 April she left Sambas again only to return to Pontianak where the ship took on a cargo of rattan and an astonishing 50,000 coconuts. She was able to have a last breakfast with her Dutch friends there. Captain van Houten surprised her with a present of insects and "a remarkably beautiful and rare plant".[258]

On the first of May 1852 Pfeiffer boarded the ship again but it took four days to weave in an out of the many sand banks in the area. One day a massive eighteen-foot python came swimming towards the ship. It had probably been swept out to sea by the tide. It swam towards the ship to get out of the water. The sailors killed and skinned it and were about to throw the body overboard.

Madame Pfeiffer standing nearby quietly advised them not to waste it, but to eat it. The sailors all laughed at her. She could eat it if she liked they playfully taunted. So she had a slice of the snake broiled and began to eat it in front of them. Impressed, and curious, one of the sailors asked to try it. He announced that it was actually quite good, so the others tried it too and soon the entire snake was cooked and eaten. Pfeiffer watched with a grin of victorious satisfaction.

A voyage of six days sailing almost due south across the Java Sea brought them to the roadstead of Batavia, the jewel of the Dutch possessions in the east. Once ashore Pfeiffer took a carriage to the stately two-storey Hotel der Nederlanden with its fine verandahs and window shutters thrown open to admit the welcome breeze. When the proprietor, Mr W. S. van Hogezand, found out that he had the famous Madame Pfeiffer as a guest, he refused to accept any payment. With a slight bow he begged her "not to spoil the pleasure he had in receiving so great a traveller".[259] It must have been quite strange to sleep in a soft bed with clean sheets and every luxury after her long adventure in Borneo. The next morning the Resident, Mr P. van Rees, to whom she had a letter of introduction from Sambas, called on her and invited her to stay at his house with his wife. Pfeiffer happily agreed.

Batavia had been established by the Dutch in the 17th century. The name came from the Roman word for what is now the Netherlands. A classical touch added to the intended status and nobility of the establishment. By 1852 the population was almost

400,000 of which 5,000 were Europeans and 50,000 Chinese. The Europeans lived around large open squares in the centre of the town. Their single-storey houses were surrounded by hedges and flowers and the whole scene gave Pfeiffer the impression of a city in a garden.

Ever the Biedermeier lady, Pfeiffer admired a set of furniture made by local craftsmen in the house of a Colonel van Schierbrandt "in the Gothic style, that he had had made in Surabaya. The chairs, sofas, &c., were most elaborately carved, and the upholstery work equally well finished."[260]

Pfeiffer toured the local institutions such as the governmental buildings on Waterloo Place, the prison and the impressive and modern hospital staffed with European doctors and native nurses for the care of all the inhabitants of Batavia. The museum was less impressive. It held "with the exception of specimens of minerals and many idols from Bali, nothing that is very remarkable, for it is in this country so very difficult to preserve specimens of quadrupeds, reptiles, and insects, that they are mostly sent to Holland."[261] Many or indeed most of the "idols" were actually from Java's Hindu–Buddhist past.

She met the famous Dutch ichthyologist Dr Pieter Bleeker. He showed her his collection of fish from all over the region, now floating motionless and bleached in bottles of preservative. He gave her some valuable fish specimens from Java. To return the favour, she would later send him further specimens. He later wrote of her in 1852:

> At the beginning of June 1852, I had the pleasure of meeting Mrs Ida Pfeiffer, the famous lady traveller, who had then just returned from Borneo, where she had visited the Dayak tribes in the river basin of the Kapuas alone and without protection, demonstrating a courage scarcely conceivable in a woman. … This remarkable woman

163

keeps herself busy with compiling natural historical collections, and with particular benevolence she passed on to me, during her stay in Batavia, a small collection of the fish from the Kapuas River, which she had gathered together in Pontianak.[262]

On 1 June 1852 she went with Mr van Rees by post horse to Buitenzorg (now Bogor), site of the magnificently opulent colonnaded palace of the Governor-General of the Dutch East Indies, A. J. Duymaer van Twist. With his high forehead and noble, almost haughty bearing, he had a reputation for being serious and taciturn. But he melted somewhat and became more talkative as he chatted with the eccentric Madame Pfeiffer in the well-appointed dining room of the palace.

Pfeiffer stayed with the Governor-General and his wife for three days and was wined and dined and introduced to all the great and the good in the area. She was taken to see a nearby cave where swiftlets built tiny cup-shaped nests with threads of their saliva. This is the principal and extremely costly ingredient in that curious delicacy, bird's nest soup. At that time, however, it was suspected that the bird's nests were made from seaweed. No one knew they were in fact eating bird spit. The eventual discovery of this fact has not dampened the popularity of bird's nest soup.

At the conclusion of her visit, Pfeiffer was sent on her way with post horses, a very unusual gift of the Governor-General. She ascended the mountains Megamendung and Pangerang, nearly 10,000 feet high, and taking advantage of the great post road, visited the town of Bandung in central Java where she was treated to a gamelan performance, though this did not please her much. At a rollicking pace she toured a tea plantation, rice terraces, coffee mills at Lembang, and climbed a recently active volcano which she noted did not erupt lava as she had seen at Vesuvius, Etna, and the volcanoes of Iceland, but instead ejected ashes and stones. She then went back through Buitenzorg to Batavia. Where she was again welcomed by Mr and Mrs van Rees.

Pfeiffer wanted very much to visit the great island of Sumatra but when she looked up the price of the steamer tickets, it was beyond her means, just as her wish to visit the great Hindu ruins of Java had been. Her host, Mr van Rees, mentioned her situation to some German merchants in the town and they chipped in to buy her two tickets from the W. Cores de Vries steamship company, to Sumatra and back. Pfeiffer was delighted and expressed her gratitude, though one starts to doubt her expressions of surprise at these frequent acts of generosity.

The following morning Pfeiffer boarded the clean and modern 120-horsepower steamer *Macassar*, under Captain Bergner, on the monthly run to Padang, West Sumatra. Halfway up the west coast, Padang was the chief town of the Dutch settlements in Sumatra. When Pfeiffer arrived on 13 July 1852, the Dutch Governor, Mr van Swieten, heard of her arrival and almost immediately came to meet and invite her to stay in his beautiful house about four miles from town.

Newspaper reports throughout the region, indeed all the way to Bombay and Australia, had informed the reading public of the movements and exploits of the celebrated traveller. This very same day a self-congratulatory report appeared in Singapore's *Straits Times* that British officials had everywhere assisted Madame Pfeiffer and thus aided "in her important researches of the countries, the inhabitants, and the works of nature in this part of the world. ... Madam Pfeiffer dreads neither fatigue nor danger in the completion of her aim—the advancement of science."[263]

In Sumatra, Pfeiffer's target was the Minangkabau Highlands far to the north. It was there that the infamous Batak cannibals lived. Willer had told Pfeiffer all about them at Pontianak. She simply had to see them. Could they really be as terrible as legend had it? But once again a familiar scene unfolded. When the Dutch officials at Padang learned where she wanted to go, they tried very hard to dissuade her. This was not just a perilous journey beyond the bounds of Dutch territory. "They told me that, in 1835, two missionaries, Messrs. Layman and Mansor, had been killed and eaten by the Battakers, and that no European could possibly venture among them without a military escort."[264] These were not idle rumours. Three years after her visit, three French missionaries attempting to penetrate the same region were similarly killed and reputedly devoured. But Pfeiffer's ears were closed to such warnings. She was confident that a woman could travel where no European man would be tolerated. Her greatest desire was to boldly go where no European man had gone before.

And so she set out on horseback on 19 July 1852. Travelling north along the government road, she could stay at the little rest houses located about a day's ride apart. The roads were busy with people. Boys walked along with proud fighting cocks under their arms. Porters carried large bundles of goods for market on their heads.

Pfeiffer always kept a close eye on her porters. She had heard a story about a Dutch mineralogist who had collected several chests of minerals which he paid some porters to take to Padang. Once on their own, the porters looked in the heavy chests and found only rocks. So, to ease their burdens, they dumped out the rocks and carried the chests to the edge of Padang where they filled them up again with random stones from the roadside. The poor mineralogist only realised that his treasures were irretrievably lost after he returned to Europe to find that he had instead several chests full of worthless pebbles.

Each day Pfeiffer started out early in the morning and could reach the next rest house by noon. After a short rest she would set off on "one of my insect and butterfly hunts". In the woods around her the colourful birds sang and lithe little monkeys jumped from bough to bough. "In the larger villages I was struck by the appearance of open halls, built of wood, and with elegantly carved roofs, painted in gay colours. These, I was told, were for the rajahs to hold their courts in, and hear complaints; and in them also all important commercial affairs are settled."[265]

She arrived at a town called Fort de Koch (Bukittinggi) on the 22nd. Here she was greeted by the Resident of the territory, Colonel A. van der Hart, a distinguished officer who had taken part in all the wars in Sumatra from 1830 to 1849. He generously showed Pfeiffer about the area. She was introduced to the village rajah and his family, dressed in their finery, at their ornately constructed home. Pfeiffer described the scene:

> The style of building in the houses is curious and original: they are of wood, painted in bright colours, and very much longer than they are broad; and each end runs together into a peak, which rises above the central part, so as to give them more the appearance of ships than of houses. The roofs are sometimes made in two or three slopes, each slope being provided with two peaks, and looking very much like a Turkish saddle. The front and side walls are decorated, often quite covered, with finely and elaborately carved arabesques. The houses stand upon piles; but these are invisible, being covered with bamboos or boards, and the whole effect is very peculiar and pretty.
>
> The interior of these ornamental-looking houses consists of one large apartment, which takes in the whole length and three quarters of the breadth of the house; and at the extremity of it is a small raised compartment that looks as if it had been added after the house was built, which is furnished with mats, carpets, cushions, &c, and is intended as a place of honour for the most distinguished woman present. The back of the house is divided into little rooms for the fires and sleeping places, but which are pitch dark, as the back

wall of the house has no windows. Opposite every house stands a miniature one, carved and painted in the same style, which serves for the preservation of the store of rice.[266]

Just three years later Colonel van der Hart was to come to an untimely and violent end. By then he had become Governor of Sulawesi (then known as Celebes) at Makassar. In May 1855 he severely reprimanded his servant, Kimping, for negligence. The man was so insulted and shamed by this that he decided to take revenge. Kimping concealed himself in the house before the family went to bed. Then, at 2.30 a.m., he crept out of his hiding place and taking his kris, mounted the stairs to his master's bedroom. Finding van der Hart asleep in his bed, Kimping stabbed at the sleeping man.

Only wounded, van der Hart leapt up and began to wrestle with his attacker. But slash after slash wounded him further and his blood splashed all over the walls of the bedroom. After receiving two kris thrusts into his chest and many other cuts, he tried to flee down the corridor. Kimping sprang after him and struck a deep gash between the Colonel's shoulders whereupon he fell to the floor and was stabbed through the right side into the heart and died.

During this horrific struggle, Kimping had received a wound himself in the abdomen. He then went after Mrs Elisa van der Hart and succeeded only in wounding her arm before she escaped through a window. She ran with her children to the house of Dr F. A. M. Schmitz, where Pfeiffer had been a guest. Meanwhile, Kimping murdered one of the children's maids before, weakened by his wound, he limped to an empty part of the house where he collapsed with exhaustion and eventually bled to death.[267]

By 28 July 1852, Pfeiffer had reached Muara Sipongi, a village about halfway to her planned destination. The comptroller, Mr Johannes Cornelis Schoggers, invited the headmen of all the surrounding villages to gather and discuss Pfeiffer's plan to visit the independent Batak territories to the north. After conferring together they were unanimous in concluding that she should abandon the idea as simply too dangerous.

But Pfeiffer, indomitable to the last, would not be discouraged. "I had tolerably well made up my mind," she recalled. And so there was no talking her out of it. There was one thing she would rather like to know, she told them. Did the Batak really "not put their victims out of their pain at once, but tied them living to stakes, and, cutting pieces off them, consumed them by degrees with tobacco and salt?" No, they answered, only criminals were treated to this particular form of tortuous execution.

Pfeiffer set about gathering all the information she could. She learned, for example, that the Batak, "like the Dyaks, appear to be destitute of any kind of religion; they do not pray, and they have neither priests nor temples; yet they believe in good and bad spirits".[268] At one time Europeans believed that although there were different religions in the world, all people believed in a god or gods. This was taken to be a powerful argument for the existence of god. The discovery of peoples who did not was unsettling because it showed that belief in god was not universal.

Pfeiffer pressed on and more days of riding followed. On 2 August she reached Padang Sidempuan where the last Europeans resided. She rested for three days under the care of the comptroller Mr A. T. Hammer. He too tried to persuade Pfeiffer not to venture into the territory of the savage cannibals. Not two years before, he told her, four local men from the Dutch territory had been seized by the Batak and subsequently "killed and *eaten*". Once again Pfeiffer replied that she would not be deterred. She would go on. She would visit the Batak and continue all the way to Lake Toba, known only from word of mouth, which no European eye had yet gazed upon.

Mr Hammer provided her with a guide who spoke Malay and the local Batak language as well as letters to some of the rajahs she would meet along the way, some of whom had occasional contact with the Dutch. By now she could speak a little Malay herself. Then she put her papers in order and gave them to Mr Hammer, asking that he send them to her family if she did not return. She then bade farewell to "perhaps the last Europeans whom in this world I was ever to see".[269]

Thus, on 6 August 1852, she set out for the final frontier. Accompanied by a single Batak guide, she rode twenty miles further north to the village of Sipirok, nestled in a small valley, where the Dutch had a coffee trading plantation operated by a Malay man. She had now traversed almost a quarter of the length of the great island of Sumatra. From this point she would leave Dutch-controlled territory. And she would also have to travel on foot. The way ahead lead through thick jungle, over steep hills and down slippery trails.

After each day's march into the outer territories she was welcomed by the rajah of a village and permitted to shelter there for the night. At a village she mistakenly called Danau, the rajah was so eager to help her that he sacrificed a buffalo calf in her honour, in order that the next stage of her journey would not be hampered by the displeasure of evil sprits. Pfeiffer noted that both men and women in this area wore their hair long and twisted up into a knot. The local girls had from ten to fifteen leaden rings in their ears. With unusual candour, Pfeiffer recorded that "many of the girls were of considerable *embonpoint*".[270] That is, they had very large breasts.

On the morning of 8 August Pfeiffer set off again in the company of her guide, the friendly rajah of Danau, five of his people and two porters. At first a large group from the village accompanied them, but only to the edge of their territory. They stopped at their border and said goodbye to Pfeiffer and wished her well, but they also pointed to her throat "giving me to understand by signs that the wild men would cut my head off, and eat me up". She remarked stoically that "this was not very encouraging". All the same she declared, "it never once entered my head to desist".[271]

The way forward was very rough; they pushed through dense forest and meadows of scratchy grass six-feet high. Every afternoon it rained and her clothes would be soaked. She was unable to change because she was never left alone. They spent the night in the woods in an impromptu bamboo shelter.

The next day it rained even more heavily and the way led through a swamp so that Pfeiffer was caked in mud up to her knees. In the evening her companions made a slight shelter of leaves and bamboo to give some protection from the rain. The firewood was wet and they barely managed to heat a meal of dirty rice and uncleaned fish. As night fell and impenetrable darkness filled the remote forest, Pfeiffer finally did become afraid. The otherwise fearless Pfeiffer really was afraid of the dark. Now she could not stop thinking about tigers, serpents or other wild beasts or wild men coming out of the darkness to attack. But in the end the night passed peacefully.

The next day's march was equally arduous. The way led through thickets of almost impenetrably tall grasses and streams and swamps to be waded through. She emerged with "my legs covered with little leeches" and on one occasion she was almost drowned. "Two [Batak] saved my life while I was crossing a deep river, the rapid current of which carried me off."[272] In such thick and entangled forest every plant seemed to be edged with thorns. Her hands and arms were covered with cuts and bled profusely. Because they were constantly wading through water and mud she had to go barefoot. "I had my feet continually pierced with thorns, and cut through by the sharp edged jungle-grass," she recalled.[273] Leeches were a constant nuisance attaching themselves to her legs and feet. When they camped each evening one of her companions would extract the thorns from her feet with surprisingly delicate flicks of the large curved blade of his parang.

The next day, at long last, they neared the edge of the forest. Suddenly they heard the yells of people ahead. Her small party stopped and kept silent. After a long pause, they crept forward stealthily. Creeping to the edge of the forest they found themselves before a river. In it were perhaps forty Batak people, almost completely naked, fishing. The rajah of Danau alone went forward to ask for permission for Pfeiffer to enter their territory. After many questions, permission was granted.

Pfeiffer's party crossed the river and walked on through a hilly terrain but now at least there were good open paths. They came to a village where they could spend the night. The group was allowed to occupy a dilapidated old hut that was in the slow process of falling down and returning to the jungle. Pfeiffer recorded the name of the rajah as Hali-Bonar. She had brought a letter in Batak to him from Mr Hammer. Hali-Bonar was particularly sympathetic and would prove a very great help to her. Two headmen then came and objected vehemently to Pfeiffer continuing into their territory. But at last they were persuaded to give their permission. Pfeiffer was certain that this was granted only because she was a woman.

The rajah of Danau and his attendants now left to return home. Hali-Bonar would accompany Pfeiffer and her guide to the next village and beyond. As each village had its own territory, it was necessary to seek permission to proceed from each village leader. It was a slow process and Pfeiffer chafed to push on.

She described the Batak people as "light brown, or brownish-yellow". The men had little or no facial hair. Both men and women wore black sarongs, sometimes trimmed with glass beads. The men wore their hair in a variety of styles. Some wore it long and flowing, others wore it short and a few had theirs sticking up all over like a brush. And everywhere the people chewed sirih. The characteristically Sumatran styles of Batak houses, although all recognisably similar, vary considerably between the dozen or so ethnic groups.

Pfeiffer asked the Batak to perform some of their dances. "The sword-dance I found, to my surprise, to be exactly the same as that which I had seen among the Dyaks in Borneo."[274] Their artefacts too reminded her of the Dyaks. Finally, the people performed the dance that accompanied, or represented, a victim or criminal being killed and eaten. Pfeiffer sat up to watch every detail of these clues to the most notorious aspect of this little-known people. A log was used to represent the victim. It was bound to a stake with a straw hat as the head. Pfeiffer described what happened next.

> The dancers lifted up their feet as high as they could, and darted their knives at the supposed victim in a most expressive manner. At length one of them gave him the first stroke, and this example was speedily followed by all the rest. They struck the head (the straw cap, namely) from the body, and laid it upon a mat spread out to receive it, taking care to preserve the blood. They then danced round it, uttering wild and joyful cries. Some raised the head in their hands and carried it to their lips, appearing to lick the blood from it; others flung themselves on the ground, and appeared to be lapping up the gore from the dripping head, or they dipped their fingers into it and sucked them; doing all this with the appearance of the greatest delight: the predominant expression, indeed, of their faces was that of pleasure rather than of cruelty.[275]

The pleasure was likely simply that of performing before an exotic foreign visitor. She reported that the nose, ears, soles of the feet, the cheeks, the palms of the hands and the liver were regarded as the finest pieces and the first three were always given to the rajah.[276]

The next day her journey continued to another village. And the following day was the same. As she eyed the villages on her way through she thought that one thing that surely characterised the Batak was their unusual filthiness. For example, they never cleaned the pot after cooking the rice. The dinners she was given consisted of a fowl torn in four pieces and throw in the fire until quite black, whereas they themselves took the entrails. To her disgust she saw that they also ate worms and beetles. This was not out of hunger as she saw they had ample harvests – but as some form of inexplicable delicacy.

"When I call them filthy," she would later write, perhaps it would be thought an exaggeration. So to demonstrate her point, and at the risk that "my readers will wonder how I could write down such a thing" she described an incident that utterly horrified the very depths of her Biedermeier sensibilities.

As Pfeiffer sat at the front of a house one day, she saw a mother sitting nearby who was busy weaving with a ten-month-old child strapped on her back. The child began to cry so the mother put it on her breast. But as the child had been stuffed full of rice not long before, the milk was too much for it. Pfeiffer recognised the signs of what was going to happen next. The child defecated all over its mother. Pfeiffer continued:

> The state of the mother's lap I need not describe. But the lady was not in the least disturbed by these accidents; she sat still, without taking any notice, but presently called a dog, and induced him to afford his assistance, and also to lick the child's person a little, holding it to him in various positions for that purpose. She then tied it upon her back again, and went on with her work as if nothing had happened, and without making any further attempt at cleansing her sarong.[277]

One day in mid August 1852, as they entered the Silindung Valley, Hali-Bonar suddenly warned Pfeiffer to stick very close to him.

Six of his men, armed with spears, marched in front, followed by Hali-Bonar, with Pfeiffer and her guide bringing up the rear. After them came a number of curious stragglers. Things were getting more complicated and the local people less willing to allow strangers to pass through their territories. Once more permission to pass was obtained. At the next village things became much, much more serious.

More than eighty men armed with spears and parangs suddenly blocked the road ahead. As Pfeiffer's little procession approached, the armed men moved around and encircled her. These were tall, muscular men and their expressions looked indescribably fierce. They yelled and shouted loudly. Pfeiffer tried to look nonchalant and sat down on a stone pretending to be unconcerned.

Then some rajahs came up to her with threatening looks. They gestured angrily and "gave me clearly to understand that if I did not turn back they would kill and eat me". Despite the fact that she could not understand a word of their language, it must have seemed unambiguous. "They pointed with their knives to my throat, and gnashed their teeth at my arm, moving their jaws then, as if they already had them full of my flesh."[278] Here she was in the middle of Sumatra, encircled by armed men who were angrily shouting at her and threatening to kill and eat her. And yet Pfeiffer somehow remained calm.

Pfeiffer had memorised a little speech in case something like this happened. She stood up and looked at the man closest to her. She slapped him familiarly on the shoulder and said with breathtaking bravado in a half Malay, half Batak phrase: "Don't eat me. I am an old woman so my flesh is very tough."[279]

This phrase, and probably her poor pronunciation, as well as her accompanying pantomime, amused the men and they suddenly began to laugh. The tension was dispelled. The circle of armed men dispersed. And yet, despite this, she was not deterred. "Rejoicing not a little at having escaped this danger, I journeyed on."[280] Another explanation is possible. The men might instead have been protesting that she could not continue because the people in the territories beyond were dangerous and would kill and eat her.[281]

The next day she was again allowed to stay in a village but the voices of discontent and dissension were getting louder and the debates about what to do with the pushy foreign woman more protracted. Every few minutes a new rajah and his spearmen arrived at the village until it was entirely filled with armed men talking and staring at the strange visitor.

At last a general consensus was noisily come to, the foreigner was to go no farther. "This was, indeed, hard!" she wailed. "So near to the goal, and after so many toils and dangers, to be obliged to turn back! According to the accounts of the natives I could not be now more than ten miles from Lake [Toba]."[282]

She begged to be allowed to go on without her guide or at least to climb the hills ahead to just get a glimpse of the great lake. It was impossible. These Batak were on unfriendly terms with the lake people whose territory that was. They assured her, through her guide, that no European had ever yet come so far as this, without being killed and eaten.

Nothing upset Pfeiffer more than not being able to pursue her chosen course, or was it to tick off another "first"? Again and again she would push on whatever the hardships, whatever the risk. It was a bitter pill indeed. But this time there was no other way.

What Pfeiffer did not know was that according to Batak tradition, the area around Lake Toba was the origin of their people and so sacred and taboo for outsiders. The following year the lake was seen by a European for the first time, a linguist named Herman Neubronner van der Tuuk. It is the largest volcanic crater lake in the world. Within it is an island, Samosir, which is almost as large as the island state of Singapore.

And so on 15 August 1852 Pfeiffer commenced her melancholy and involuntary journey back, but by a different route. But she would not go home empty-handed. In addition to her unique experiences she took away a few artefacts including a finely carved magic staff, a *tunggal panaluan*, which she would eventually sell to the museum in Vienna. It still survives there. *Tunggal panaluan* were said to be carved from trees to which a human victim had been bound and then killed. A more common tradition is that they represent a mythical tree into which multiple people and animals had been absorbed. A *tunggal panaluan* was believed to be imbued with supernatural powers and was used by the shamans for performing rituals and divinations.

At one village along the way a very tall and ferocious looking rajah came forward. Again Pfeiffer was encircled by spearmen. The rajah shouted angrily and barely allowed those who accompanied her to speak. He pushed her several times and gestured that she should follow him into his large house on stilts. "But Hali-Bonar gave me a look, that I understood, not to do so, but to remain close to him. It was not till after a very long and fierce dispute that he obtained permission for me to pass, and it was evident my life was hanging by a hair."[283] When they were at last allowed to leave, Hali-Bonar told her to walk as fast as she could. Once they were out of sight of the village they ran through the forest until they reached another village that seemed less hostile.

Day followed day like this, trekking from village to village. Pfeiffer counted more than fifty of them during her journey back. On the 19th they reached a village she called Bolanahito. "Here I took leave of my true friend Hali-Bonar, to whose powerful protection I certainly more than once owed my life."[284] Then there was just the thick and unforgiving forest to traverse.

Finally, on 21 August 1852, Pfeiffer reached the village she called Danau where the people were astonished to see that she had returned alive. Her guide, with whom she was by this time utterly exasperated, suddenly made himself scarce. She suspected that he had somehow contributed to her failure to reach Lake Toba. Perhaps he had conspired to get her to turn back so that he could get out of the territory of the Batak as quickly as possible. Pfeiffer would later complain of him bitterly to Mr Hammer.

On the 23rd she reached Padang Sidempuan where Mr Hammer fed and nursed her for a few days until she was rested and had regained her strength. By 9 September she was back in Fort de Koch but there she was struck with fever for the first time. It was almost certainly malaria which would not be formally identified until the end of the century.

Once Pfeiffer was sufficiently recovered from her bout of fever, she headed off on another expedition, this time to Payakumbuh, to the north east, where a German botanist, Dr Bauer, was stationed. She added to her collections and together with other friends she and Dr Bauer ascended the great volcano, Gunung Merapi or Fire Mountain, now the most active volcano in Sumatra. When they reached the brink of the crater at over 2,800 metres, they looked down and could see that "thick black columns of smoke were rising from two openings … and an incessant hiss and roar gave warning of the activity of the fires beneath".[285]

On 7 October she was back in Padang where she was struck by the fever again. She was carefully and tenderly nursed by a Dutch family with whom she stayed. After twelve days she had recovered sufficiently to take the steamer back to Batavia. Sumatra had been one of her greatest triumphs and the unstinting welcome and assistance of the Dutch officials with information, lodging, guides and horses was everything she could have wished for. She left with feelings of particular fondness for them.

In addition to her Batak artefacts she had accumulated a good collection of natural history specimens. She gave several of her freshwater fish to Dr Bleeker in Batavia. Two of these, a lizard loach (*Homaloptera gymnogaster*) and a checker barb (*Puntius oligolepis*), he described as new species in his great work on the fish of the archipelago.[286] Another, a new species of ray-finned fish, he named *Cobitis pfeifferi*.[287] Her specimens were particularly valuable to him because she recorded details of the habitat where the fish were collected. Bleeker thanked Pfeiffer for her contributions in a scientific paper: "I owe them to a large degree to the famous woman traveller Mrs Ida Pfeiffer, whose friendship I consider to be an honour and whose achievements do not need my praise."[288] And, with her typical range of captures, she also came away with what was said to be a new species of red-eyed crab.

Back in Batavia Pfeiffer stayed with a different family so as not to impose too much on the kindness of Mr and Mrs van Rees. Ever restless, she made enquiries about seeing more of the Dutch East Indies. There were two mail and passenger steamship companies in Java, one belonging to Cores de Vries and the other to Maclain Watson and Co. She called on the directors of both to see if they would consider giving her cheaper tickets. Once again her fame and uniqueness produced very valuable dividends. Both directors issued her with a special note that provided unlimited first-class passages.

Thus equipped, a week later she was off again, this time on the steamship *Koningin der Nederlanden*, under Captain Henri Chevallier, bound for Semarang in the middle of Java. There she visited a large tobacco factory and at Grobogan she learned about the terrible famine there of 1849 when an estimated 120,000 people perished. As the tragedy unfolded, several people wrote to Batavia to call for help. But the government seemed to believe only intelligence from its own officers. So an official report was requested from the Resident of Semarang who, inexplicably, denied that anything was wrong. By the time the truth was realised, it was too late for many thousands.

Pfeiffer was horrified as she reflected on this tragedy:

> Could not a confidential agent have been immediately sent to ascertain the truth? But there were only human lives to save! Had anything so important as the arrears of taxes been in question it would probably have been done ... And what punishments were awarded by the Government to the servants who had so shamefully neglected their duty, and abused their trust? These! The Resident was pensioned with a handsome yearly salary; the Assistant-Resident received an appointment as *Resident* to another province.[289]

Even three years later traces of disaster were still evident with empty and dilapidated houses everywhere.

Pfeiffer left Semarang on 26 November, and travelled only forty-eight miles to Magelang to see the ruins of the great ninth-century Buddhist temple of Borobudur. The ruins were rediscovered in 1814 by men sent by Sir Thomas Stamford Raffles, then Lieutenant Governor of Java, during the Napoleonic wars when the British had taken over the Dutch territories to keep them out of the hands of Napoleon.

The temple was mysteriously abandoned sometime in the fourteenth century. In 1835 the monument was fully cleared of vegetation and volcanic ash revealing the astonishing structure, the size of a hill. It has over 500 statues of Buddha and 400 bas-reliefs lining the walls as one walks around the structure towards the top. It is now the most visited tourist site in all of Indonesia. Strangely, Pfeiffer was not very impressed with the architecture which she thought was "nothing very remarkable". When she visited it, however, it was still in ruins unlike its fully restored appearance today. She noted that "the building is crowned by something like a great bell, beneath which is seated an image of Buddha, purposely left unfinished, because the Holy One cannot be completed by human hands".[290] She was able to compare this Buddhist monument with the various temples she had visited in India.

> The sculptures here, both figures and bas-reliefs, appear to me much more accurate and tasteful in their execution than those I saw at the temples of Elora, Adjunta, and others in British India; but the arabesques, bells, &c. are finer there, as well as more colossal in size. The architecture of the building itself, can certainly not be compared with that of the grander specimens in Hindostan. In the mode of building without mortar, and the formation of a kind of arch by the projection of one stone beyond another, they appear to be the same.[291]

Her countryman, a forty-year-old engineer named Frans Carel Wilsen, had been commissioned by the Dutch government to copy the statues and reliefs in pen and ink drawings on vellum. Just before Pfeiffer's visit he had completed the enormous labour which had taken him four years of kneeling and sweating against the dry stone walls to copy the scenes of Buddhist stories inscribed in stone.

Working in the ruins was still dangerous. Sometimes the stones, which have no mortar, would come falling down without any apparent reason. His dedication and perseverance, like the efforts of Captain Gill at the Ajanta caves in India, were the result of governmental decisions far away. The incentive was to collect and record comprehensive collections of data. A more cynical view today might be that they wished to record their colonial possessions or exercise some sort of power, but at the time those involved, such as Wilsen and Gill, thought they were preserving precious and possibly yet-to-perish ancient monuments for posterity. They believed that the monuments would continue to degrade and ultimately be lost. Wilsen was anxious lest a large earthquake topple the remains of the temple at any time.

During the following week Pfeiffer visited the two independent sultanates of Yogyakarta and Surakarta. Each ruler granted her an audience at his palace. Along the way she visited the ruins of the eighth-century Buddhist Sewu temple complex. It was known locally as the "thousand temples", a slight exaggeration as there are 249.

On 4 December 1852 Pfeiffer boarded the small steamer *Amboyna* which in two days reached Surabaya, on the eastern end of Java. Pfeiffer stayed in the "magnificent" house of the courteous fellow Catholic, Resident Pierre de Perez. He was one of the more liberal figures in the Dutch administration. Unfortunately the rains had set in and Pfeiffer was not able to do her usual sightseeing or collecting. Instead, she spent her time comfortably indoors writing letters. One of these was a detailed report of her travels to Petermann in London. He, in turn, published much of it in the *Athenaeum*.

With the rainy season in Java in full swing, Pfeiffer decided to take the next Cores de Vries steamer, the *Banda*, to Makassar on the multi-limbed island of Sulawesi (Celebes) to the northeast. Makassar had been the chief Dutch settlement on that island since the late seventeenth century. It was also one of the busiest ports in the whole archipelago.

The *Banda* dropped anchor on 17 December 1852. Pfeiffer thought the town, set in the middle of a vast plain, "a small, almost European-looking, town, with a fort. The Government-house is small and insignificant, and the Europeans live in poor-looking little stone houses, lying close together, along the side of a beautiful piece of meadow land, called *Hendrik's-pad*."[292]

Makassar gave its name to two new English words in the nineteenth century. The first was Macassar oil, a hair treatment made from coconut oil that gave a gentleman's hair a glossy and tidy appearance. When everyone wore a hat outdoors, greased down hair was particularly convenient. However, the oil on men's heads began to soil the tall backs of upholstered chairs. In the 1850s the "antimacassar" came to the rescue. These often embroidered cloth covers were laid over the backs of chairs to protect them from soiling. Even today the white squares on the back of airline or first-class train carriage seats are still called, though few remember the name, an antimacassar.

But December is also the rainy season in Makassar. To Pfeiffer's frustration, the rains were duly unceasing. Further exploration of the area was out of the question. So, with her free ticket in hand, she boarded the *Amboyna* on the 21st to take a passage east to the island of Banda in the Maluku Islands, the famous Spice Islands. Banda is the original home of nutmeg; originally it grew nowhere else. In three days the little steamer reached the beautiful harbour amidst the tiny group of islands dominated by the perfectly conical volcano Gunung Api with a column of steam rising gently up into the clear tropical skies.

Almost as soon as the ship arrived, a man came on board to report some shocking news. Just four weeks before a terrible earthquake had struck the island. As the residents stood the following day blinking at the ruins of their little town, a second earthquake hit. The water in the bay suddenly drained eerily away leaving the bottom of the sea exposed to the air and light. Then, just as suddenly, a great and unstoppable tsunami twenty-four feet high came rolling over the bay and up onto the shore. The boats and small vessels were tossed about like toys, smashing against the rocks or trees further up the beach.

People ran inland in terror but many could not escape. More than eighty were drowned. A large ship that lay at anchor was twice grounded. She was still under repair. The second earthquake not only destroyed many buildings but also thousands of nutmeg trees which were killed by the salt water that had washed up into the orchards.

While the *Amboyna* lay at anchor, Pfeiffer stayed in the town with a German military physician named Krause. Exploring the town revealed the devastation of the earthquakes. The buildings were almost all either destroyed or in a precarious condition. People had thrown up hasty wooden shelters beside them, afraid to sleep in their houses lest another earthquake collapse their damaged homes onto them as they slept. Pfeiffer toured some of the large nutmeg plantations. Here in its native home she found that the trees grew much greater and stronger than the ones she had seen in Singapore.

On 27 December the *Amboyna* steamed on towards her namesake, the island of Amboyna (Ambon), the Dutch capital of the Maluku Islands. This island is the native home of cloves. In past centuries cloves were traded from island to island, from town to town and across Asia, some of them making it all the way to Europe. Of course by that time their price had gone up hundreds if not thousands of times. It was to gain access to these immensely valuable spices, literally worth more than their weight in gold, that Europeans had sailed in their precarious fifteenth- and sixteenth-century ships to these faraway islands in the first place.

The little town at Ambon only had about 1,500 inhabitants. The local people here were Christians, as they had been since the time of the Portuguese occupation in the sixteenth century. Since the coming of the Dutch in 1605 they had converted from Catholics to protestants.

In order to properly see the island, Pfeiffer walked from one end of it to the other and spent days collecting insects. Another bout of the Sumatra fever slowed her down somewhat. New Year's Day 1853 was celebrated with other Europeans at the surprisingly modest home of the Dutch governor of the Maluku Islands, Mr C. M. Visser. Wallace would celebrate the New Year in the same house five years later. He remarked, "Tea & coffee were presented as is almost universal during a visit as well as cigars for on no occasion is smoking prohibited in the Dutch colonies, & the ladies stand the fire most heroically."[293]

But Wallace met a different governor because Mr Visser was by then dead. Just two years after Pfeiffer's visit, Visser tragically fell from an enormous waterfall at lake Tondano on Sulawesi and was killed. Wallace later visited this waterfall and left a vivid description.

> The river enters a gorge, very narrow and tortuous, along which it rushes furiously for a short distance and then plunges into a great chasm, forming the head of a large valley. Just above the fall the channel is not more than ten feet wide, and here a few planks are thrown across, whence, half hid by luxuriant vegetation, the mad waters may be seen rushing beneath, and a few feet farther plunge into the abyss. Both sight and sound are grand and impressive.[294]

The waterfall is sadly no more. It has been replaced by a hydroelectric power installation. This in turn leads to increasing accumulation of sediments in the lake and the increase in algae and water hyacinths and thus less fish.

On 11 January 1853 Pfeiffer sailed over to the small nearby island of Saparua where there was a small Dutch fort and an Assistant Resident. From here, on the 18th, she sailed in a native proa to the large island of Seram a few miles further north. Seram was not occupied by the Dutch and was little known, perfect for Pfeiffer.

"I wished to visit the interior of this island, which is inhabited by the wild Alforas, more enthusiastic collectors of human heads, I understood, than even the Dyaks. Hitherto only two Europeans had ever ventured among them, and one of these had taken 150 men with him for his protection."[295] The Alfuros of Seram were the other exotic tribe, in addition to the Batak, that had been described to Pfeiffer by Thomas Willer in Borneo.

At the village of Makariki, Pfeiffer met the local rajah and passed on the request of the Dutch governor that he assist her. It was agreed. Twenty men, mostly Malays but also some Alfuros, were gathered. They set out on foot into the interior on 20 January. They slowly climbed the jungle-shrouded mountains ahead of them. Pfeiffer was not satisfied with the sago bread and bananas they had brought as provisions. Fortunately, her native companions caught a wild boar and on one occasion a man climbed a tall tree and clubbed a cuscus which was eaten for dinner.

On 22 January they reached an Alfuro village of about thirty houses on stilts. It looked abandoned. There was not a soul in sight. The guides told Pfeiffer that the village was indeed inhabited but the Alfuros were so shy that as soon as they heard approaching voices or steps they hurried into their houses and locked the doors. As they looked around the village for a sign of life, a heavy rain shower suddenly erupted. They knocked on doors but no one would open so Pfeiffer's little band sheltered underneath the houses until the rain died away.

On the 23rd they reached the Malay village of Passanea on the other side of the island. From here Pfeiffer took a proa to the settlement of Wahai where the Dutch had their only station on Seram with a small fort and thirty men. "I remained in the proa, while I dispatched my letter of introduction from Mr Visser, to the Commandant Lieutenant J. W. C. Kern, who would not believe my messenger, when he informed him that a European woman had made the journey overland, and repeatedly assured me afterwards that 'he should not have been more surprised if the sky had fallen.'"[296]

Mr Kern had been living at Wahai for two years. He confirmed that the Alfuros were indeed headhunters. In fact, during her stay news came in to Mr Kern that one village had attacked another and taken five heads. Surely this was exotic enough to satisfy Madame Pfeiffer. For six happy days she collected insects in the surrounding forest, quite unafraid of losing her head. She discovered a new species of trap-jaw ant which was later sold by Stevens to the British Museum.[297]

Mr Kern then took her by boat to Saway to visit two Alfuro villages. Pfeiffer naturally undertook her usual domestic inspections. She reported to her readers:

> The huts of the Alforas are small, and built, like those of the Malays, on piles. The walls are made of the ribs of the sago leaves, and the roofs of the leaves themselves. In the interior you find only a few mats and earthen pots, a parang, bows and arrows, a lance, and a wooden shield four feet long and six or eight inches thick.[298]

The people were almost completely naked. Their appearance was very different from the Malays. They had a light brown complexion, "fine black eyes" and thick black curly hair. But these people did not seem as remote and untainted by the outside world as the village Pfeiffer had seen high in the mountains.

When she headed back across the island she took with her a rajah who promised to be able to get the mountain Alfuros to come out of their houses. When they eventually reached the village the rajah did not have much success and finally resorted to dragging and pushing people outside so that Pfeiffer could see them.

Face to face at last, the notorious headhunters were terrified by the pale-skinned lady in woollen trousers and petticoat. "The children ran from me screaming as if for their lives; and it was as much as the Rajah could do to induce the grownup girls to stay and hold out their hands to me."[299]

Now able to look inside, Pfeiffer found that some of their houses were indeed decorated with human skulls. Inside one of the larger houses she counted a long garland of 136 skulls and innumerable jawbones of wild hogs and deer. To satisfy Pfeiffer's curiosity, her rajah friend demonstrated, with an elaborate pantomime, how a head was taken. He laid down in the bushes to ambush a victim. He then quietly got up, flung his spear and then immediately rushed forward brandishing his parang and with a swift stroke, decapitated the imaginary victim. The rajah then smilingly presented Pfeiffer with a stone, in lieu of a head. Pfeiffer breathlessly described what happened next.

> I begged the Rajah to introduce to me the most renowned *headsmen* of his tribe, and he pointed out some of the men who were sitting round me; and told me this one had conquered two heads; that one three; but *he himself only one*. My astonishment when I heard of this fact, and looked at the mild, good-natured face of this man, can hardly be expressed. The other heroes, too, looked as modest and complacent when their deeds were alluded to, as if the most amiable and praiseworthy actions had been in question. The cutting off a head is, in their eyes, what the winning a battle is in that of a European general, or sabreing his enemy in that of a soldier. Is there, in fact, much difference?[300]

Pfeiffer and her small procession continued their march on down the mountains back to the coast whence they had come. Her provisions of rice had been damaged by moisture and became inedible so she ate from the sago cakes and plantains that the porters had brought with them.[301]

During their first night on the forest trek all had fallen asleep except for one man assigned to keep watch. Late at night he quietly woke the others and pointed into the forest, "to our terror, we saw a faint light glimmer". The men sprang up and gathered their weapons as dark figures with torches approached.

It was half a dozen Alfuros. They said they had seen a large group of men moving through the forest, perhaps only to cut sago, but they urged Pfeiffer's men to be cautious. These Alfuros continued on into the forest. Pfeiffer's Malay guide from Saparua had the last embers of their campfire extinguished and ordered the men to keep watch in a circle around Pfeiffer. Others he sent to lie in hiding a little distance away. But the fatigue of their march through the forest had been too much to maintain their vigilance for long. Despite the danger, every one of the party fell fast asleep.

Pfeiffer did not lose her head and she returned safely to Ambon. Reports of her extraordinary overland crossing of Seram would soon pass back to the urban centres and make exciting press reports in Java and Singapore. Even Wallace, when he later visited Seram, barely made it a short way up one mountain trail and then turned around again because the collecting wasn't good enough. He thereby missed a great many endemic bird species which remained long unknown to science. Pfeiffer brought away her own varied collections. She discovered a new species of giant ant which Stevens sold to the British Museum.[302] She sent ten species of fish as well as butterflies from Ambon.[303] One snail from Seram, for example, was later named after her (*Helicina idae*) and found its way into the Berlin Museum. Similarly, a species of longhorn beetle she collected was named *Pascoea idea*.[304] The Museum also purchased five species of fish, three species of cockroaches as well as butterflies, moths, earwigs and other insects.[305] In the eventual published list of the British Museum Pfeiffer and Wallace were listed side-by-side as collecting the same species of butterfly there.[306] This was only one of many occasions when their names shared the same page of museum catalogues.

On 3 March Pfeiffer left Ambon on the monthly mail steamer. The ship chuffed and churned 260 miles north to a string of beautiful volcanic islands to Ternate, once the centre of a great clove-powered sultanate.

189

Ternate is an almost perfect volcanic cone. At its base was a small town dominated by a massive seventeenth-century Dutch fort. Most of the island was still ruled by the sultan, Taj ul-Mulki Amir ud-din, though pensioned by the Dutch. The steamer lay in the bay for a day and a half while Pfeiffer visited the Dutch Resident, Mr Goldman.

In the evening they were invited to visit the sultan at his palace on the other side of town. The eighteenth-century stone palace was built in a hybrid European style on a hillside overlooking the sea. It had a large wooden verandah supported by thick columns with an attap roof. The interior was full of European furniture. It still stands today, little altered. The sultan even sent his carriage to fetch them.

This was not to be just any carriage ride. The carriage had been a gift from the King of the Netherlands to the sultan. But the Dutch king was unaware that there were no horses on Ternate. The good sultan rectified this omission by having the carriage pushed and pulled by upwards of twenty men. Pfeiffer thought that the carriage moved just as fast by man power as it would have by horse power. At the palace, Pfeiffer was entertained by pretty dancing girls in costumes festooned with golden jewellery. At the end of the evening the sultan led Pfeiffer to the carriage on his arm.

Some of the insects Pfeiffer collected in the Maluku Islands would eventually find their way to Samuel Stevens in London. He was able to get excellent prices for them. These were large and very rare creatures and the collectors and museums of Britain were more than eager to acquire them. News of these captures reached Wallace. He thought that if an inexperienced collector like Pfeiffer could find such treasures, this gave "good promise of what a systematic search may produce".[307] He was right.

Five years later Wallace would also come to Ternate on the monthly mail steamer. Unlike Pfeiffer, he arrived as an obscure and unknown collector and received none of these signs of recognition or honour. But Wallace would immortalise the name Ternate in the history of science forever. It was there, in February 1858, that he lay in his dilapidated old house on the lower slope of the volcano sweating with a bout of tropical fever.

Suddenly he had a new idea about how new species could evolve. Since it was believed that species were constantly giving rise to new daughter varieties (or races), and these were randomly different than their parent species, when the environment changed some would do better than others. Indeed, if the environment changed too much, the parent species and all but one of the daughter varieties could go completely extinct. But if one of the daughter varieties happened to be suited to the new environment – it would survive and prosper and be considered a new species. And it would be adapted to fit that environment. There was no way this variety could revert back to the form of the parent species, since that form no longer fit the new environment. It was Wallace's independent version of what Darwin had called "natural selection".[308]

As soon as he recovered from his fever, Wallace began drafting an essay to explain his ideas, drawing heavily on his reading notes and notebook speculations from the past few years.[309] But when he finished it, he hesitated. He was an obscure collector with no prospect of a job when he returned home. And to publish a paper arguing for the then ridiculed idea of evolution was extremely risky. Although he had long been convinced that species must change, he had carefully concealed this belief in his scientific publications.

When the mail steamer arrived that March, he received a letter of reply from his correspondent, the eminent and respected naturalist Charles Darwin. The letter was one of the most flattering Wallace had ever received. Not only did Darwin praise Wallace's earlier article of 1855, he mentioned that Wallace's hero, the great geologist

Sir Charles Lyell also found it interesting.

Wallace now had a new possibility before him. He knew from their letters that Darwin was working on evolution too. Since Wallace did not plan to send his new essay to a journal, he could send it to Darwin and ask him to forward it on to Lyell if it were "sufficiently interesting". That was a Victorian euphemism for, if Darwin approved or thought it publishable. And, at the same time, Wallace had put the suggestion so politely that Darwin was under no obligation to publish what he might not approve of. Wallace wrote Darwin a letter and enclosed his so-called "Ternate essay" and left it at the post office before setting off on a great expedition to the wild shores of New Guinea in search of exquisite and lucrative Bird of Paradise.

When the letter reached Darwin, on 18 June 1858, he was quite shocked.[310] Wallace's theory seemed to him to be exactly the same as his own. As Wallace knew, Darwin was then only about a year or two away from finishing his big book on evolution. He had come up with his own theory twenty years before Wallace. But he felt honour bound to do as Wallace requested, so he forwarded the essay to Lyell the same day. Lyell could have chosen to publish it right away, or send it back with comments. It was up to him now.

Lyell, quite a high-society snob by all accounts, couldn't be bothered to reply for some time. In the end, he advised Darwin to just publish an overview of his own theory now. That was perfectly fair game after all. Darwin could publish his own older views any time he wished. But Darwin's conscience would not let him. He kept asking if Lyell was sure this was the best course of action. In the end Lyell's last letter of advice was passed by (at Darwin's request) their mutual friend, the botanist Joseph Dalton Hooker.

Hooker had a different idea that would be both fair to Wallace and extricate his friend Darwin from the awkward position of receiving, unasked for, a potentially competitive manuscript. Hooker decided to present Wallace's essay together with some older documents by Darwin at the same scientific meeting under his own (Hooker) and Lyell's names. And thus the modern theory of evolution by natural selection was first made public. These brief papers made little impact and apparently not a single convert. The following year however, Darwin would publish a heavily condensed version of the big book interrupted by Wallace. It was entitled *On the Origin of Species*. The world would never be the same again.

Ida Pfeiffer had no scientific eureka moment on Ternate. She left on 7 March 1853 and steamed across to the northern arm of Sulawesi. Like most European visitors, she was struck by the remarkable beauty of its long valleys and the pretty and tidy villages of the Minahassa region.

> All that I saw of the country pleased me extremely: it is rich in natural beauty, has a moderate climate, and a good productive soil. The villages are handsome and cleanly, the houses, though built on stakes, spacious, and as well kept as I have ever seen in these countries. Many of the native houses, though built only of the ribs of sago leaves, were so large and neat, that I took them for the habitations of Europeans.[311]

She took a journey into the highlands to see the famed fine scenery. The winding roads lead over 2,300 feet up to a vast plateau bejewelled by the pristinely beautiful Lake Tondano. While there Pfeiffer suffered her seventh attack of the Sumatran fever. She recovered in the house of a German missionary. In the evening she was sufficiently recovered to walk to see the dramatic Tondano waterfall as it cascaded eighty feet down a sheer cliff. It was here that Governor Visser would one day perish.[312]

On 10 April 1853 she took the steamer back to Makassar. Only the town and an area extending two miles around it was Dutch territory. The rest of the island was divided amongst the princely states of "Bonni, Goa and Sidenring". Pfeiffer of course wished to visit them. Governor Pieter Vreede Bik gave her letters of permission to enter the territories of Goa and Sidenring, but not Bonni as they were not at that time on the best of terms. Accompanied by a local interpreter and a porter, Pfeiffer set off on horseback north across the vast plains planted with neatly tended rice paddies. Her first stop was at the small locality of Maros where she stayed in the well-appointed home of Assistant Resident Count E. F. Bentheim Teeklenburg Rheda and his family. In the background a series of vertical limestone hills thrust abruptly out of the surrounding plains. She managed to collect thirty-seven species of fish which she sent to Dr Bleeker in Batavia who later published descriptions of them and thanked Pfeiffer generously.[313]

After six days of rain she was ready to ride on northwards to the native states. Against his better judgement, the Count sent additional people to keep Pfeiffer out of trouble. More personnel added to the logistical troubles of her type of travel, but it could not be helped.

On the 25th they reached Tanette (Bone), an independent principality on the eastern coast. Pfeiffer, being a lady, was allowed to inspect the palace of the queen or datu, We Tenri Olle. It was not very impressive in Pfeiffer's eyes. She next visited the principality of Barru which was ruled likewise by a queen, who was only eighteen years old. Pfeiffer was able to witness the chilling ceremony of the young queen having her teeth filed into a more fashionable shape.

The country was everywhere fruitful and productive. Water buffaloes were very plentiful. These strange beasts with their inwardly curved horns often reacted erratically on the appearance of westerners, as the naturalists Wallace and Albert Bickmore reported. Wallace wrote in his diary on Sulawesi of "those horrid, ugly brutes, the buffaloes, they could never be approached by me; not for fear of my own but of others' safety. They would first stick out their necks and stare at me, and then on a nearer view break loose from their halters or tethers, and rush away helter-skelter as if a demon were after them, without any regard for what might be in their way."[314]

Pfeiffer reported no stampeding buffaloes but she was quite annoyed by her interpreters as they would not obey her. "The fellows would not even carry my butterfly-net for me," so she was obliged to carry it herself.[315] It is possible that the men understood themselves to be assisting as interpreters and not as her servants. With language difficulties and unfamiliarity with one another's culture, such misunderstandings were all too likely.

Pfeiffer next visited the kingdom of Sidenreng and was warmly received by the king in his thatched palace of bamboo and wickerwork. To Pfeiffer's Austrian eyes the ragamuffin place looked more like a decayed barn than a palace. Among the fruits she was served here was perhaps the most extraordinary fruit in the world, the inscrutable durian. It is called by some the king of fruits and described by others as smelling either like a sewer or rotting garlic with onions – opinions vary widely. The British surveyor John Turnbull Thomson was introduced to durian at Malacca and wrote an eye-watering account:

> I look and see a rough looking substance full of yellow yokes or seeds borne forward to the table. But what is this odour? I looked about me furtively, and my friend smiled. I took a momentary glance at the lady, and she laughed outright. The fruit is placed on the table. Shades of Cloacina! [the Roman goddess of sewers] What is this? I give a piteous glance to my host: he laughs immoderately. I look at the contents of the fruit dish, and learn that the atrociously foetid odours come from it … I would have held my nose did good breeding allow it, but I resigned myself to my fate, and looked on.

My host proceeded to open up the disgusting entrails of the horrid-looking vegetable, and they send forth an odour of rotten eggs stirred up with decayed onions ... that my polished friends should eat such an abomination as this, was beyond my conception.[316]

Durian is the only fruit that is banned from public transportation in several Asian countries. Pfeiffer was told that if she could just become accustomed to the smell, the taste is incredible. "Though I made several attempts," she confessed, "I never could succeed in liking it,—the perfume was too powerful." Wallace, on the other hand, eventually overcame his initial repugnance at the stench of durian. He would later describe it, "as producing a food of the most exquisite flavour it is unsurpassed".

Once she had seen the people and the landscape, Pfeiffer was eager to return to Makassar. During the final leg of the journey she literally wore out the young men sent to accompany and assist her.

We had to cross such deep morasses that at one place they had a good deal of trouble to drag me through. I sank in at every step almost to the waist, and they had to pull me out again; yet on the following morning I was so entirely recovered from my fatigue that I rode thirty-two miles, through roads as bad as those of yesterday, and the same deep marshes, which, even for travellers on horseback, are very toilsome. I got to Maros, nevertheless, in quite good condition, but my two interpreters were so affected by the fatigue that they were unwell for several days.[317]

On 13 May she rode back in to Makassar. There was one more princely state to visit, Goa, just a few miles to the south. A merchant named Mr J. G. Weijergang accompanied her. Pfeiffer was impressed by the palace of Sultan Abdul Kadir Moh Aidid, which was much handsomer than those of the other monarchs of Sulawesi. Its exterior was adorned with ornate wood carvings. And yet the sultan was in the midst of having a new house built.

The old one was in perfect condition. Pfeiffer learned that the Sultan "would not inhabit it any more because his father had died in it".

On 20 April 1853 Pfeiffer left Makassar on the steamer *Banda*, heading back to Surabaya, Java. Some of the collections she made in Sulawesi were eventually purchased by the British Museum. These included ten species of Homopterous insects, an earwig, a moth, a butterfly and other insects.[318] She discovered two new species of land snail, one of which was named after her *Vitrina idea*.[319] She also collected two species of beetle that were new to science. One of these was named *Schizorhina idea*.[320]

Unfortunately she fell ill with "an affection of the back". She assumed it was brought on by "the toils and hardships I had undergone in my many wanderings in the Moluccas and Celebes".[321] It may well have been a recurrent attack of malaria. When she recovered she was able to do a little sightseeing around Surabaya including a beautiful mosque that had been recently built by a Dutch architect, and a nearby Malay village where, as usual, she inspected the interiors of the houses finding them dirty and wanting. She had to admit that after more than a year in the Malay archipelago that Malays were not as unattractive as she had at first thought, "habit had begun to manifest its levelling influence," she confessed. The nearby Chinese village pleased her much more as she admired the pretty houses and the, to her all-important, "remarkable cleanliness".[322] She was particularly impressed with the Dutch hospitals and prisons.

Pfeiffer was told a strange story of a house in Java that the local people said was full of ghosts. Some invisible agent was said to throw stones and spit sirih juice near people who entered the house. There was so much talk about this haunted house that the government sent a trustworthy officer to investigate. He had the house surrounded with soldiers and sat inside on a chair. The shower of stones and red spit was said to have duly occurred. The house was entirely searched and no one was found. The officer then tried a sagacious experiment. He marked the stones and had them buried a considerable distance from the house. The following night he went in again. To his astonishment, the shower of spit and stones happened again and the stones were the very same ones he had cunningly marked. But, Pfeiffer noted wryly, "At last, however, the Dutch Government proved more than a match for the ghost, and checkmated him by having the house pulled down."[323]

In 1868, when Wallace had returned to England and was writing up his great book, *The Malay Archipelago*, he read the works of other travellers in the region including Ida Pfeiffer's. For some reason, he never mentioned Pfeiffer in his book or any of his scientific publications. By the late 1860s he had been swept up by the Victorian craze of spiritualism with its séances, mediums and table rappings. He could not resist quoting Pfeiffer's account of the haunted house on Java so he sent a short notice of it to the *Spiritual Magazine* and thereby gave us our only evidence that he read Pfeiffer's book.[324]

Pfeiffer returned to Batavia, unsure where to go next. She was still not too keen to try Australia as it would likely be too expensive for her to travel there. Serendipity once again filled the breach. Anchored out in the roadstead was a ship bound for San Francisco. The American consul, Mr Alfred Reed, spoke to the captain of the ship to see if a cheaper passage for Pfeiffer could be negotiated. But her fame was the best negotiator. The captain offered to take her all the way to San Francisco for free. So it was settled.

Pfeiffer was sad to leave behind the Dutch friends who had so aided and honoured her. "It was with almost melancholy feelings that I took leave of the Dutch Indian settlements," she recalled.

The Dutch had made her so welcome and given her every possible assistance for her travel and adventure, and she had thus been able to see "many of the magnificent wonders of nature".[325]

As far back as 1848, when she visited the American missionaries at Urmia, she had said that she would visit North America during her next journey. This may or may not have been politeness. But it was now to become a reality. The United States of America would be her next stop.

On 6 July 1853 Pfeiffer sailed on the three-masted ship *Seneca*, commanded by Captain Feenhagen, for a voyage across the Pacific and almost halfway around the globe. For two long months the ship sailed eastwards with nothing to see but sky and featureless ocean in all directions.

When at last the coast of California came into sight, Pfeiffer's Austrian standards of what constituted a pleasing view were not impressed. "This coast did not make a pleasing impression on me, but, on the contrary, rather a melancholy one. It was, beyond all description, desolate and dead. Naked sand-hills rose steeply on all sides. No tree, no shrub, not so much as a blade of grass, varied the melancholy colour of the corpselike waste."[326]

The *Seneca* sailed through the Golden Gate strait and dropped anchor in the crowded and bustling Bay of San Francisco. California had first been sparsely colonised by the Spanish in the mid eighteenth century. It had then become part of Mexico after its independence from Spain in 1821. By the late 1840s Mexico had lost the territory to the USA. This was just in time for the discovery of gold there in 1848 and the wild juggernaut of frantic mass immigration of the 1849 gold rush that followed. California became a state of the union in 1850.

The news of her arrival soon spread around the city, the state, and around the world with newspapers from London to Sydney reporting Pfeiffer's sudden appearance in California. Before she could find a cheap hotel, an invitation was sent to her on board from the English firm of Colquhoun, Smith, and Morton for free accommodation during her stay.

The frontier town was not the sort of place to please Pfeiffer. Its streets, which still had no street signs, were dirty, often muddy, and full of disorderly traffic. In a letter to Petermann she described the streets as covered in dust half a foot thick, with rubbish strewn all over including "boxes and barrels, wheels and bottles, clothes, washing and parts of shoes, dead dogs and rats".[327]

The houses were small and their tiny rooms overly crammed with furniture and clutter. The churches and public buildings were unworthy of notice. Hardly more interesting was the Spanish Dolores Mission, built of adobe brick in 1776. Its flaking plaster gave it a very shabby and worn appearance but the church had a fine altarpiece, she thought.

Another German was just establishing a west coast branch of the family dry goods business in San Francisco to cater to the burgeoning population. His name was Levi Strauss and his company would later introduce denim blue jeans.

Pfeiffer explained to her European readers that in the parlance of the place, the term "American" was used only for citizens of the USA and, to her surprise, did not include other inhabitants of America such as Mexicans or Peruvians.

One evening she toured the gambling houses. The smoke-filled saloons with loud piano music, so familiar to us now from the caricatured image of Hollywood films, utterly shocked Pfeiffer with their raw licentiousness. The clientele was decidedly mixed. At one table you could see a "daintily dressed gentleman" beside a miner in his red flannel shirt and muddy boots and then a sailor, fresh from his ship, with tar still on his hands.

With respect to the furniture and decorations of these houses, it is obviously intended not only to encourage directly the passion for gaming, but also to intoxicate the senses, and entice to all kinds of sensuality. Noisy music resounds through the spacious saloons, licentiously seductive pictures hang on the walls, and beautiful girls are seated as lures here and there at the tables, I have travelled far and wide through the world, and have been among many nations … but such open and shameless enticements to evil I have never seen anywhere else … Of the other places of public entertainment and the dancing-rooms, I will not speak.[328]

In a newspaper interview not long after, Pfeiffer said: "Of all the countries I have ever visited, of all the vile, immoral places I have ever seen or heard of in savage or civilised lands, the gambling saloons in California are the worst."[329]

The now legendary lawlessness of the Wild West was all around her. On one occasion she was walking along the street when someone shouted out to her, "A bear! A bear!" She was confused but looking behind, there really was a bear running down the street towards her! She just had time to step out of the way. The animal had in fact a rope around its neck but its tether was so long that it could cover a wide area of the street. Its owner seemed quite unconcerned.

In August the decapitated head of the infamous Mexican bandit Joaquin Murieta and the severed hand of his notorious sidekick, Three-Fingered Jack, were displayed at the Stockton House for the entry price of $1. A fictional biography written the following year by John Ridge would begin an ever snowballing legend about Murieta as a Mexican Robin Hood that continues to grow as a mythical hero in films and TV to this day.

Just a month before Pfeiffer arrived, a gun duel was fought between the southern sympathising US Senator and millionaire mine owner William Gwin and Joseph McCorkle, a judge. The classic western image of men quick-drawing pistols is, however, an invention of Hollywood movies. The real duel of the west was derived from the European duel. And indeed six-shooters were not the norm. In this case, Gwin and McCorkle were armed with rifles and separated by thirty yards. At a word from a spectator, both men turned and fired. There were three shots in total. Neither was injured but a donkey standing innocently nearby was killed.

A gentleman whom Pfeiffer knew in San Francisco actually shot and killed his servant while she was in town. The victim was drunk and threatened his employer. "Either I will shoot you, or you shall shoot me," he said.[330] Then he came at his employer with clenched fists. So the gentleman shot him down. He told his version of the story to the local sheriff and was locked up for a day.

Pfeiffer was disgusted to see for herself that the infamous American habit of chewing (and spitting) tobacco was as widespread as legend had it. But as bad as this was, Pfeiffer found another still worse. "They had another practice, however, if possible still more abominable; namely, though they carried a pocket-handkerchief, of making use of their fingers instead of it."[331]

She made excursions further inland, first by steamer to Sacramento on 3 October, where the local newspaper gave a full account of "this remarkable lady" who was described as "rather short, thin, and spare, with a constitution capable of undergoing great fatigue. The expression of her countenance, in conversation, is mild and pleasant, at the same time the eye evinces a keen sense of observation; a quick ear; her hair is dark, and tinged with the frosts of fifty winters."[332]

Her next stop was Marysville and the gold mines of the Yuba River. The California State Telegraph Co. would connect San Francisco with Marysville for the first time a month later. She met the stout Swiss-born John Sutter who owned the eponymous "Sutter's Mill", where, as generations of Californian school children would learn, gold was first discovered in 1848, thus ushering in the famous gold rush.

Pfeiffer visited Crescent City and made a short expedition to see the so-called Rogue River Indians. Once again she was warned that she could only venture into such wild places with an armed escort as the people she wished to see were "very savage". Pfeiffer went anyway. Fortunately, she found a German sailor, named Karl Braun, who had lived some months in the area and who had traded with the Indians and knew many of them. He agreed to accompany her into Indian territory. They proceeded away from the settlements of the Americans along the Smith River. The deeper they went into Indian territory the less clothing the Indians wore until at last they were almost naked.

As so often, Pfeiffer found the people themselves rather ugly and dirty. "They are extremely filthy, almost too much so to describe. I have seen them, for instance, searching in each other's heads for vermin, and presenting all the specimens they found conscientiously to the owner, who actually devoured them!"[333] What she may not have appreciated was that these people were not in their prime, but a people under great pressure from invaders.

Pfeiffer and Braun visited a succession of villages as they travelled east and spent three nights sleeping on the ground in Indian wigwams. During their last night Braun had a very close shave. Pfeiffer slept in a wigwam with several Indian women. Braun slept in another by himself.

> In the middle of the night he heard a rustling among the boughs with which he had closed the entrance, and soon saw an Indian come crawling in on hands and knees. His enemy was just in the act of raising himself up, and with a drawn knife in his hand, when

203

the sailor sprang upon him and presented a pistol at his head. Thereupon the Indian drew back, pretending he had only come to see whether there was wood enough to keep the fire up.

Reflecting on the way the Americans described these Indians as "treacherous, cowardly, and revengeful", Pfeiffer, as an outsider, thought it perfectly natural that the Indians should attack an American when found alone.

> What other means of attack have they against the well-armed whites—the domineering race from which they have had so much to suffer. Revenge is really natural to man; and if the whites had suffered as many wrongs from them as they from the whites, I rather think they too would have felt the desire of revenge.[334]

She noted that it was well known that the tribe was fast diminishing, especially those that lived near the Americans. Neither she nor apparently anyone else understood that it was Old World diseases, more than all the other causes, that were reducing their numbers.

Her final trip was to visit Santa Clara and San Jose in the company of Eduard Vischer, the Austrian Consul. Vischer, forty-four, had lived in California since 1842. He was a talented artist who made hundreds of pencil sketches of Californian landscapes, missions and rural scenes throughout the 1860s and 1870s. He later published several volumes of enchanting drawings.

Ida Pfeiffer next wished to visit Panama, in central America. The Pacific Mail Steamship Company operated a service from San Francisco to Panama City. She tried to get her usual discount by having a word with one of the officers of the company. He applied to the head office which granted Pfeiffer a free passage to Panama.

On 15 December 1853 she boarded the paddle steamer *Golden Gate*, under Captain Johans. Pfeiffer had "never in my life seen a finer vessel". The ship entered the San Francisco to Panama City service in 1851. She was 269 feet long and 40 feet wide, with two oscillating steam engines giving a cruising speed of ten knots, burning fifty tonnes of coal per day and could carry up to 1,000 passengers. Less than a decade later, in July 1862, disaster struck the *Golden Gate* when she caught fire in the engine room near Manzanillo, Mexico. After an hour the ship was engulfed in flames and run aground; 213 of the 338 people on board perished. Only a portion of the treasure of gold on board was ever recovered.

After stops at San Diego and the Bay of Acapulco, the *Golden Gate* steamed into the port of Panama, of the Republic of New Granada, on 23 December. The other passengers hurried ashore to hire the best mules for the expensive overland crossing of the isthmus. The Panama fever was a constant danger to those who lingered. Pfeiffer stayed on in the city, touring its houses, churches and hospitals and observing the dress and behaviour of the local people.

Just a week after New Year's Day 1854 she left on the steamer *Bolivia*, under Captain Strahan, bound for Lima, Peru. On 12 January they stopped at Guayaquil in the Republic of Ecuador. Pfeiffer went ashore. The town was fringed with fine wooded hills and in the background were the mighty Cordilleras. This was finally a view which an Austrian could respect. She toured the bazaars and markets and approved of the single-storey houses whose balconies facing the street formed a shelter from the sun for pedestrians. She somehow managed to collect a new species of stick insect which would find its way to the Vienna Museum.

On 19 January 1854 the ship arrived at the port of Callao, Peru. Twenty years before, Charles Darwin thought it "a most miserable filthy, ill built, small sea-port".[335] But by Pfeiffer's day it was only a short train journey up the hills to the capital, Lima. The train did not even need to use its engine to return to the port, but merely coasted back down. Pfeiffer was hosted at the home of the Hamburg consul, Hermann Georg Rodewald. This was particularly helpful as she had not yet learned Spanish.

Peru had been independent from Spain since 1824. Its large capital had a population of almost 100,000. The inhabitants were an astonishing mix of "Indian, European, and African blood". Unsurprisingly, Pfeiffer found that "all whose complexions approach at all to white call themselves 'Old Spaniards'; a race with which they are eager to claim kindred".[336] Some of the women of Lima she thought very beautiful. The famous habit of women wearing a long black robe over the head with only a single peep hole for one eye had gone out of fashion in recent years.

Despite being in both the tropics and a desert, the climate was surprisingly mild. The sky was often grey and fresh breezes kept things pleasantly cool. Pfeiffer walked about the city taking in the sights. She thought the "Plaza grande is a fine quadrangle", and around it was the cathedral and episcopal palace. There was also a museum, an academy of fine arts and a library to visit. But she was not very impressed. "There is no public building in Lima worth mentioning except the churches; and, on the whole, the city does not make a very advantageous impression on the stranger." She found the museum "one of the most deplorable that I ever saw". No longer quite as scientifically naïve as she once had been, she noted the shortcomings of the collection.

> Every species of natural production is represented by some specimen poor in itself, and spoiled by neglect, and the insects and crustacea are wanting altogether. Instead of Peruvian insects, there are half-a-dozen boxes with the most ordinary Chinese beetles, and of marine productions there is nothing at all. The most valuable things in it are some very well-preserved mummies in a crouching posture, as they were taken from the graves of the Incas; as well as a tolerably large collection of ancient Peruvian drinking cups and other vessels.[337]

This critique suggests that Pfeiffer expected a museum to display the range of living things as well as local productions.

In the town one day she saw llamas for the first time. These charming creatures were used as beasts of burden to carry salt into the mountains. She thought they were "beautiful gentle animals" with "slender necks, gentle eyes, and stately bearing", but, she warned, they "have a nasty trick of spitting".[338]

Lima lies in a seismically active zone and earthquakes are all too common. During her five-week stay there were three earthquakes. Each time, the people all ran instantly out of the buildings and into the streets. Many fell to their knees and cried out "Misericordia!" (mercy).

Pfeiffer took a tour beyond Lima with Mr Rodewald. They visited the hilltop temple complex of Pachacamac, lying in utter ruins after the Spanish destroyed it along with the Inca empire. Pfeiffer reflected on the fate of the native peoples who had built and worshipped at these once magnificent temples. She told her readers the story of the site's destruction as far as she could learn.

> Pachacamac (Creator of the Earth) was the most powerful deity of the Yunhas; and, when they were overcome by the Incas, their idols were cast out of the temple, and replaced by images of the sun; and certain royal virgins were appointed to maintain the sacred fire; but, as the Incas had banished the Yunkas' gods, and forced them to worship the sun, so did Pizarro subsequently treat the Incas themselves when he conquered their country. The Christians, however, behaved much more cruelly than the heathens had done; the virgins of the sun were given up to the outrages of rude soldiers, and the people driven by fire and sword to adopt the new religion, which they could hardly do otherwise than detest, when they saw its professors thus guilty of every kind of violence and crime.[339]

Pfeiffer's original plan had been to cross the Andes and sail down the Amazon to the Atlantic coast. But the so-called "liberal revolution" of 1854, led by Ramón Castilla, saw fighting across the very area she wished to traverse. Pfeiffer explained the troubles as she understood them to her readers. "For several years Peru has had the misfortune to be governed by covetous and grasping men, whose chief care has been devoted to the filling their own pockets." Despite the hugely valuable guano deposits that had been mined at enormous profit to the state for the past years "nothing had been done either for the public benefit or towards the liquidation of the national debt. The President is accused of having appropriated to himself and his party a considerable portion of the riches of the country."[340] Some things never change. Indeed this sort of 'scandal' has occurred so many times over the past few centuries it is a wonder anyone ever regards it now as surprising or shocking.

While Pfeiffer waited in Lima she wrote letters to friends and family. On 26 January she wrote to her friend Petermann in London. She told him she was now in Peru, having abandoned her earlier plan to enter the USA from either Mexico or the West Indies. If crossing the Andes was impossible, she might try visiting Quito and Panama. Her letter to Petermann was summarised in the *Athenaeum* of March 1854.[341]

Some of her acquaintances had advised her to try Quito in Ecuador. In particular Mr Muncajo, the charge d'affaires for Ecuador. He promised Pfeiffer that she would find all the assistance she could desire there. "He told me the President was his particular friend, and that he would give me letters to him, as well as to other persons holding high and important offices; and, he added, that he did not doubt the President would himself be greatly interested in my journey, and afford me every assistance."[342]

Full of buoyant expectation, Pfeiffer boarded the rather filthy and chaotically crammed steamer *Santiago* and headed north for Guayaquil, the main port of Ecuador. Such was the state of international communications by 1854 that only a month after Pfeiffer left Lima for Guayaquil, this fact had been reported to the readers of *The Times* in London.[343]

She arrived on 1 March and for once had no letter of introduction. There were no hotels or inns so it was essential to find someone to take her in. Fortunately the Hamburg consul, Ernst Wilhelm Garbe, welcomed her to stay at his house.

It was the midst of the rainy season which lasts from December until May. The roads inland were said to be so bad at this time that all transportation came to a halt except for the mail carriers, and these could barely make it, often having to cross widely flooded areas. As usual, Pfeiffer was undaunted. If a mail carrier could do it, she was convinced she could too. Besides, these reports were probably exaggerated. But her old bane the Sumatran fever struck again and for three weeks she was bedridden.

Once recovered, she set off for Quito by boat up the Guayas River on 22 March with a letter carrier. Mr Garbe persuaded her, because she knew no Spanish, to take a servant. It was against her better judgement, and she would later regret it.

From the start of her journey she was cheated out of small amounts of money from those she stayed with or who sold her food or supplies. At Botegas she hired mules. Her servant, who was going to Quito anyway, got his wares loaded on an extra mule at her expense.

The roads really were execrable and often flooded but not nearly as bad as she had been told. Along the way she managed to collect gaily coloured butterflies and dragonflies. "As a good sportsman is never to be found without his gun, I take care always to have my butterfly-net in readiness; and, as we rode very slowly, I could make prisoners without dismounting."[344]

As the road climbed ever steeper into the desolate mountains, the road seemed to grow worse. Loose stones, pot holes and mud made riding impossible, she dismounted and walked beside her mule. Pfeiffer slipped and fell and called to her servant to help, "but I was only a woman, and unfortunately his mule was already paid for; so he quietly went on his way, and left me to my fate".[345]

At the town of Guaranda, located in a deep valley in a pass high in the Andes, they changed mules. From there it was possible to see Mount Chimborazo, the extinct volcano that in her youth was believed to be the highest mountain in the world at 6,268 metres (20,564 feet). Although Mount Everest attains a higher altitude, Chimborazo is in fact the furthest point on the Earth's surface from its centre. This is because the Earth is slightly thicker near the equator.

Alexander von Humboldt had climbed Chimborazo to 5,875 metres, higher than any previous attempt, in 1802. His book and diagrams showing the ecological zones that are determined by altitude had made Chimborazo a scientific icon. Seeing this famous mountain with her own eyes marked, as Pfeiffer wrote, "one of the most remarkable days of my life".

They had reached 2,668 metres (8,753 feet) and the thin mountain air was beginning to give her chest pains. From this plateau the vegetation seemed to cease and there were no more farms. Soon the landscape would be dotted only with spiny cactus and succulent aloes.

"On the small plateaux of the Chimborazo bleak violent winds often blow, that drive sand and stones in the travellers' faces; and it is therefore customary for them to provide themselves with silk masks, with small pieces of glass over the eyes."[346] To protect herself from the sand, Pfeiffer had a blue silk full-face hood with protruding glass lenses to see through, a bit like a burqa with integral goggles. She retained it in later years.

The road ahead was now downhill but constant rain and rough winds made the ride torturous. In the evening they reached a "miserable" empty roadside rest house.

> I do not think I was ever in my life so tired as on this evening. I suffered also much pain in my chest, my teeth chattered with cold, and I was so stiff that it was the utmost I could do to drag myself from my mule to the place where I was to sleep. I was covered with mud, my hands and face not excepted; but my servant brought me no water to wash, and I was quite incapable of fetching it for myself: so, wrapping myself in my cloak, I sank down on the sleeping-place.[347]

As the journey to Quito continued, Pfeiffer suffered a succession of some of the most appalling accommodation she ever encountered in all her travels. At one house she was shown to "a sleeping apartment that had certainly not been cleaned within the memory of man". In another she was just about to fall asleep when, "I sprang out again, literally and truly covered with vermin, and passed the remainder of the night on a chair. In the morning my skin was marked all over with red spots, as if I had had an eruptive disease."

These may have been Vinchuca bugs. Charles Darwin wrote of them in his *Beagle Diary* in 1835: "At night I experienced an attack, & it deserves no less a name, of the Benchuca, the great black bug of the Pampas. It is most disgusting to feel soft wingless insects, about an inch long, crawling over ones body; before sucking they are quite thin, but afterwards round & bloated with blood, & in this state they are easily squashed."[348]

On 2 April, as she plodded along on her little mule, she kept her eyes on the surrounding volcanoes which were giving off smoke. At one moment she happened to look back just in time to witness one of the most stupendous sights of her life. In the distance the volcano Cotopaxi suddenly erupted.

Thick, heavy clouds of smoke burst up, through which flames darted like forked lightning rose high above the smoke into the sky, and then poured down a fiery rain upon the earth. What a spectacle would it have been at night! But as it was I was abundantly satisfied, and thanked God that, among the many wonders of nature, I had been permitted to see this surpassingly beautiful one.[349]

Alexander von Humboldt had been the first European to attempt to climb Cotopaxi in 1802 but the thin atmosphere at that altitude defeated him. Its summit was not reached until 1872.

Quito was finally reached on the 3rd. The entire town consisted of single-storey buildings with red-tiled roofs. Pfeiffer found it not at all to her liking.

The streets are full of puddles and filth, and grievously offensive to one's olfactory organs; the people clothed, if you may call it so, in the most disgusting rags. They not only stared, but laughed and pointed with their fingers at me as I came along, and sometimes ran after me, for strangers are rare in this forgotten country; and, if they are not dressed exactly like the natives, as I was not (for, although I had the poncho, I had not the little straw hat), they become objects of mockery to the populace.[350]

But she could not help admiring a view that was surrounded by mighty mountain peaks.

There was not a single inn so she took one of her letters of introduction to the house of a local gentleman. Unfortunately the house had been vacated. As she stood before it wondering what to do next, the local people gathered around the strangely dressed foreigner "laughing, screaming, and asking all kinds of curious questions. They seemed to think that, as I was without masculine protection, they might give full swing to their impertinence."[351] Pfeiffer was unaware that the way she was dressed sent mixed signals, combining forms of clothing that were exclusively worn either by upper-class ladies or peasants. Luckily, she was later hosted by the

American charge d'affaires, Philo White.

As she toured the town, she found little that pleased her. Everything was dirty, shabby and neglected. The hospital and the asylum were utterly wretched hovels. The churches were the only sights at all worth seeing. She stopped by an apothecary to buy some spirits of turpentine to preserve her specimens. The apothecary scanned his shelves of unlabeled bottles for a quarter of an hour. Only by unstoppering and smelling their contents could he find the right one. And then the cost was ten times what it would have been in Europe. She reflected that at these prices the local people could hardly afford any medicine.

Her letters of introduction from Mr Muncajo appeared worthless as most of those she sent them to did not even bother to reply. Without the support of local politicians and administrators it was impossible for her to continue on to reach the Amazon. "To my great vexation I had to renounce all hopes of this journey," she wrote bitterly. Added to this disappointment were the many occasions when she was cheated by local tradesmen and servants. She angrily and revealingly declared, "the severest toils and hardships are never sufficient to spoil my enjoyment of a journey; but to have to do with people of this sort is beyond my patience. I was incomparably more comfortable among the cannibals of Sumatra than amongst the *soi-disant* Christian rabble. Alas! that I should so often have to declare that some of the worst people I have ever met with have been called Christians."[352]

While Pfeiffer was chafing in Quito, on the other side of the world a young English naturalist, Alfred Russel Wallace, arrived on the P&O steamer at Singapore. It was the start of his eight-year expedition in the region that would see him and his large and ever changing team of assistants collect an astonishing 125,000 natural history specimens. He would visit many of the same islands as

Pfeiffer and occasionally refer to her in his letters home.

On 25 April, Pfeiffer left Quito, again by mule, heading back to Guayaquil. Along the way she continued to collect beetles and butterflies. The roads were even worse than they had been a few weeks before because they were often very steep and careful footing was necessary to avoid tumbling downhill. "The animals slipped and stumbled at almost every step, and continually fell into holes, of which the road was full. Just as I was on a very steep declivity, down went my mule into one of these; and my saddle-girth breaking at the same moment, I was flung, saddle and all, right over his head. My amiable companion the arriero [muleteer] burst out laughing, and appeared to enjoy it amazingly, and fortunately I suffered no serious damage."[353]

Far worse was to come. The last stage of her journey was a three-day voyage in a small boat down the river Guaya from Savonetto to Guayaquil. Unfortunately, she stepped too close to the edge of the boat, slipped, and tumbled into the river. Never mind that the river was full of caiman, Pfeiffer could not swim. As soon as she bobbed up to the surface spluttering, she thought of course the boatmen would save her.

> After this I was conscious of rising twice to the surface, so that they must have seen me. The caymans I had forgotten. When I rose the first time, I looked vainly round for help. I could see the boat, and also that no one in it stirred, and then I sank again. Now, indeed, I felt terror, but, luckily, did not lose my senses; and, remembering to have heard that in such a case you ought to put out your hands before you and use them as oars, I did so as far as my strength permitted. I was beyond all human help; but behold! when I rose for the second time, I found myself quite close to the boat, and had only to cling to it. The boatmen contemplated me, indeed, with the most perfect tranquillity, and no one put out so

much as a hand or even an oar to help me; but, fortunately, one of the fellow-passengers, an Indian, took compassion on me, and assisted me into the boat; and I was saved.[354]

It was one of the closest calls she ever had and years later she would still feel "a cold shiver all over" when remembering it. Presumably the boatmen did not realise that she could not swim. Perhaps she was so close to the boat and did not call out for help so that no one understood that she was in real danger.

From Guayaquil, Pfeiffer took a steamer back north to Panama City. Since she could not sail down the Amazon, she would pursue the main artery through Panama to the southern United States. She made the 117 mile overland crossing of the isthmus to the small port of Aspinwall (now Colón) which had been established by Americans four years before as the Atlantic terminal of the railway being constructed across the isthmus. From there, on 31 May 1854, she boarded the fine mail steamer *Eldorado*, under Captain A. G. Gray, bound for New Orleans.

On board the *Eldorado* Pfeiffer noticed a very beautiful young lady, about twenty years old, "with a dazzlingly fair skin, and fine black hair, which showed a very slight tendency to curl, just enough to give a sharp observer some suspicion of the purity of her white blood".[355] The young beauty disappeared as soon as the ship got under steam and didn't appear again during the voyage.

In those days passengers dined together at a long dining table in the central saloon. Pfeiffer was curious. Where could the young lady be? Pfeiffer mentioned this to one of her fellow passengers, an American man, who replied with a scornful air in a Southern drawl, "How could a coloured dare to join our company? Every one of our ladies would have left the table in a body if she had."[356]

Pfeiffer was disgusted. "And the ladies who would have been guilty of this stupid inhumanity do nothing all Sunday but go to church and read the Bible! Truly, I think they must enter as much into the spirit of it as a parrot does into that of the speeches he utters so fluently."[357] Pfeiffer was not well prepared for what she would see next.

Long before the Mississippi River could be seen, the sea around the steamer became yellow with the tonnes of silt washed many miles out to sea. Once the mouth of the great river was reached it took the steamer a further five days to churn the last ninety miles against the current to the port city of New Orleans. It was the wealthiest and third most populous city in the United States and it was still booming and expanding. The river was lined with warehouses and the water was crowded with an armada of steamships, steamboats, flatboats and sailing ships.

Here the beautiful young lady came on deck at last. Although she was shunned by the other passengers, Pfeiffer spoke to her. The young lady was very sweet and well educated. Pfeiffer remarked with an icy sting that many a young "white" lady could only wish to be so intelligent. When the *Eldorado* docked and passengers began to go ashore, Pfeiffer was shocked by the example of American "equality" she observed. The young lady had scarcely set foot on shore when she was stopped by a police officer and taken away to gaol on suspicion of being mixed race. Pfeiffer was told that the young lady would have to wait there for her relatives to claim her and to show that she was free and not a slave.

Even Gray, the ship's captain, did not escape from the effects of slavery. Dr Henry Daret, from his stylish residence at 908 St. Louis Street, submitted to the Second District Court of New Orleans a petition on 2 May 1854 for compensation of over $400 from Captain Gray for harbouring his runaway slaves on board the *Eldorado*. The petition was denied, appealed and finally reversed.[358]

For once Pfeiffer stayed in a hotel, and one in an "astonishingly grand style", the St. Charles Hotel with its Palladian frontage and lavishly furnished rooms, halls and reading rooms. There was little monumental architecture to see in New Orleans, except for the grand hotels. Pfeiffer informed her readers that the streets in American towns were formed into regular quadrangles called "blocks". The streets were frightfully filthy and Pfeiffer had to hold her handkerchief over her nose because of the stench of sewage gurgling along the gutters.

New Orleans had the largest slave market in the domestic slave trade since the international trade ended in 1808. Out of curiosity for the foreign and exotic, Pfeiffer paid these strange institutions several visits. She was therefore able to give her readers an account of what she observed.

> At the slave-dealers' the slaves were waiting in court-yards for customers: they were well-dressed, and not doing any work; and as I wished to see them, I talked as if I were likely to make a purchase of a cook and a man-servant, and immediately the dealer rang a bell to summon the slaves, and placed them in two rows, the men on one side, and the women and girls on the other, and then began to describe and extol his wares. For a good cook he asked 1,200 dollars, and for one that was, as he said, not completely trained, 1,100.
>
> These slave-dealers are, inconsistently enough, despised and avoided by every one, so that they are almost excluded from human society. But since the gentleman slaveholder buys and sells slaves as well as the dealer, since he equally lives upon the labour of these poor creatures, and regards them equally as mere cattle, I am really at a loss to conceive on what ground he can regard the dealer as so much viler than himself. But society is full of these capricious distinctions![359]

She stayed for a few days at a nearby plantation and was surprised to see that the slaves were not treated there as badly as she had expected. Nevertheless, she remained adamantly anti-slavery.

> I am, of course, like every person with the ordinary feelings of humanity not warped by early prejudice, an enemy to slavery; I regard it as a disgrace to our common nature, and hold that a willing owner of slaves can have no claim to the title of Christian, if indeed he has to that of man. Hating slavery everywhere, I most especially detest it in a republican country, where people value so highly their freedom and equality of rights that they would think themselves justified in shooting any one who should attempt to detract from them, but who yet thus openly set at nought every principle of religion and morality.

Pfeiffer was echoing the old sting of Dr Johnson in one of his political tracts of 1775: "how is it that we hear the loudest yelps for liberty among the drivers of negroes?"[360]

The fact that Pfeiffer remarked upon seeing slaves in Brazil and the USA that they were not as badly off as she had expected does not reveal any sympathy with slavery, rather it probably suggests that the sort of anti-slavery literature she was familiar with focused particularly on cases of cruelty and torture in order to create sympathy for the cause of abolition.

After a three-week stay in New Orleans, Pfeiffer boarded the magnificent new paddle steamer *Belfast* to journey upriver. Captain Taylor, who owned the vessel, heard someone say the name Pfeiffer. Addressing her, he said he was well acquainted with her name from the newspapers and declined to take any payment for her passage.

She was very happy to be leaving. "To a stranger entering the United States by New Orleans the impression made can hardly be a very favourable one," she chided. And although those who hosted her had been very kind and gracious, she was still "most heartily glad nevertheless to get out of it. ... This, too, is called a city of wonders, and not the least wonderful thing in it is the hearing slave-owners and slave-dealers talking aloud about human freedom and the rights of man."[361]

The *Belfast*'s paddle wheels churned and swished against the current as they departed on 23 June 1854. It was the classic age of the river steamboats. This was the Mississippi of Tom Sawyer and Huckleberry Finn. All around bloated twin-funnel riverboats ploughed majestically up and down the waters of the great river. "The internal arrangements of this steamer were very splendid," Pfeiffer noted with approval.

> Rich carpets covered the floors and enormous looking-glasses the walls; and velvet-covered chairs and sofas and a beautiful piano adorned the saloon. Sleeping-cabins, beds, &c., left nothing to wish on the score of either convenience or luxury; and there were four rich and abundant meals, with pastry, ice, and so forth; yet the price was very reasonable, namely, for the passage from New Orleans to St. Louis, above 1200 miles, only twenty-five dollars....[362]

The view from the steamer for the first 100 miles showed an endless succession of cotton and maize plantations stretching over wide alluvial plains bordered at the edge of sight by forest. After a three-day voyage, the *Belfast* called at the little town of Napoleon on the west bank, at the juncture of the Arkansas River. Napoleon was hastily built on flood plains and so later destroyed by floods. Today it is a ghost town.

Pfeiffer alighted with her carpetbag. The next day she took the little steamer *Thomas P. Roy* for Little Rock up the Arkansas River. Pfeiffer found the landscape along the Arkansas much more pleasing to her romantic eye. The view of native forests was punctuated by the occasional hill or mountain. Sometimes a small log cabin could be spotted amongst the trees with wisps of smoke curling from its chimney. These scenes prompted serene reflections.

> There is something in the deep solitude of the yet untrodden wilderness, where even the smallest villages are few and far between,

and where not even the sound of the falling axe is heard, that is impressive and almost sublime; and the impression is not lessened, perhaps rather heightened, by the contrast of one of the greatest works of human art—the steamer—rushing, foaming through for a moment, and disturbing the solemn silence which, as soon as the sound of its paddle-wheels has ceased, settles down again as death-like as before.

Her fellow passengers, however, were far from sublime. Truly, with apologies to Jean-Paul Sartre, hell is other tourists. She tried to put it delicately: "The company on the boat did not appear to be of a very refined or highly intelligent class." The steamer occasionally stopped to take on wood to fuel its ever hungry engine. During these stops Pfeiffer went ashore to collect insects in the primeval woods. The other passengers laughed heartily at her for this unheard of pastime.

These brash Americans also bombarded her with endless impertinent questions about her family, connections and religion. They even had the indecency to ask where she got the money to travel. The annoyance was not limited to talk. Some of the passengers even entered her cabin to look at her insect collection, some actually handling them and spoiling some.

And if hell is other tourists, then the very lowest circle of hell is the children of other tourists. Pfeiffer observed with knowing disapproval as the children "screamed and roared if their parents did not immediately comply with all their wishes, and do just what they pleased. Unluckily, they sometimes refused at first and afterwards complied, which is, I think, the very worst plan they could have adopted. With children it should be always 'Yes' or 'No,' and the word once spoken should be maintained. In this way, as a child soon learns that its screaming answers no purpose, and does not help it to what it wants, it soon ceases to scream."[363]

Despite the unmatched number of educational institutions for women in the USA, the knowledge and education of the young ladies Pfeiffer met was "extremely superficial". They could boast of little more than playing the piano and singing a French song. Indeed they constantly vied to show off these great accomplishments by playing one after another at the piano in the steamer's saloon.

Pfeiffer was continually asked where she was born and which country she had come to the USA from. She replied Vienna and Peru. To her astonishment, her questioners did not know where either place was. Pfeiffer later attended American school examinations in geography and found that the questions did not go beyond the USA, "so that one might have thought there was no other country in the world".[364]

From Fort Smith she planned to ride to Fort Gibson to visit the Cherokee Indians. But the Sumatran fever visited her once again and she had to abandon the plan. She returned by the brand new passenger packet steamer *Crescent City*. Three years later, Samuel Clemens (Mark Twain) stood his first pilot watches on this boat. Pfeiffer travelled again on a free ticket due to her fame and a captain's generosity, to Napoleon, and continued on to St. Louis. She was hosted at the home of a local judge who invited her to stay when he learned Pfeiffer was in town. Pfeiffer described his domestic slaves as well dressed, treated almost like members of the family, and with little enough work to occupy them.

For tourist sites, Pfeiffer consulted the local directory. Being a Catholic, she looked up the cathedral and read:

The cathedral of St. Louis can boast no rival in the United States for the magnificence, the value and elegance of her sacred vases, ornaments and paintings, and indeed few churches in Europe possess anything superior to it ... decorated with the original paintings of Rubens, Raphael, Guido, Paul Veronze [*sic*] and a number of others by the first modern masters of the Italian, French and Flemish schools.[365]

Her visit to the cathedral did not live up to these promising expectations. Instead of a fine picture gallery, to her "infinite astonishment" there were only four oil paintings, only one of which could possibly be attributed to one of the old masters. She was not amused and later penned: "It is common enough to find exaggeration and colouring in the statements of travellers, but such a piece of downright falsehood as this I had not before met with."[366]

While staying in a nearby town Pfeiffer visited the still untouched prairies. For once her Viennese criteria for a good view were overruled. "I could never have imagined that a landscape without river, mountain, or lake, could have been half so beautiful," she said. For a time she lingered to cast her eyes over the endless gentle landscape. American farms were also visited which were clearly modern and profitable but Pfeifer was surprised that, unlike in Europe, the farmers' wives only helped with domestic labour rather than working in the fields.

Pfeiffer continued on in the beautiful steamer *Excelsior*, as she turned into the clear waters of the Missouri River where they joined the cloudy Mississippi. Here again Pfeiffer's diary returns to examples of the indecorous behaviour and bad manners of her fellow passengers. Worst of all was the noisy and pushy way the overly zealous Christians importuned her. Scarcely did they spot her then they would ask which church she belonged to. "'Really, Sir,' or 'Madam,' I used to reply, 'I do not wish to question you about your Church, and I should be glad if you would follow my example.'" If she asked someone for a book to read she was handed the Bible or a religious tract. This was very off-putting. "I must own this rude and abrupt manner of forcing their opinions upon me, gave me anything but a favourable opinion of them, and did not at all dispose me to listen to what they might have further to say; indeed, I used to shun these proselyte-makers as I would a pestilence."[367]

Finally on 7 August 1854, Pfeiffer could escape the religious zealots when the steamer reached St. Paul, the capital of the territory of Minnesota. The town was only a few years old and Minnesota would only become a state four years later. The weather was cold, cloudy and rainy.

For this destination Pfeiffer bore a letter of introduction to a "Mr Hollingshead" (possibly the lawyer William Hollinshead) who kindly hosted her in his pleasant house built just outside the town. He took her for a drive in his carriage to see what her hosts called one of the most remarkable scenes, the falls of St. Anthony. "I was soon standing on the edge of these renowned falls, and I certainly was beyond measure astonished; not, however, at their grandeur, but their insignificance," she explained.

Pfeiffer found that the Americans constantly praised many things in the most superlative terms, the same things she found to be utterly unremarkable and mundane. "I think only those who have seen very little could extol so highly," she concluded.[368] More interesting for Pfeiffer was a group of wild-looking fur trappers she happened to see. They lived for weeks or months at a time in the woods and married Indian wives.

Pfeiffer pushed on again. She proceeded first by river and then stagecoach in the direction of Lake Superior. The coach rattled through very pretty countryside with park-like meadows and small lakes. Through the window, Pfeiffer noted these signs of natural beauty with approval. At one stagecoach stop a woman entered who, dressed in a silken gown and an abundance of jewellery, looked like a wealthy lady. But Pfeiffer soon found that this was a false first impression. If it were not the bruises on the woman's face from a recent fight, it was certainly the mass of chewing tobacco she went through, spitting with gusto out the window. Then, taking a bottle of brandy from her pocket, she uncorked it and took a good swig or two. She had the politeness to then offer the bottle around to the other passengers. The woman talked familiarly to everyone in a loud voice but, not being sufficiently entertained, asked the driver to stop and moved outside to sit with the men. When the stagecoach stopped at a roadside inn for dinner, Pfeiffer sighed to find that, because the vulgar young woman was "white", they were therefore "compelled to endure her company at table; another instance of the wisdom of classing people by the colour of their skins".[369]

On 20 August Pfeiffer reached Chicago by steam train. She thought the town on the edge of windy Lake Michigan was notable primarily for its rapid growth over the last two decades. She took a small steamer across the lake to Milwaukee. There she met some people involved with the underground railway, an organisation helping, in breach of the law, escaped slaves to reach the safety of free Canada. Pfeiffer was even introduced to their leader, Sherman Booth. Earlier that year Booth had instigated a mob of 5,000 abolitionists who broke into the Milwaukee gaol and effected the dramatic release of Joshua Glover, an escaped slave from Missouri. Glover safely made his escape to Canada.

At Lake Superior, Pfeiffer was able to see many Chippewa and Sioux Indians. For once she did not describe different peoples as ugly, in fact "they were strong handsome men, and much taller than those I had seen before in the south-western countries", though their skin colour still struck her as ugly. She described it as "dirty-yellowish" and was baffled why the Americans called them "Redskins". Although some wore European clothes and could read and write, these "savages" of the cold north, she observed, were just as unwilling to work as those of the warm south.

Her journey continued to Fond-du-Lac on other end of the great lake. The new villages in the area were just log cabins surrounded by woods. Once again fellow passengers offended her with importunate questions about her religion. "Whereupon I felt so wrathful as to reply, 'Certainly not to the same as you and the rest of the ladies here; for my religion would have forbidden me to insult an unoffending fellow creature.' I suppose this explanation was satisfactory, for they did not ask me any more questions."[370]

Pfeiffer was just one of many nineteenth-century European travellers to complain about American manners. De Tocqueville, Mrs Trollope, Harriet Martineau and Charles Dickens would all make similar condemnations. Even Oscar Wilde quipped, "I believe the most serious problem for the American people to consider is the cultivation of better manners. It is the most noticeable, the most painful defect in American civilization."[371]

Pfeiffer passed through Lake Huron and Cleveland and on 9 August 1854 arrived at Buffalo. She was very eager to rush straight on to the celebrated Niagara Falls that night. But the Sumatran fever struck once again so she was forced to convalesce. A local remedy was given to her. It consisted of a teaspoonful of cayenne pepper and sugar mixed in half a tumbler of good brandy. Two teaspoons of this fiery cocktail were taken every hour before an onset of the symptoms were expected. Her fever did not return for another two months. She took the American remedy when she suffered another attack and the fever abated.

When she did finally visit the famous falls she described how the "enormous mass of water falls over a vast, broad, perpendicular wall of rock, and sends up such clouds as if the whole river were dashing itself into spray. During sunshine, beautiful rainbows are formed over both Falls in the clouds of spray." Here the romantic spirit of her youth was fully awakened. "This was a day never to be forgotten in the annals of my life—one of those which brilliantly rewarded me for all the toils and hardships by which they were purchased; for on this day I beheld one of the most sublime and wonderful scenes of God's beautiful world—the Falls of Niagara!"[372]

But the awesome power of nature not only inspires, but kills. A story was told to Pfeiffer of three men rowing upriver not long before her visit that had proved disastrous. Somehow the current swept their rowboat towards the falls. One of the men managed to grab hold of a tree branch sticking out of an island in the middle of the river but his companions were swept away. From the shore faint cries for help from the island were heard. Only in the morning could the stranded man been seen. The roar of the torrent was too great to communicate so that people on shore wrote in large letters on a board that they were sending help. After many failed attempts, they managed to float a tethered boat close enough for the man to clamber into it. The men on shore heaved on the rope and began drawing the boat across. Just then a large wave struck the boat and the sudden strain snapped the rope. There was nothing anyone could do. The boat and the poor victim were swept with terrifying speed to the edge of the falls and then plummeted down into the misty abyss. No trace of either man or boat was ever found.

Pfeiffer's next destination was Montreal in Canada. It had 75,000 inhabitants and most of its houses were made of stone with steep lofty gables showing some French influence. She proceeded to the best hotel in town and asked for a room. The man behind the desk looked suspiciously at this lone woman in her weather-beaten travel clothes and finally replied that there were no vacancies. Pfeiffer wasn't fooled. "The cause of this uncivil reception was, I knew perfectly well, the circumstance of my coming alone and with merely a small carpetbag, instead of having half a dozen trunks and bandboxes dragged after me." She had the same reception at the next hotel. This time in response she slapped a $10 gold piece on the counter. That did it. "When I went into the streets of Montreal and asked my way, I either got no answer at all, or the person I addressed endeavoured to get rid of me as quickly as possible with 'I don't know'. Certainly it did not appear to me that courtesy to strangers could be numbered among the Canadian virtues."[373]

Next she went to the offices of the principal newspaper to ask for information. The editor had never heard of her, and treated her accordingly. Pfeiffer was yet again offended and formed a very ill opinion of the Canadians. In the USA, in contrast, she "never found an editor of a newspaper who was not acquainted with my name, not even in the smallest town". Pfeiffer was coming to expect recognition wherever she went, and rather resented it when she didn't find it.

Next she travelled to Quebec but could find no vacancies there either and was again offended that the gentleman to whom she had brought a letter of introduction did not offer her a room in his house. Pfeiffer had become so accustomed to acts of kindness and generosity as a lone lady traveller that when these were not forthcoming, she put it down to rudeness. With nowhere to stay, she was forced to leave Quebec on the steamer that evening. She decided to head next to New York.

Pfeiffer arrived in New York City all alone. It was a rather formidable prospect since she knew no one in the vast metropolis of 600,000 people. For the first time in all her travels, she saw signposts warning against the danger of pickpockets. Once again serendipity served her well. She met a kind gentleman, a Mr Wutschel, and in the following days three other gentlemen invited her to stay in their homes. In this way she divided up her time amongst these hosts. One of these was the journalist William Cullen Bryant who wrote in a private letter on 26 September 1854: "Mrs. Ida Pfeiffer called on me this morning – a little thin woman, with a very dark complexion and pretty good teeth. She wanted to see the public institutions and I gave her letters."[374] It was common in the 18th and

19th centuries for respectable visitors to tour houses of correction, hospitals, schools and madhouses.

New York City was the busiest and most populous city she had seen in the USA. She found many imposing-looking buildings, "but their beauty consists chiefly in their size" she felt. The multistorey houses of the wealthy New Yorkers were equipped with every modern convenience. There was gas lighting and speaking pipes in every room. These allowed one to speak with ease directly to servants downstairs. Pfeiffer saw that shopping was a great pastime. The shops were very grand and ladies in their bulging bell-shaped crinoline dresses bent forward to peer eagerly into shop windows.

There was not much to see in the way of museums and picture galleries as far as Pfeiffer was concerned. There was the private "American Museum" of P. T. Barnum (later of circus fame). She thought it was more of a freak show which in addition to natural history objects, drew in the public with "a collection of stuffed birds and beasts, Chinese dresses, a dwarf, some remarkable animals, a mummy in good preservation".[375] Nevertheless it managed to attract hundreds of thousands of visitors per year.

She attended the theatre which was presenting a peculiarly American genre of entertainment, "Black Minstrels". That is, "white" singers were painted black and performed a peculiar genre of singing and performance. After this came a comedy. But Pfeiffer was completely lost: "the wit and sense of [the comedy] was to me profoundly mysterious" she confessed. The audience, which seemed very well to do and fashionable, appeared very satisfied with all of this and laughed prodigiously. She described her surprise in this way to indicate that she thought the supposedly discerning audience was easily satisfied with a very low standard of entertainment.

Pfeiffer also toured some private girls' schools. She was surprised to find the girls were taught a little Latin. Why Latin? she enquired. The answer was that it was useful in learning the modern Romance languages such as Italian, French and Spanish. Pfeiffer was very surprised because she was certain that their rudimentary Latin was seldom used for this purpose. Indeed, she noted, "I have in no country found fewer who were familiar with foreign languages." Pfeiffer attributed the appalling "superficiality of the ladies' knowledge" in the USA to the low standards of the schools.

After visiting many schools across the country, studying educational materials, exams and questioning teachers and students, Pfeiffer concluded that it was held down to such a low standard by an unhealthy dynamic between children and parents. The children would complain to their parents if the school was too difficult or they were pressed uncomfortably to work hard or learn. The parents would then either criticise the school or move their children to another. The teachers, caught in this situation, were compelled not to work the children beyond what they liked, and so the result was that the standard was rock bottom.

In fact the education of American women struck Pfeiffer as far too much like that for men. The "feminine" subjects and skills were neglected. This seemed to Pfeiffer to be one main cause for "that uneasy longing for what they call emancipation that characterises American women". In her critique, Pfeiffer gave her most detailed account of what she felt women ought to do. Education was fine and good, but women had practical responsibilities that should not be neglected, she held.

> They might begin, one would suppose, by emancipating themselves in their own houses: Domestic occupations must, after all, be attended to by somebody; and surely it had better be by the women than the men. It is not necessary that they should perform the offices of servants; but, if they do not understand how work of the

domestic kind ought to be done, the servants of the house will ere long become the masters. The girls in my own country also study foreign languages, music, history, and so forth; but they find time too to make themselves acquainted with womanly duties.[376]

How far she had come from the tomboy who so persistently resisted learning the feminine arts. As for women working, Pfeiffer had her own idiosyncratic opinions. If women wished to pursue a career, they should be free to do so.

In the exceptional cases where girls have at the same time an aversion to feminine employments and a strong vocation towards some art or science, and are likely to carry it to perfection, they should be allowed to pursue it; but then they should not do so by halves, but, if they desire to become doctors and professors, renounce all thoughts of being wives also; for it is difficult, if not impossible, to perform at the same time the duties of man and woman; and let the advocates of this kind of emancipation not forget, that there is no sphere of action more beautiful and noble than the one they have turned away from. In the hands of every mother lies one of the most precious treasures of every state. It is the mother who must inspire her child in its tenderest years with the love of duty and of virtue, and first lead it in the way by which it may become a worthy and perhaps a great and important member of the social body. A wise and thoughtful housewife, and a rational and loving mother, will, after all, remain the ideal of feminine perfection.[377]

Here is a strange mix of the modern and traditional. The roles are inherently sexed, yet women are free to chose which they want to pursue. This is why Pfeiffer was decidedly no feminist, nor even some sort of proto-feminist. Is there some trace of the young Ida in these remarks? Was she herself not one who had "an aversion to feminine employments and a strong vocation towards some art or science"? Unlike the Vienna of her youth, the women of the

USA had "the greatest freedom, and the greatest independence of thought and action".[378] But she did approve of the fact that mothers breastfed their babies rather than relying on wet nurses as was most common in Europe.

Some might accuse Pfeiffer of a double standard, since she travelled the world alone for pleasure, as only a man would normally do. To these critics she would later write: "Perhaps it may be objected to me that, in leaving my home and travelling about the world as I have done, I have in some measure emancipated myself from the duties of my sex; but I beg it may be borne in mind, that I have only done so when my children were grown up and settled, and had no longer the slightest need of my care; and when I had really no longer any household duties to perform."[379]

Together with a local journalist, Pfeiffer visited the "Tombs", the city House of Detention. Pfeiffer was shocked by what she witnessed there.

> I saw, to my deep sorrow, many women and young girls; and there often came, I was told, as many as thirty or forty in a day. The whole number brought during the preceding year amounted to 6,000. Whoever would wish to see this vice in the full horror of its degradation should come here. How it is possible, with such examples as this before their eyes, for the people of America to treat this vice with so much misplaced indulgence, is what I cannot understand.

The vice she alluded to was drunkenness. The journalist later reported that Pfeiffer told him that: "in all her travels she never saw so mournful a spectacle. She was moved to tears."[380]

Perhaps the highlight of her visit was to pay a call on the eminent American author, Washington Irving, then seventy-one years old. They got on very well and Pfeiffer was deeply impressed with the quiet dignity of the bachelor sage.

A writer for *Harper's New Monthly Magazine* met Pfeiffer at this time and gave a full description of her appearance.

> Imagine a plain, weather-beaten, little old woman—with features showing the wear and tear of hard luck in many lands—a complexion colored with as deep a brown as that of any ancient mariner by frequent battling with the elements—a dress of rustic homeliness in all its details—a general air of earnest, but perplexed curiosity— tones of voice that betray a rough experience of practical life, rather than the culture of polished society—and the complete absence of every thing like presumption, pretense, or affectation—and you will have a tolerable picture of the renowned lady-traveler.[381]

After three weeks in New York, and having seen what a tourist could see, Pfeiffer's friends recommended that she visit Boston, Philadelphia and Washington. She was not convinced. "But, to say the truth," she later confessed to her readers, "nothing wearies me more than visiting in succession several great towns, especially in America, where they very much resemble one another."[382]

On 10 October 1854 Pfeiffer left New York and headed for Boston. She was well received by some there, but not by all. Pfeiffer had brought a letter of introduction from New York to one of the leading businessmen in Boston. When the gentleman addressee saw Pfeiffer arrive in her plain dress, and on foot no less, he looked her sceptically up and down and gave her a very cold reception. Even after he read the letter he asked her in a guarded tone what she wanted, as if he were suspicious that she might need money. Here, she observed, was a prime example of an arrogant local elite such as can be found in so many parts of the world. Perhaps she remembered her cool reception in Iceland. She mused:

> Their pride and arrogance are far more unsupportable than that of the real aristocratic class, who generally have at least the grace of deportment, that is often wanting to the former. In Boston these

purse-proud people are said to hold together more than anywhere else; they scarcely associate with any but their own class, marry amongst themselves, and even live almost all together in one street.[383]

Boston had a population of 150,000 and Pfeiffer noted approvingly that, unlike New York, it was "perfectly clean". But to her disappointment as a demanding tourist "in the way of museums, public galleries, and so forth, there is not much worth seeing".

But the celebrated naturalist Dr John Collins Warren showed her his outstanding collection of fossils which included the complete skeleton of a mastodon, a giant extinct creature related to living elephants. Warren was one of those who had first introduced ether as an anaesthetic. Pfeiffer had witnessed its sadly botched initial introduction to India.

As usual she toured other institutions such as schools, an institute for the blind, an asylum and the prison. The General Hospital of Massachusetts impressed her so much that she said it was about as good as those at Surabaya and Semarang in Java. "Higher praise I could not give it." At Harvard University she met the eminent naturalist Louis Agassiz. She had stayed with his relative in Canton in 1847. Unfortunately Agassiz's outstanding collection of insects was packed away at the time so Pfeiffer was unable to inspect it. Agassiz was instrumental in establishing that the earth had once had an ice age or ice ages. He is principally remembered today as a staunch opponent of Darwin and his theory of evolution, especially as he was one of the last holdouts after the rest of the scientific community had accepted evolution to be a fact.

In a surviving notebook are some of the testimonials signed by those Pfeiffer met. The mayor of Boston, physician Jerome Van Croninsfield Smith, signed the book as follows: "Boston, U.S. America. This certifies that Madam Ida Pfeiffer, arrived in this city Oct. 11th.

and has inspected the institutions, and received the attentions and hospitalities of the citizens. J.V.C. Smith. Mayor. Oct. 17t. 1854."[384]

A month later Pfeiffer left the United States on the "splendid" steamer *Pacific*, under Captain Nye, bound for Liverpool. Once again she was generously given a free ticket by a kind-hearted gentleman, this time a Mr Curtis of New York. She reflected on all she had seen in the country that she "had so long ardently desired to visit". While admiring American declarations of "freedom and equality" for its people, she criticised its principal injustices. These were: "Slavery in some states,—the exclusion of free negroes and coloured people from society, and from political and civil existence in others,—the cruel law by which fugitive slaves are hunted and caught like wild beasts......and, lastly, the puritanical observance of the Sunday, which denies to those chained all the week to their work the privilege of cheerful and innocent recreation."[385]

After ten days crossing the Atlantic, the *Pacific* arrived at Liverpool on 21 November 1854. Captain Nye himself accompanied Pfeiffer to the Adelphi Hotel, where, as she was fast coming to expect, any payment for her stay was declined.

In London she stayed again a few weeks with naturalist George Robert Waterhouse and his family at the British Museum. She had suffered another bout of fever during the Atlantic crossing and it took her some time to recover. The "American remedy" – cayenne pepper, sugar and brandy – did the trick however.

Before returning to Vienna, however, Pfeiffer resolved to visit her son Oscar who was living on São Miguel in the Azores. She had not seen him for six years. There was no easy way to get there so in the end she took a passage on a small fruit schooner, the *Royal Blue Jacket*, that regularly made the passage to bring oranges and fresh fruit to Britain. She agreed with the master of the ship to pay £3 for the journey, without board. When she was prepared to depart, however, the owner of the vessel demanded £5 instead. Pfeiffer pointed out that the price had already been agreed. The owner, a Mr Chessel of Bristol, said if she did not pay the £5 she could take her bags off the ship. Pfeiffer was so incensed by this "extortion" that she made sure to name and shame him near the end of her book. It was hardly pleasant shipboard accommodation at any rate. There was no provision for passengers so Pfeiffer had to be content to sleep in a tiny bunk meant for the ship's cook. But she was used to cramped quarters anyway.

The *Royal Blue Jacket* reached São Miguel on 31 December 1854. The island struck her as extremely pretty with its many green hills and mountains. Here Pfeiffer would stay with Oscar for a few months. She continued to collect natural history specimens. Some of the fish she collected turned out to be new species and were purchased by the British Museum.[386] But most of her time was spent adapting her travel journal to the book on the second world journey.

In the middle of May 1855 she and Oscar sailed to Lisbon on a little Portuguese vessel of 110 tonnes, the *Michaelense*. Pfeiffer was very surprised and much annoyed at the border arrangements. First health officers came on board to inspect the passengers, then came the customs officers who would not allow them to leave with even a small bag, then the ship police inspected and then the harbourmaster and finally officers came to examine their passports, which cost a fee. Pfeiffer fumed. "Considering how proud we are of European progress, it seems strange to find a European government thus endeavouring to throw all possible hindrances in the way of travelling."[387]

Pfeiffer saw little of Lisbon as she fell very ill and was bedridden until it was time to leave. She boarded the steamer *Iberia* on 9 June bound for Southampton. The steamer was run by an English company, Pfeiffer's least favourite. She complained about the overpriced ticket and the deplorably cramped and uncomfortable shared cabin. It was worse than the little Portuguese vessel from São Miguel.

Reaching Southampton on 14 June 1855, she arrived in London later the same day by train. "I was once more cordially welcomed by the kind family of Waterhouse, and took up my abode with them in the British Museum. And herewith ended happily my Second Journey Round the World."[388] But not quite.

She spent some of her time to make arrangements with the publisher Longman, Brown, Green, and Longmans for an English translation of her next book. The earlier translations were probably pirated and earned her no money. Foreign translations and editions were almost a free-for-all in the nineteenth century. In all she stayed for a month in London and then made an indirect return journey to Vienna via Hamburg, Berlin and Prague.

In Berlin she again met with Humboldt. She made new scientific contacts including the professor of mineralogy, Gustav Rose. To the zoologist and conchologist Friedrich Paetel she sent a sample of land snails collected in the Malay archipelago.[389]

Once back in Vienna at the end of July 1855, Pfeiffer completed her book and sent it to the publishers. *My Second World Journey* appeared in German in 1856. It was dedicated to "The Dutch and the Dutch Governmental Authorities of India" in gratitude for all of their help and generosity during her sojourn there. It was clearly one of her most fondly remembered times. In the same year her signature was lithographed so that it could be purchased by autograph collectors as was then common for prominent figures.

The English translation of her book published by Longmans, *A Lady's Second Journey Round the World*, actually appeared in 1855, before the German edition published by Gerold in Vienna. For the first time one of her books carried the declaration that the right of translation was held by the author. A Dutch translation appeared in 1856 followed by French in 1857. A combined edition of both world journeys appeared in Polish in 1860. A Russian translation was published in 1876. Selections of her accounts of Sumatra, Borneo and the Maluku Islands were translated into Malay from 1877–1907.[390]

The book was well received and reviews appeared around the world. *Carinthia* (now the oldest Austrian magazine still in print) devoted an entire issue to the story of this "interesting" but "strange lady".[391] The Frankfurt newspaper *Didaskalia* called her "the famous Viennese lady, who is unmatched amongst her kind".[392] The *Neue Münchener Zeitung* reproduced part of a letter from a captain Lamprecht, long resident in Sumatra, that indicated that Pfeiffer's journey amongst the Batak cannibals was even more dangerous and astonishing than her own account revealed.[393] Further articles on Pfeiffer appeared in *Die Donau, Ost-Deutsche Post, Ungarische Post, Frankfurter Konversationsblatt, Illustrierte Zeitung* (Leipzig), *Pester Sonntags Zeitung* and *Le Spectateur* (Paris).

The Edinburgh Review applauded "that enterprising, courageous traveller Mrs. Pfeiffer".[394] The American literary magazine *Criterion* described the amazing Ida Pfeiffer to its readers as:

> An Austrian lady of advanced years and limited means, with, we need not say, a passion for change of air. She makes the longest voyages, climbs the highest mountains, rides the hardest trotting horses, and wades through the deepest mud with an indifference to discomfort and a persistence of purpose, which, had there remained any undiscovered continent or so, would have resulted in a more than Columbus fame.[395]

Another American periodical, *Putnam's Monthly Magazine,* declared that with all of her astonishing adventures one would think that Pfeiffer was an Amazon. It was unbelievable that at a time of life when most people would start to slow or settle, Madame Pfeiffer had embarked on a completely new career. The reviewer was, however, annoyed at Pfeiffer's descriptions of American ladies as uncultured.[396]

In Britain, the *Athenaeum* also reviewed the latest book by this "indefatigable *touriste*". It quoted the eminent German geographer Carl Ritter, who had said of Pfeiffer, even before the second circumnavigation:

> Frau Ida Pfeiffer, as a single she-traveller, undoubtedly took the first rank among her sex as to the range and extent of travelling; and that, indeed, in this respect she even surpassed the most celebrated of travellers of the middle ages, Marco Polo, the Venetian, Ibn Batuta, the Mahommedan, and others; for she had not only, like these men, explored and traversed in various directions the three continents of the Old World, but also those of the New World … and also crossed all the great oceans.[397]

The British Catholic periodical *The Rambler*, perhaps finding in Pfeiffer's views on emancipated women an effective reply to these new demands of American woman, offered a lesson.

> Her example shows that, in journeys for scientific purposes among savage tribes, a woman may travel with much more security than a man: and we beg to hint to some of our blooming sisters of the United States, that by following Madame Ida Pfeiffer they may establish their claims to equality of strength much better than by the adoption of short petticoats, long trousers, and transcendental theories of the rights of woman.[398]

Pursuing science was often seen as a safe practice that would keep people out of trouble and not ruffle established society. Here at least women could actually make unique progress, and it was a welcome antidote to the sort of anti-feminine "emancipated" women some writers disliked.

Pfeiffer's first book is heavily laced with expressions of religious piety, which she claimed was the motivation (or excuse?) for her journey. This did not seem to get much sympathy from readers and reviewers. The remaining voyages were justified as motivated, in part, by the study of nature and man. This worked incredibly well as can be seen not only by the approval of readers and reviewers but by the support of the Austrian government, elite scientific societies of Prussia, France and Britain, the support of so many eminent men of science, and it paid.

And, never to be outdone, the satirical London magazine *Punch* published a spoof new year's resolution about Pfeiffer. She needed a mountain of writing materials to be got ready because she was about to set off on a third world journey. *Punch* was poking fun at both her copious writings and her copious travel.

> Beginning of the New Year Well.
> Ida Pfeiffer (*spricht*). Here, Minna, child, listen and attend to me. You must run directly, and get me fifteen reams of paper, one quire of blotting ditto, six quarts of black ink, and five hundred Magnum Bonum steel pens. To-morrow is New Year's Day, and I intend starting on a trip round the World for the third time. You must call me at five o'clock.[399]

The Scottish journalist James Hannay penned an even more hurtful (if also more witty) poem about Pfeiffer.

> Through regions by wild men and cannibals haunted,
> Old Dame Ida Pfeiffer goes lone and undaunted;
> But, bless you!—her risk's not so great as it's reckoned,
> She's too plain for the first, and too tough for the second.[400]

Pfeiffer might be admired, much talked about and even an object of public ridicule, but her scientific collections and observations were treated with essentially the same respect and value as those made by men. The collections she made during the second world journey were certainly impressive, but the full extent and range is not known.

Of her Bornean specimens, some were named after her including the very striking dead leaf mimic orb-weaver spider (*Poltys idea*), a spindly stick insect (*Lonchodes pfeifferae*), a freshwater prawn (*Palaemon idae*) and a sea snail (*Vaginula idae*).[401] The British Museum purchased rare fossil shells that Pfeiffer collected in Java. Asiatic soft-shell turtles in spirits collected in Ambon and Seram were also purchased along with rare butterflies. The Berlin Museum acquired many specimens including an orange-brown snail (*Pupina superba*) from Sumatra. An even rarer specimen was a human skull, likewise bought by the British Museum, listed as collected at "Mailura" presumably Madura, an island just off Surabaya.[402]

Wallace, writing to his colleague Henry Walter Bates in 1856, mentioned that the British Museum had some beetles from the Maluku Islands which had "recently been obtained by Madame Pfeiffer [which] give good promise of what a systematic search may produce".[403] Wallace, of course, meant to head there to do the systematic search himself. In December 1857 he arrived on the island of Ambon where he met a thirty-one-year-old Hungarian physician named Carl Ludwig Doleschall. The young doctor was an enthusiastic entomologist who had studied at the Vienna Museum for a year before setting out for the Dutch East Indies. Amongst the specimens in the museum, Doleschall had studied those collected by Pfeiffer, including a huge hairy spider. He reported in a Dutch scientific journal that her specimens were far larger than any he had been able to procure. "I have seen specimens of *Mygale javanensis*, sent by Mrs. Pfeiffer to Vienna, which were over 2½ inches long. Personally I have only obtained immature specimens."[404] Even Charles Darwin cited Pfeiffer's authority in his *Descent of Man* (1871) to the effect that "in Java, a yellow, not a white girl, is considered, according to Madame

Pfeiffer, a beauty".[405] Collecting thus resulted in a completely different fame from travel alone.

The earliest known photograph (daguerreotype) of Ida Pfeiffer, date and photographer unknown (Lebzelter 1910). Her clothing suggests this must be the early 1840s. She is wearing a lace day-cap (not a bonnet). These were worn by married women.

Lithograph of Ida Pfeiffer by Adolf Dauthage, 1855. (Stökl 1920)

William Henry Bartlett. (Bartlett 1842)

Title page of the English translation of A Visit to the Holy Land. *(Pfeiffer 1852b)*

Ida of Arabia. Frontispiece to Reise einer Wienerin in das heilige Land, *1846, 3rd edn., vol. 1.*

The Women's Tower outside the monastery of Mar Saba. Women were not allowed to enter the main compound. (Bartlett 1851)

An artist's rendition of the attack in Brazil during which Pfeiffer was stabbed in the arm. (Pfeiffer 1885)

The broken handle of Pfeiffer's parasol broken during the attack in Brazil. (Honsig 2012)

An oil portrait of Ida Pfeiffer by Emilie Marie Schmück, c. 1845. (Honsig 2012)[491]

Pfeiffer's passport for her first world journey. (Honsig 2012)

Pfeiffer being led to the "great geyser" by a drunken Icelander. (Stökl 1920)

An artist's rendition of Pfeiffer visiting Purí Indians in Brazil. (Pfeiffer 1885)

The serpent in Singapore. (frontispiece to Pfeiffer 1852f)

Pfeiffer in Baghdad. (Pfeiffer 1885)

*Pfeiffer on a tiger hunt in India. She is
armed with a knife. (Pfeiffer 1885)*

*Pfeiffer's Babylonian "seal".
(Honsig 2012)*

*Alexander von Humboldt, c. 1857.
Engraved by D.J. Pound, 1859.*

Fashionable dresses that appeared opposite the image of Pfeiffer's travel costume. Pfeiffer's image was probably the most unusual the magazine ever published.

Pfeiffer in her travel costume. Drawn from life by Adolf Dauthage. (von Gayette 1856)

Photograph of Pfeiffer by Franz Hanfstaengl, 1856. A globe made a handy prop to symbolise the world traveller.

Pfeiffer calms the cannibals in Sumatra. (Stökl 1920)

The rajah's house and rice barns at Fort de Koch.
(Rijksmuseum, the Netherlands) Pfeiffer probably
visited this house.

Pfeiffer crossing a Dyak bamboo bridge, Sarawak,
with butterfly net in hand. (Pfeiffer 1856c, vol. 2)

Eine gelehrte Reisende.

A caricature of Pfeiffer entitled "A learned traveller."
It was published with the following caption:
Ida: "Don't run, I am not afraid of savages."
Indian: "But I am!"
(Wiener Telegraf, (15 Sept.) VII, 1855, nr. 215)

The Madagascar buzzard (Buteo brachypterus) discovered by Pfeiffer in Madagascar. (Grandidier 1876)

The Diademed sifaka (Propithecus diadema) discovered by Pfeiffer in Madagascar. (Grandidier 1875)

Pfeiffer playing the piano at the royal
court in Madagascar. (Anon. 1880)

Monsieur Lambert.
(Chartier & Pellerin 1888)

The silk dust mask Pfeiffer wore to
protect herself from the sand while
climbing in the Andes.
(Honsig 2012)

Pfeiffer on Madagascar. (Stökl 1920)

Proof of the unissued Ida
Pfeiffer banknote.[492]

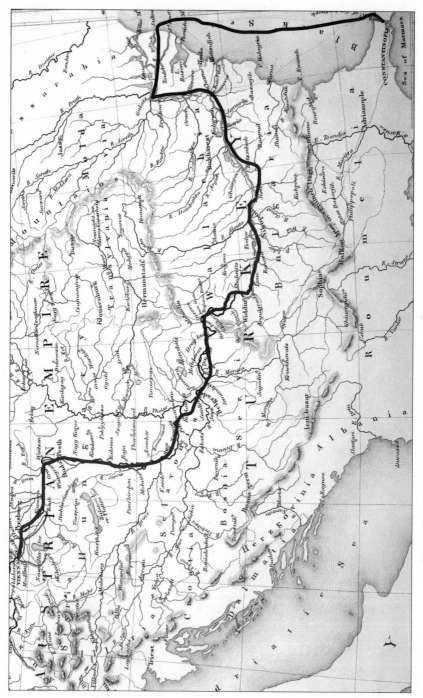

Map of Pfeiffer's journey from Vienna to Constantinople. Map based on Bartlett 1844.

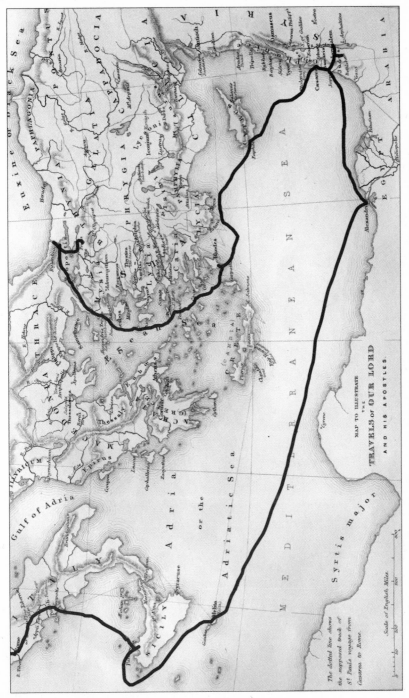

Map of Pfeiffer's journey from Constantinople to Palestine, Egypt and Italy. Map based on Bartlett 1844.

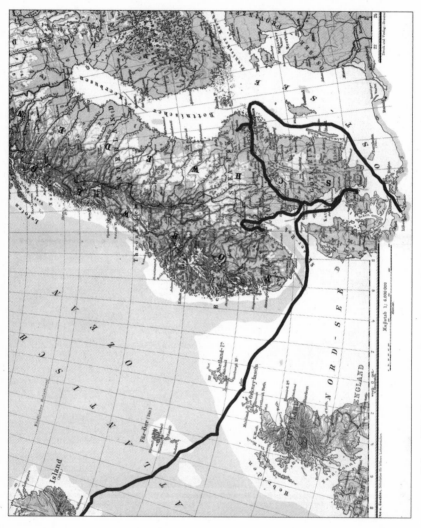

Map of Pfeiffer's journey from Copenhagen, Iceland, Norway, Sweden and Germany.
Map based on Gaebler 1896.

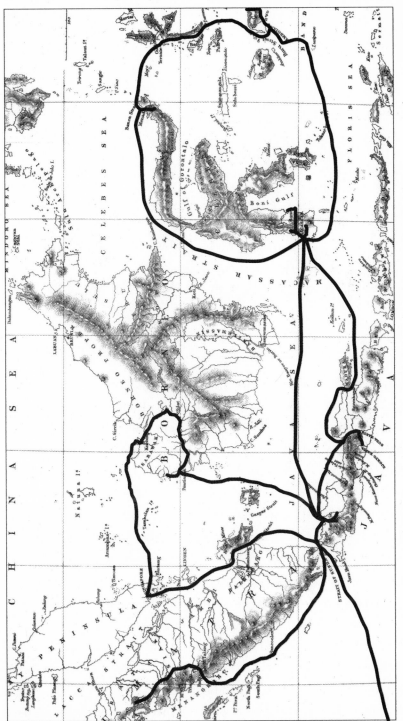

Pfeiffer's 1851–1852 route through Southeast Asia. Map based on Bickmore 1869.

CHAPTER 6

QUEST TO MADAGASCAR
(1856–1858)

"I found no one to accompany me, and was determined to go;
so I trusted to fate, and went alone."
Ida Pfeiffer, 1852

In mid 1855 Ida Pfeiffer had finally returned home to Vienna after her lengthy second journey around the world. She had become the first woman ever to circle the globe alone twice. Her collections, some shipped from abroad, were unpacked, sorted and organised. She set up an impromptu "Private Museum" of her collections in a flat on Graben, one of the most genteel streets in central Vienna.[406] On tables were displays of butterflies and beetles. The ethnographic items included Chinese artwork, Dyak bark cloth, earrings, a belt, spears and a basket festooned with human hair in which the Dyaks carried severed heads. Equally macabre was a necklace composed of 150 human teeth from fallen enemies. From the Batak of Sumatra she brought a six-foot-long magic staff or *tunggal panaluan*, a rattan bag, a woven cloak (*ulos*), a book (*pustaha*) written in the unique Batak script and a calendar (*porhalaan*) made of two pieces of carved wood.[407] Some items were for sale. Pfeiffer complained in interviews with journalists that her fellow Viennese had too little interest in science. Most of these items eventually found their way into the Natural History Museum Vienna, the Museum of Ethnology in Vienna and the Heimatmuseum in Waidhofen an der Ybbs.

Natural history specimens were sent to Vinzenz Kollar, of the Royal Museum of Vienna, which occupied many halls in the Hofburg palace. The museum purchased 2,500 specimens which earned Pfeiffer 1,971 guilders.[408] Duplicates were sold on the commercial market. Many specimens found their way to the Berlin Museum.[409] Her collections were surprisingly varied, including everything from Bornean beetles, Javan crustaceans and Tahitian seaweed to Ecuadorian snail shells. Many other specimens were sold through Samuel Stevens to the British Museum in London and presumably private collectors too.

Perhaps at this time, Samuel Stevens wrote to her with the advice of one of his most ingenious collecting clients, Alfred Russel Wallace, who was diligently collecting in the Malay archipelago. Wallace wrote to his sister in June 1855: "I expect [Pfeiffer] will set up regular collector now, as it will pay all her expenses & enable her to travel where she likes. I have told Mr Stevens to recommend Madagascar to her."[410] Following on from the profitable success of her recent collections, should she chose to travel again, Madagascar would prove particularly profitable as it was largely terra incognita for European museums.

No suggestion could fall on more fertile soil. Madagascar was a land almost wholly unknown and mysterious to Europeans, sure to produce a wealth of valuable natural history specimens, which could themselves propel yet further travels around the world – perhaps to Australia, New Guinea or Japan. Perhaps even a third circumnavigation of the world could result; what could tick more boxes for Ida Pfeiffer?

The prim lady readers of the Austrian fashion magazine *Die Wiener Elegante* begged for a portrait of the famous world traveller who had sprung so unexpectedly from their midst. The magazine normally published dress patterns and illustrations of the latest top hats and large hoop skirt dresses then in fashion. When approached by the journal's editor, Pfeiffer replied "people would find it laughable if I allowed myself to be depicted in my travel costume".[411] And yet, she was told, that is what the world wanted to see. Reluctantly, Pfeiffer agreed to don her well-worn short trousers, petticoat, conical hat, butterfly net and a vasculum for collecting plants hanging from her shoulder. And thus we have a fascinating glimpse as to what she looked like in the wilder parts of her travels.[412] The conical Balinese hat, Pfeiffer said, was the lightest and most comfortable travel hat she had ever found. The magazine informed its readers that her "grey and black checked linen dress is light and airy".[413] Pfeiffer's costume was, above all, determined by practicality, but it was still a compromised version of feminine attire. She did not don men's clothes.

The accompanying article was written by Jeanne Marie von Gayette, author of *Mädchenwelt. Gegen die falsche Frauenemanzipation* (1848), which could be translated as Girl World: Against the False Emancipation of Women. Clearly the author was no fan of emancipation, but Pfeiffer was not objectionable on this count. Von Gayette described the strange double personality of Frau Pfeiffer. She was "in her homeland feminine, timid and shy, but she has the courage of a hero and the strength of a martyr against the dangers of the wide world, no emancipated woman, no Amazon, no mannish woman (*Mannweib*), an original type, a breed of her own".[414] The drawing was reproduced as the frontispiece to the German edition of *A Lady's Second Journey* (1856) and as a carte de visite.

In March 1856 Pfeiffer was elected an honorary member of

the Berlin Geographical Society, the first woman to receive this distinction. Even the Austrian Archduke himself, Ferdinand Maximilian, honoured her with two invitations to visit the palace.

As pleased as she was with all of these attentions, they could not satisfy her for long. The itch to travel was insatiable. She must push on, ever onwards, towards new and distant horizons. At the end of May 1856 she was ready for her next, and as it happened, her last great journey – to Madagascar. Can it be a coincidence that Wallace had recommended this destination through Stevens and it was this place, of all the world, that she chose to visit next?

She was fifty-eight years old, thin, and now slightly bent. With a free ticket provided by the steamer company, she left home on 21 May 1856. She travelled via Salzburg to Munich where, among other things, she was presented to King Maximilian II.

Local hosts took Pfeiffer from one sight to another. There were museums and art galleries crammed with fine paintings and the sturdy twin-towered Frauenkirche whose silhouette is still the symbol of the city's skyline. This tourist visit led her to make one great if not very original observation shared by countless millions of footsore tourists wearily treading pavements, ruins and museums around the world: "Nothing is more tiring, or more exhausting to the mind and body, than crowding a large amount of sight-seeing into a limited time."[415]

She was photographed by prominent Bavarian photographer Franz Hanfstaengl who also photographed the likes of King Maximilian II, Franz Liszt and Richard Wagner. She attended the great Artists' Festival then being held in Munich. Afterwards, when she asked some strangers on the street for directions, they offered to show her the way, not knowing who she was. Which is why she was so amused when the strangers asked, "Oh you were at the festival, did you see the 'great traveller,' Ida Pfeiffer, there?" Press reports claimed, "This very simple woman drew all the attention away from the beautiful young ladies."[416]

On 1 June she proceeded to Berlin where her arrival again engendered great interest. Far greater, in fact, than in her native Vienna. But then, as always, a prophet is not regarded in his own country. In Berlin, everyone was eager to see this extraordinary creature. She was shown the sights by or introduced to the likes of Prince von Pückler-Muskau, the romantic author Countess Bettina von Arnim and the opera composer Giacomo Meyerbeer. The King of Prussia, Frederick William IV, awarded her the gold medal for science and art. The celebrated geographer, Carl Ritter, invited her to a meeting of the Geographical Society, to which she had recently been elected. She was led by the president of the Society to a seat of honour prepared for her.

A lengthy report and interview appeared in the avant-garde magazine *Unterhaltungen am häuslichen Herd* (Entertainments for the Homely Hearth), which was modelled on Charles Dickens's successful *Household Words*. Rumour had it that after spending so much time with savages, Pfeiffer had become half wild herself, with an appetite for human flesh and she knew how to scalp an enemy. In fact, the magazine testified, Madame Pfeiffer was a plain, simple, honest lady. She was not affected, not pushy or disagreeable. And yet when it came to travelling and exploring, she had accomplished vastly more than anyone else. And why? Pfeiffer told the journalist, "I was born with this travel- and wanderlust."[417] Perhaps her only really special skill, it was suggested, was an unparalleled ability to mimic and hand gesture. She had, after all, travelled amongst many peoples with whom she shared no language whatsoever. In these situations, a proficiency with hand signing must have been irreplaceable. Apart from experiencing adventure, there was a virtuous result of her travels, she was furthering science. "With tireless patience and care she had collected brightly coloured butterflies, beetles, sea urchins, scorpions and many other exotica of the animal and plant world for our museums."[418]

Pfeiffer gave the grand old man of European science, Alexander von Humboldt, an advance copy of her new book. He was full of praise and promised to cite her in the next volume of his great attempt to unify the sciences – *Kosmos*. He kept his promise and cited her as "our admirable, courageous and world travelling Mrs Ida Pfeiffer".[419] When he heard about her next travel destination, however, he was emphatically opposed to it. Madagascar was far too dangerous, even for a man. Pfeiffer had heard this tune many times before, and always remained steadfast in her determination to go anyway.

Nevertheless, Humboldt provided her with an open letter of introduction addressed to anyone in the world who knew of his name and work and bade them assist Madame Pfeiffer who was "famous not just because of her noble endurance which she exhibited in so many dangers and deprivations, which took her twice around the world" but also her noble character and the "inextinguishable energy of character which she has everywhere shown, to wheresoever's she has been called or better put, driven by her unconquerable passion to study nature and man".[420]

After enjoying the transient rush of being a celebrity globetrotter, Pfeiffer spent a fortnight touring the Netherlands which, neat and tidy as it was, she found almost as delightful as their eastern possessions. Pfeiffer praised the simple and orderly prettiness of the country though it was too flat for an Austrian to find it a truly beautiful or satisfying landscape. There were simply no mountains to complete the view. She was hosted and honoured by some of the colonial administrators she had met overseas, Colonel Steuerwald and Mr van Rees. Usefully, she was given more free steamer tickets.

After touring Amsterdam, Utrecht, Leiden ("a very dull place") and Rotterdam, she headed on to London on 2 July 1856.

Pfeiffer turned up at the offices of a British steamer company to buy a ticket. When the owner learned who she was, he refunded her ticket price. Pfeiffer was astonished as she had never before received free passage on a British steamer. (Something that she had complained about in her books.)

Pfeiffer spent about four weeks in London, lodging with her friend the naturalist Waterhouse and his family at the British Museum. She sought out the great African explorer, and fellow German, Heinrich Barth, for information.[421] She then crossed the channel again at the beginning of August. In Paris she sought more information about travelling to Madagascar. It was the French, far more than any other European nation, that had had the most to do with Madagascar and would ultimately bring it into their colonial fold. During her stay in the French capital, Pfeiffer was showered with honours as in Berlin and elsewhere. Her contact Carl Ritter facilitated an invitation to attend a meeting of the Geographical Society of Paris and she was duly elected an honorary member. This touched Pfeiffer as a particular honour because "my old tutor, who had taught me history and geography" was also a member. This was her first, and apparently only love, Trimmel. He became a corresponding member of the society in 1829. This was the only time Pfeiffer ever mentioned him in her published travels. According to the entry on Pfeiffer in the *Neu Deutsche Biographie*, Trimmel supported Pfeiffer's travel reports.[422]

What about travelling to Madagascar? Once again Pfeiffer was advised to forget it. Everything about such a voyage looked discouraging. War seemed imminent and it was at any rate judged to be extremely dangerous for a European to travel there without armed protection. The British and French governments were vying for control of the region and nothing seemed as yet secure. Somewhat disappointed, but not entirely discouraged, she returned to London on the 12th. At the very least she had received a letter of recommendation from the French admiralty.

In London she continued her enquiries. One of those whom she met for information about travelling to Madagascar was Henry Norton Shaw, diplomat and Secretary of the Royal Geographical Society. He could not provide much. And otherwise he seemed a little embarrassed during their meeting. At last he explained that he regretted that his society was unable to offer her the same honour as the societies in Berlin and Paris because the statutes expressly forbade the election of women to a fellowship. Women would not be admitted until 1892 and not as full fellows until 1913.

Much better news, and certainly more practical for the ever cash-stretched Frau Pfeiffer, was the decision at a meeting of the British Association for the Advancement of Science to award £20 "to Mrs. Ida Pfeiffer, the celebrated female traveller, to assist in her researches into the natural history of Madagascar".[423] Augustus Petermann, who was a member of the Association, may have helped with this award. Not long after one of the more arresting headlines to bear Pfeiffer's name in the press appeared as: "H.R.H. PRINCE ALBERT AND MADAME IDA PFEIFFER." This was not the announcement of a scandalous affair but coverage of the fact that when Prince Albert heard that the British Association had awarded Pfeiffer £20, "His Royal Highness immediately forwarded to Professor Owen a further sum of £10 for the adventurous lady".[424]

But the perpetually moving Pfeiffer was by that time no longer in London to read these gratifying headlines. She was already pursuing her merry way. Since Madagascar seemed impossible to enter or even reach, she would happily continue to investigate the Dutch East Indies. So she had sailed for Rotterdam on 22 August

1856 to seek a Dutch ship back to the East Indies. She was once again obligingly offered a cheaper ticket by the owner of a ship. The 700-tonne sailing ship *Salt-Bommel*, under Captain Juta, turned out to be one of her most uncomfortable vessels. The ship was full of children bound for domestic work at the Cape of Good Hope. They had been collected from all the poorer parts of the Netherlands. Pfeiffer exclaimed, "in all my life I never saw such an amount of riff-raff collected together ... the whole community swore like the sailors."[425]

It was going to be another nightmare voyage. And on a ship, as on a plane today, there is no escape from fellow passengers. Not only were the young people dreadfully behaved but even her own cabin became uninhabitable when the woman she was sharing it with actually gave birth in it. Pfeiffer was given a narrow settee in the lounge to sleep on which was so narrow that when the ship rolled she almost did too, onto the floor.

Day after day she sat on deck hoping to enjoy the fresh sea air and the anticipation of a new voyage ahead. The young people were obviously having a whale of a time, but Pfeiffer was appalled. The girls flirted with the sailors all day. The whole pack "shouted, laughed, and screamed like denizens of the lowest public houses".[426] Mercifully for Pfeiffer, on 16 November 1856, the *Salt-Bommel* arrived at Cape Town.

The following morning Pfeiffer was packing up her things to go ashore when a gentleman came on board and enquired for Madame Pfeiffer. It was a Frenchman named Joseph-François Lambert, a trader and civil engineer who had for some years been based in Mauritius. He had visited Madagascar about two years before and was personally acquainted with its sovereign, Queen Ranavalona. He had recently written to the queen from Paris requesting permission to make a second visit. As part of a new isolationist policy, foreigners were forbidden from entering the kingdom of Merina without the queen's consent. He expected to receive a letter of permission at his home in Mauritius. He had read in the newspapers about Pfeiffer's planned trip to Madagascar and, since he had actually been there, and was soon to return, he offered his assistance. Once back at his home on Mauritius he would write to the queen asking permission for Pfeiffer to come too. It must have seemed like another one of those many propitious meetings that had furthered her travels so often in the past. Lambert's steamer was leaving for Mauritius the following day. Pfeiffer had to decide right away. Here was a chance that would never come again. This might be her one and only opportunity to reach Madagascar. She would go.

But it was a terrible mistake. Monsieur Lambert was in fact a former slave trader, an unscrupulous adventurer and a rogue. If there were a villain in the story of Ida Pfeiffer, Lambert was it. Born in Brittany in 1824, by the age of twenty-two Lambert had arrived in Mauritius and married a wealthy widow. Thereafter he engaged in transporting black African "labourers" between Mozambique and the isle of Bourbon (Réunion). In 1854 he relieved the Merina garrison at Fort Dauphin with a shipment of rice from the siege of coastal tribes hostile to Merina rule. This apparent service secured Lambert an invitation to meet the queen at her capital, Antananarivo, in the central highlands of Madagascar. Also in Antananarivo at that time was another Frenchman and long-term resident, Jean Laborde, who was producing weapons for the Merina military. Some of his canon remain on display today. The two men became friends.

Queen Ranavalona has quite possibly the worst reputation of any queen in history, although she was not quite the gymnastically oversexed and sadistic monster portrayed in George MacDonald Fraser's novel *Flashman's Lady* (1977): "When Queen Ranavalona came to the throne (by murdering all her relatives) in 1828, she'd broken off all traffic with the outside world, forbidden Christianity and tortured all converts to death, revived slavery on a great scale, and set about exterminating all tribes except her own [and] she went through lovers like a rat through cheese." Some in the nineteenth century described her as a modern Messalina, the "female Caligula" or just "l'horrible Ranavalo".[427] Even Pfeiffer would eventually describe her as certainly one of the "most cruel women on the face of the earth … her whole history is a record of bloodshed and deeds of horror".[428]

But the queen's extreme views were not shared by her mild-mannered son and heir, Prince Rakoto. Lambert had joined Laborde and other conspirators to seek to remove Ranavalona and replace her with her more moderate, amenable and pro-European son. Lambert convinced Rakoto to sign a document asking Napoleon III of France for protection. This amounted to a request for French assistance to overthrow the present monarch and place Rakoto on the throne in return for French trade access. And just as importantly, Lambert and his business associates were to be granted exclusive rights to minerals, timber and unoccupied land in exchange for a ten per cent royalty on the profits. It was later claimed that Rakoto could barely understand the French document that he was pressured to sign, and indeed thought it entailed only an account of the hardships his people were suffering under the queen's policies.

Armed with this so-called charter, Lambert returned to Europe and approached Napoleon III in Paris and later Lord Clarendon, Britain's Foreign Secretary, for assistance. The latter refused to assist and the French would not act alone. Undeterred, Lambert set off for Madagascar to try his luck anyway. He brought with him from France a treasure trove of gifts to help sweeten deals in Madagascar.

Lambert was returning to Madagascar intent on instigating a coup d'état of his own. He felt sure that he and a few fellow conspirators would be enough to topple the corrupt government, a rashly overconfident sentiment rather like that of Adolf Hitler who said of the Soviet Union, "We have only to kick in the door and the whole rotten structure will come crashing down."[429] Lambert was inviting the innocent and inoffensive Ida Pfeiffer along as cover.

Like the Galapagos Islands, Mauritius was so isolated in the Indian Ocean that humans never reached it until recent times. When the island was first discovered in the sixteenth century, the birds were so oblivious to the danger humans presented that they could simply be killed with a stick. There were two species of giant tortoise. But Mauritius is most famous for the non-existence of another aboriginal inhabitant, the dodo. When Europeans first arrived these stodgy flightless birds were blissfully unaware of the fate that awaited them. In about a century the species was utterly extinguished forever. The dodo is sometimes, and quite unfairly, represented as an icon of stupidity or doomed inferiority. By the early nineteenth century it was the first and for many years the only species recognised by western science to have been driven extinct by man. In fact it was only a particularly conspicuous and recent example of a very, very long line of species driven to extinction by man, the super predator.

The island was occupied by the Dutch in the seventeenth and eighteenth centuries, followed by the French until it was captured by the British in 1810. The island's population remained primarily French together with the descendants of imported slaves and labourers from Africa, India, and Madagascar.

HMS *Beagle* visited Mauritius in 1836. As Darwin would later explain in *On the Origin of Species* (1859), Mauritius had no native frogs because "these animals and their spawn are known to be immediately killed by sea-water, on my view we can see that there would be great difficulty in their transportal across the sea, and therefore why they do not exist on any oceanic island". Frogs were introduced to Mauritius by man in the late eighteenth or early nineteenth century and flourished to the extent of becoming a nuisance. Since the island was therefore obviously ideal habitat for frogs, but none had existed there before man, Darwin pointed out, "Why, on the theory of creation, they should not have been created there, it would be very difficult to explain."[430]

On 18 November 1856 the handsome new steamer *Governor Higginson* bearing Pfeiffer and Lambert quitted the Cape. What sweetened the deal even more, Lambert, who owned the controlling share of the ship, declared that she was now his guest and thus need pay nothing for the voyage and could stay gratis at his country house on Mauritius until the weather would permit a voyage to Madagascar in about four months. Pfeiffer had long since come to expect such acts of generosity as her due, so there was nothing to be suspicious about. So all promised well for her journey. After steaming 2,400 miles and burning 375 tonnes of coal, the steamer dropped anchor at Port Louis, Mauritius on 2 December. Just as European newspapers had reported that Pfeiffer was heading for Madagascar via Mauritius within two months of her leaving Cape Town, the local newspaper in Port Louis soon announced the arrival of the famous lady traveller.

> One of the greatest living travellers—perhaps the greatest—arrived here by str. *Governor Higginson*, Madame Ida Pfeiffer, a German lady has made we believe three voyages round the world, and has visited almost every known country ... We express the wish of a number of ladies as well as gentlemen when we say they are desirous of paying their respects to Madame Pfeiffer, and we trust she will not refuse to be "at home" to them during her short stay in this town. ... Madame Pfeiffer is particularly anxious not to attract attention ... But Madame P. will allow us to say that hers is now a world wide

fame, and she ought not to wonder that she has many admirers among her own sex in the ladies of Mauritius. ... It is very natural that everyone should be anxious to pay their homage to a lady of so much merit, enterprise and renown.[431]

Another newspaper writer tried to explain the essence of what made Ida Pfeiffer so unique – her wanderlust. "An irresistible, impulse impels this wonderful lady to wander over God's vast and beautiful world, and to visit the great variety of races of men."[432]

Pfeiffer settled in to Lambert's large and luxurious country house, "Les Failles" (The Shambles), seven miles from the town of Port Louis. Despite the enforced halt to her progress, she was at least quite comfortable. There were plenty of servants and Lambert went to work each morning and only returned in the evenings, leaving Pfeiffer free to do as she pleased.

Pfeiffer would make her stay on the tiny island count. The specimen collecting was pursued with her usual diligence and imagination. She was surprised by the comparative scarcity of ants on Mauritius. "I could sometimes leave the insects I had collected for half a day together on the table, and the ants did not get at them, while in other hot countries these depredators would be devouring their prey within a few minutes."[433]

In the end her collection included reptiles, a freshwater fish, two species of worm, three species of crustaceans and twenty species of molluscs. Her greatest bounty was the insects. She found 122 new species as well as four species of spider. A species of fish she collected ended up in a Hamburg museum and a cricket in the British Museum.[434] One of her new discoveries was a species of termite that fed on the largest trees of the island. Pfeiffer even included the larvae and part of the nest in her collection. Another one of her finds was an unknown species of insect, which, Pfeiffer reported in a note with the specimen, did great damage to the trees and had only appeared on the island in recent years. Another new species she collected was a type of seaweed that came to be named after her, *Sargassum pfeifferae*. Two days after Christmas 1856, she wrote to one of her contacts at Batavia that, after Madagascar, she planned to return to Java and from there travel to Japan or New Guinea to continue collecting.[435]

The primary commercial crop of Mauritius was sugar cane and it covered vast tracts of the island. Many of the fields belonged to her host Lambert. "Sugar, and nothing but sugar, is to be seen in this island," she wrote in despair. "Every undertaking has reference to sugar, and all the conversation is about sugar. Mauritius might be called the sugar island, and its coat of arms should be a bundle of sugar-canes and three sugar-bags rampant."[436]

Society was essentially divided between the French, the English and the creoles. Like oil and vinegar, they did not mix very well. Pfeiffer rolled her eyes at the unnecessary formality and stiffness observed by the inhabitants of this remote outpost, eager to convince themselves that they were still in civilisation. Pfeiffer found the interminable dinners the worst. "At table, one is frequently seated between two perfect strangers, and after suffering the horrors of ennui for hours, a move is made at past nine o'clock into the reception-rooms, there to suffer ennui for some time longer." This human phenomena has no doubt been suffered in all ages as it still is today. And here she wrote something quite curious in her diary. "I received many invitations" to dinners and parties, but "most of these invitations I declined". Yet it was exactly the lack of such invitations that had so disappointed and disgusted her in Iceland and elsewhere.

Pfeiffer did make many English friends, several of whom hosted her at different parts of the island or took her to see various sights. Pfeiffer thought she was ignored and snubbed by the French families. She attributed this to her spending too much time with the English. For example, they gossiped that the many valuable presents that Lambert had brought from Paris for the Queen of Madagascar had some sinister purpose: "it must be some secret political movement of the French cabinet", Pfeiffer heard with disdain.[437] Some even whispered that the British government had found out and had sent Pfeiffer to poison him. The "creoles", on the other hand, were seen by the local Europeans as dirty, money-grubbing and stupid.

But the rumours and intrigue were not limited to the creoles and the French. Near the end of her stay Pfeiffer called again on the governor, Sir James Macaulay Higginson, for his promised letter of introduction to the Queen of Madagascar. But now he had changed his mind and declined to provide one and sought to dissuade her from going. To Pfeiffer's astonishment and disbelief "he pronounced my companion to be politically a dangerous man". How ironic, she reflected after she had returned to her room, "the French took me for an English spy, and the English governor for a spy of the French government!"[438] Sadly, Pfeiffer seemed almost immune to warnings.

Unbeknownst to Pfeiffer, the British Consul in Mozambique, John Lyons McLeod, had heard news and even minute details of the Lambert plot. Learning that the famous Madame Pfeiffer was travelling with Lambert, McLeod wrote her several letters, directed to Mauritius, in an effort to warn her.[439] If she received the letters in time, they had no effect in changing her course.

Madagascar

At the end of April 1857 the monsoon winds had turned and it was possible to sail west to the virtually unknown island of Madagascar.

Once again Pfeiffer's fame procured her a free passage, this time courtesy of the owners of the brig *Triton*. Captain A. Benier told her that the *Triton* fought the French at the battle of Trafalgar. This was not actually true, but in any case the tired old war horse was now only a vessel for transporting oxen. The *Triton* was so completely modified for this purpose that there was no other cabin but the captain's. He graciously offered it to his female passenger and resolved to spend the voyage sleeping in a corner amongst the miasma of oxen.

Madagascar is the fourth largest island in the world. It is the home of lemurs, bulbous baobab trees and the fan-shaped traveller's palm. In David Attenborough's BBC series and book *Zoo Quest to Madagascar* (1961) the viewing world was first shown these strange creatures in their native home. Attenborough even procured the broken fragments of a complete egg of the extinct elephant bird, the largest bird ever to walk the earth. Its egg was also the largest egg ever laid, far larger than a dinosaur's. The elephant bird is believed to have inspired the myth of the roc, a bird so gigantic it could carry away and eat elephants. Such stories were dramatically portrayed in *Sindbad the Sailor* and by Marco Polo. By the mid nineteenth century only strips of the coast and tiny pieces of the interior of this peculiar island world were known to Europeans.

After six days sailing the *Triton* dropped anchor at Madagascar's chief harbour, Tamatave (Toamasina), on the central east coast. There was only one other ship at this seldom-visited port. Pfeiffer was taken directly to the customs house or rather, the officers at once took her into custody and proceeded to disembowel and inspect every item of her baggage. Pfeiffer watched bemused, knowing she had nothing objectionable. Once out of their clutches she was free to explore the large but clearly impoverished village.

As so often on her travels, Pfeiffer was not impressed with the local physiognomies. She found the people repulsively ugly. They were so unsightly that she repeated this impression in her diary several times over the next few weeks. They were an "ugly and indolent race". For readers of her travel writings the Malagasies (as natives of Madagascar are known) would have the unenviable distinction of being the ugliest people Pfeiffer had ever seen.

Their dwellings were shabby and they kept many slaves. Pfeiffer recorded that their single-room houses were built of wood or bamboo on poles from six to ten feet high and their steep gabled roofs were thatched with grass or palm leaves. She did not recognise the similarity of these dwellings to those in the Kalimantan region of Borneo. It is now known that the ancestors of some of the Malagasies somehow settled Madagascar from Borneo about 2,000 years ago. Their manner of building and a few other cultural traces, such as burial above ground, still survive from their ancient Bornean ancestors.

The people ate mostly rice and a spinach-like vegetable. The favourite beverage was rice-water. Water was added to a pan with burnt rice crust on the bottom and boiled until the liquid became black as coffee. She did not observe the local people to smoke, instead both men and women took their tobacco by placing pinches of snuff in the mouth.

Curiously, Pfeiffer again felt that the local slaves were not treated as badly as one might think. They seemed to have little work to do, were seldom punished and ate as well as their masters. They were not protected by law, however, so they could be beaten, even to death.

In Pfeiffer's opinion, the few Christians there didn't set a good example for the superiority of their religion as they lived just like the local people. By this she meant they cohabited rather than marrying and changed partners when they pleased and sometimes had two "wives" at a time. The more she saw of the local customs, the less she liked them. "I dare not trust my pen to chronicle the many immoral customs which prevail," she wrote. "I can only say that female virtue is looked upon as quite valueless, and that the laws regarding marriage and progeny are of a stranger kind than any where else in the world."[440] In the end she would conclude, "I have never met with a more immoral people than the inhabitants of Madagascar."[441] But at least the women had freedom, more she thought than even the women of the USA. And perhaps strangest of all, from Pfeiffer's perspective, was the apparent lack of any local religion. As far as she could learn: "Incredible as it may appear, the [Malagasies] have no religion at all—not the slightest idea of a God, of the immortality of the soul, or even of its existence."[442] Her account does not seem accurate. At any rate, modern anthropologists would not agree in defining religion based only on the belief in the existence of a god or gods.

Lambert had not yet arrived from Mozambique where he was attending to some business. He had arranged for Pfeiffer to stay with his friend, Mademoiselle Julie. To Pfeiffer's astonishment the French-sounding "Mademoiselle" was a Malagasy widow with several children. But at least she spoke perfect French. She was also a shrewd businesswoman who owned several local properties. Her accommodation, however, was of a wretched standard that only someone like Ida Pfeiffer could endure. The Austrian traveller was given a small dirty shack which was furnished solely with an empty bedstead. Mademoiselle Julie refused to provide any bed linen. Pfeiffer would have to sleep wrapped in her cloak for weeks. In this and many other matters Pfeiffer was inwardly shocked. But worst of all was the fact that the shack had no lock on the door. One day Pfeiffer returned to find that her precious watch had been stolen. When Pfeiffer asked for help, Mademoiselle Julie seemed to think it was a matter of course that such a thing would be stolen if left lying around. She didn't even bother to question her servants.

Lambert finally arrived on 13 May 1857. Preparations were made to travel to the capital, Antananarivo, in the island's highland interior. The hoard of presents Lambert had brought for the queen and her court had to be carefully packed to withstand the trek. There were valuable works of art, musical clocks, barrel organs and other European gadgets. Lambert said that he had bought them all himself. Pfeiffer entirely sympathised with and believed every word of her wealthy benefactor.

To carry this queen's ransom, a small army of 400 porters was assembled and then a further 200 men to carry three Europeans in palanquins and their baggage. The capital was 215 kilometres southwest, but up on the highland plateau of the interior. The straggling and struggling chain of porters snaked up into the mountains that block the rains that feed the east coast from the interior uplands. For days they marched past lakes and along rivers and occasionally by "a few wretched villages". Pfeiffer admired the strength and skill of the porters who persevered despite their crushing loads. "The bearers, whose duty it was to transport my little meagre figure, were the most lucky," she thought.[443] They also carried boats to cross many lakes and rivers. In this way they crossed the green eastern belt and climbed up onto the highlands plateau. As she surveyed the almost treeless landscape, Pfeiffer could only see that it would look very fine if under busy cultivation. That, combined with hills in the background would make a fine view. Further on were districts dotted with the strange raffia palm, with all of its long leaves emerging out of the top of the trunk like flowers in a narrow vase.

There were also stands of the native traveller's palm. The tree supposedly has this name because water collects at the base of the leaves so that someone travelling can reliably go to them for a drink. The local people, however, told Pfeiffer that this tree only flourished in damp soil in places where there was plenty of water. "Unluckily, I had no opportunity of investigating the subject, so as to judge of the truth of these reports; but I hope the time will come when botanists will roam at pleasure through this great island, and settle, not only this, but many other doubtful questions in geography and natural history."[444]

The houses in the last villages before they reached the capital were not built of wood or bamboo like those on the coast, but earth and clay with thatched roofs. These houses generally had only one room with no furniture. No interior furnishings was a shock for the Biedermeier lady. The people had a few plaited straw mats and an iron or clay pot in which to cook their rice. Pfeiffer supposed that never having seen more possessions, they could hardly feel the want of them. The last day of their march became a sort of "triumphal progress" as locals, who somehow knew that the wealthy Lambert was coming, excitedly joined the column.

Antananarivo was a modest but bustling city of 100,000 with houses of wood or bamboo. Most of the larger structures had been fitted with lightning rods by Mr Jean Laborde. The procession finally stopped at the large house of Laborde whom Pfeiffer described as "a very warm friend of Mr. Lambert's, and who is also a great protector of every European that arrives at Antananarivo". Two Catholic missionaries were also staying with Laborde. Since Christian missionaries were forbidden, the men were disguised as a physician and a tutor.

Laborde had his own colourful story. He was shipwrecked on Madagascar in 1831 and was, like all foreigners stranded there, to be sold into slavery. The queen heard of his skill in manufacturing weapons and other goods so she offered him his freedom if he would serve her for five years. He soon produced several excellent manufactories. "In spite of her general hatred toward Europeans," Pfeiffer reported, the queen came to rely heavily on him.[445] After he was given his freedom Laborde stayed on and amassed a wealth of goods and properties and married a local woman.

Not long after their arrival the queen's twenty-seven-year-old son, Prince Rakoto, paid them a visit. He warmly embraced Lambert. Pfeiffer had endless praise for this kind, gentle, and benevolent young man. He was so much the opposite of what she had heard from Lambert about the diabolical mother.

There followed a few days of visits and feasts. After four days of waiting, according to court etiquette, Lambert and his friends including Pfeiffer, were invited to an audience with the seventy-five-year-old queen. Pfeiffer described her as having a "rather dark complexion, strong and sturdily built".

Lambert had told Pfeiffer many stories about this evil queen and the account by the English missionary William Ellis seemed to confirm these atrocities.[446] Pfeiffer recorded in her diary with unusual passion: "This cruel, bloodthirsty woman began her rule by the execution of seven of the nearest relatives of the late king … not only were all killed who belonged to [the previous king] Radama's family, but those nobles also who stood near the throne, some of whom Ranavola feared might advance a claim to it."[447] On one occasion she was said to have massacred 25,000 prisoners after conquering their territory. Those deemed to be enemies of the state were executed by the hundreds. Some were hurled off cliffs, others were burned, beaten to death, had their limbs hacked off, or were sewn up in mats and left to rot in the sun.

Another infamous practice sounds almost like a scene from *Monty Python and the Holy Grail* where learned medieval men conclude that a witch must weigh the same as a duck since both float on water. In Madagascar, according to European reports, in order to determine the guilt or innocence of people accused of a crime, there was the infamous "tanghin ordeal". Tanghin is a poison made from the seeds of the "suicide tree" (*Cerbera tanghin*). The seeds of this small evergreen coastal tree contain a toxin called cerberin that stops the heart beating and is now believed to cause more deaths by suicide than any plant in the world (especially a related species found in India and Southeast Asia). For the ordeal, the accused was not allowed to eat anything for twenty-four hours. Powdered cerberin was applied to three pieces of chicken skin and these were fed to the accused. If he vomited up all three pieces, and lived, he was declared innocent. If all three were not forthcoming however, the accused was despatched with a spear or by some other means. Very often, however, the poison itself proved fatal. And, voila tout, guilty as charged.

Shortly after she came to the throne in 1828, Queen Ranavalona was said to have asked her advisers how they could keep the loathsome Europeans out of Madagascar forever. Then, as now, dreams of closing borders led to some strange proposals. One ambitious suggestion was to build a wall around the entire island. Or perhaps they could construct a machine bearing an enormous iron plate which would ricochet the canon balls of European ships back against themselves, thus destroying them with their own firepower. Another idea was to forge giant scissors and place them over the roads leading out of the harbours. Any Europeans who attempted to enter the island could thus be simply cut in half. Snip snip. These stories may be entirely apocryphal, but they reveal the sort of contemptuous stories that Lambert told about Ranavalona and her ministers.

Pfeiffer later learned that Lambert was not as universally popular as she had at first supposed from all the adulation connected with their arrival. Obviously he had many friends in Antananarivo, but he also had enemies in court circles. Once back at the house, Lambert explained that he had been very pleasantly surprised to see how honoured and welcomed he was by the queen. He had feared that during his absence, his detractors could have succeeded in blackening his name. Now that Pfeiffer believed so entirely in Lambert's version of the state of Madagascar, he began to take her into his confidence.

French connection

Lambert told Pfeiffer a version of events which, as always and everywhere, made his own motives sound pure, unselfish and humane. During his first visit to Madagascar, he saw how cruelly and mercilessly the people were treated. He wanted only to "free the unhappy people from this tyrant". He explained something of the "treaty" that had been signed by Prince Rakoto to this end. Lambert had gone to Paris and London to secure military force to help free Madagascar in vain. "And now, for the first time," Pfeiffer later wrote, "I got an insight into Mr. Lambert's real plans and intentions."[448]

There was more, Lambert went on. Members of the meddling London Missionary Society were acting like spies reporting all of his doings to the British government. They were afraid that if the French gained the upper hand then the island would become Catholic and not Protestant. Heaven forbid. Thus they sent a missionary to tell the queen that Lambert was really a French agent seeking her overthrow.

There really had been an English missionary. His name was William Ellis. He wrote voluminously about his trips to Madagascar. Pfeiffer had even read his first book, *History of Madagascar* (1838). Needless to say, Ellis's own account of his visit to Madagascar, and his discussions with the queen, differs greatly from Lambert's and Pfeiffer's.[449]

One evening, after a splendid dinner at Laborde's house, Lambert whispered to Pfeiffer that she should feign feeling unwell to break up the party early, so as to get rid of the guests, except Prince Rakoto. She did not want to lie but did as requested. Later she suspected that she had been used to make it appear the evening's party had been for her, rather than as a pretext to meet privately with the prince.

Lambert and Laborde took the prince into another room. They invited Pfeiffer to join them. They now unfolded their secret plot to overthrow the queen and install the prince on the throne. According to Pfeiffer, Prince Rakoto himself confirmed to her that he wanted Lambert to come and help depose his mother, who would remain free and with all her possessions. The point was not to enrich himself, the prince pointed out, it was solely to prevent his aging mother from causing the people more suffering. The Frenchmen then showed her a room stacked high with weapons of all kinds, ready for the conspirators. The moment of truth might come at any time.

Back in the private stillness of her room, Pfeiffer confided to her diary in German: "I confess that a strange feeling came over me when I found myself thus suddenly involved in a political movement of grave importance." And yet she had been warned of this on Mauritius. Indeed, she had occasionally entertained a few suspicions before but, as so often, "my wish to obtain a knowledge of Madagascar was so great that it stifled all fear".

Exhausted from the excitement of the evening's revelations, she soon fell asleep. But vivid dreams troubled her slumber. "I dreamed that the plot had been discovered, and that the queen had summoned Mr. Lambert and myself to the palace."[450] In the dream they were forced to submit to the tanghin ordeal. In the paralysing horror of the dream, Pfeiffer was just about to take the poison when she awoke.

As the days passed, all seemed normal and genial, at least on the surface. One of Lambert's other uses for Pfeiffer was as a pianist. The queen had been given a player piano but she had never seen anyone play it with their hands. Pfeiffer had not played for more than thirty years, ever since her enforced feminine training in Vienna. In the midst of the foreign strangeness of the palace at Antananarivo, Pfeiffer sat down at the instrument but found it was horribly out of tune and many of the keys stuck or no longer worked. Unable to do anything but do as she was bid, she "played the first part of a waltz and the second of a march, in short, any thing and every thing that came into my head".[451] To her surprise the audience of the court and queen were delighted with her rusty performance.

The following day Pfeiffer wrote a letter home which somehow reached her aunt in Trieste and was published in a local newspaper. The news was reprinted from London to California and Tasmania.

> According to a letter from Madame Ida Pfeiffer, dated Tana-nariva (Madagascar), June 23rd, and communicated by a Trieste paper, the well-known traveller was very happy there, and highly content with her reception. On the day previous to her writing, she had been summoned to court, to play on the piano, which she had done with so much success that the Queen sent her a quantity of fowl and eggs, as a mark of her satisfaction.[452]

Despite the brave face Pfeiffer put on her situation in letters home, in just two days the plot was to be executed and a coup d'état unleashed on Madagascar. The plan was simple. The several conspirators were to go to the palace at 2 a.m., armed. The commander-in-chief of the army would have the gates open with only sympathetic men standing guard. The conspirators would then rush the palace and arrest the queen without loss of life. Thus the conspirators would free the wailing masses of Madagascar from their long-endured reign of tyranny.

But before the plan could be set in motion, the commander-in-chief sent word that he was unable to help. In other words, he got cold feet. And so nothing happened. Two days later, on 22 June, Pfeiffer penned in her diary, "To-day we received very bad news: the queen has received information of the plot." Pfeiffer penned resignedly, "At any rate, I consider our cause is lost; and Heaven knows what the queen may intend to do to us."[453] Perhaps it was just a rumour because again nothing happened. Over the next ten days, more and more co-conspirators drifted away and Pfeiffer felt that "traitors and spies surround us on all sides".[454] The secret plot was now leaking like a sieve.

On 8 July Pfeiffer scribbled breathlessly in her diary: "We have just learned that, since yesterday evening, every one has been prohibited, on pain of death, from entering our house. Mr. Laborde now no longer ventures to appear in the streets."[455] For thirteen days the small group of Europeans were encircled and besieged in their house, at least by fears of what would happen next. The slightest sound outside sent shocks of adrenaline through those inside. The days of intense uncertainty, fear and suspense were almost unbearable. The house slaves brought news that Christian converts were being sought and rounded up throughout the capital and the surrounding countryside. Pfeiffer heard that on 11 July an old woman was denounced as a Christian and dragged to the marketplace where she was brutally executed by having her backbone sawn through.

On 17 July 1857 suddenly and without warning, the wait was over. There was a great commotion in the large courtyard before the house. The Europeans were summoned to come out. They did so not knowing what to expect. Would they be tortured and killed?

Arrayed before them in the courtyard were "more than a hundred persons—judges, nobles, and officers—sitting in a large half circle on benches and chairs, and some on the ground; behind them stood a number of soldiers".[456] The half dozen Europeans stood silently. As they waited in defenceless suspense, the horror of the tanghin ordeal seemed to hover in the air. Pfeiffer whispered to a European next to her, "I believe our time has come."[457]

At length an official rose and declared that it had become known to the people in Antananarivo that they were conspirators who wished to overthrow the government and that they were fraternising with and abetting Christians. The people were thus so incensed that the Europeans were in danger of mob violence. The *people* demanded their execution. It was for this reason, the official said, that the queen had kept them secluded and housebound for their own protection. It was a brilliant bit of spin. Furthermore, the official went on, the queen had decided not to execute them and indeed, as Pfeiffer recorded, "in her magnanimity and mercy she had accordingly decided to limit our punishment to perpetual banishment".[458]

Lambert, Pfeiffer and the three other Europeans were to leave within the hour. They were permitted to take their belongings. The group was to be taken to the port and put aboard the first ship sailing from the island. On pain of death they were never to return to Madagascar.

Pfeiffer was relieved beyond description. It was said that although the queen routinely executed countless thousands on quite trivial grounds, she was unwilling to kill the foreigners because she feared reprisals from the great European powers.

Things went far more darkly for the local conspirators, they were all ruthlessly executed. His devoted mother could not believe that Prince Rakoto had willingly been part of the conspiracy, so he remained safe. The once privileged Laborde was given an extra twenty-four hours to prepare to leave and was to be escorted behind the others, always a day apart from them.

In the end the lazy soldiers assigned to the duty did not come for them until the following morning. Lambert thus had more time to hurriedly pack up as much of his haul of remaining gifts, many of which had been returned. No doubt their recipients were more afraid of the danger to their lives than of losing their treasures.

On 18 June 1857 the Europeans were taken out in the custody of soldiers. With crowds of the curious looking on, the Europeans and their escort left the capital. On their way they passed the place where Christians were being executed by stoning and decapitation. Pfeiffer's final view of Antananarivo was one of blood-soaked horror. She hoped the queen had not given secret orders for the people to kill the Europeans as they were marched out.

Pfeiffer and Lambert had both begun to suffer from the early signs of the notorious "Madagascar fever", presumably a form of malaria. Pfeiffer described it as "perhaps, one of the most malignant of all diseases, and in my opinion it is far more formidable than the yellow fever or the cholera ... Violent pains are felt in the lower parts of the body, frequent vomiting ensues, with total loss of appetite, and such weakness that the sufferer can hardly move."

Unfortunately the procession of the banished wound through a long and circuitous route. Pfeiffer noted, "It was very dangerous for us to stay long in the low-lying lands, where we were inhaling deleterious gases." It was then still thought that such ailments came from bad air – hence the name mal-aria, literally bad air.

The journey was in fact a death march. The queen had not dared execute them publically, but by ordering her soldiers to take such a long route, it was expected that the Europeans would perish of fever before they could leave the country. Instead of taking eight days, as the journey inland (and uphill) had, this journey back to Tamatave took a ghastly fifty-three days. For much of it Pfeiffer's fever grew worse and worse. "My sufferings were beyond description during the last three weeks, when I was unable even to raise myself from my bed and totter a few paces."[459] She had to sleep in the same shelters as the men. With no privacy, Pfeiffer was unable to change her clothes for fifty-three days. "At Befora [Beforona], one of the most unhealthy places on the whole line of march—a squalid little village, so entirely surrounded by morasses that it was impossible to advance fifty paces on firm ground — we were detained eighteen entire days."[460]

A European visitor described the area five years later as "a valley approximately five miles long and half a mile wide, entirely enclosed by hills. The valley is very marshy and a fair-sized stream runs across it. Noxious fumes escape from it incessantly and are visible in the form of a thick mist, in the morning and evening."[461]

Yet even as she lay in the shelter, almost at death's door, Pfeiffer could not resist wondering what natural productions lay all about her unobserved and uncollected. She begged her guards to go into the nearby woods to take some specimens for her, but they would not help. And yet, in the end, she somehow managed to collect a few things.

On 12 September 1857 they finally reached Tamatave. They remained prisoners until a ship was ready to sail for Mauritius on the 17th. This happened to be the barque *Castro*, under Captain M. Schneider. Although she was frail and weak, Pfeiffer had an overwhelming sense of triumph. The evil queen had not had the satisfaction of seeing them die.

It was already dark on the evening of 23 September when the *Castro* reached the safety of Mauritius. It was cloudy so the captain decided to wait for a steam tug to bring them into port in the morning. They were just about to drop anchor when the rudder struck a submerged rock with such violence that it was totally destroyed. A shudder went through the entire ship. The crew of twenty scrambled. Pfeiffer was already in bed. Amidst the confusion, the second officer shouted down, "Come up this moment, Madame Pfeiffer, if you want to be saved; the ship is broken in two, and sinking." She wrapped her cloak about herself and hurried on deck. She was helped into one of the ship's boats and told to stay there where she would be safe.

Fortunately, after closer inspection, it turned out to be a false alarm. The ship had not even sprung a leak, the rudder alone had been damaged. The next morning the ship was safely towed into harbour and inspected by the boarding port officer, N. Cartier.

The French naturalist Justin Goudot had been in Madagascar at the same time as Pfeiffer but she did not mention him in her book. He had first travelled to the island in the 1830s and had married a Merina woman. He arrived in Mauritius on the same ship as Pfeiffer and was listed on the port officer's report on arrival. Lambert was not listed.[462]

Pfeiffer's local friends were very surprised to see her. Reports of the failed coup had already reached Mauritius. Rumours were rife.

> Some people gave out that Queen Ranavola had caused all the Europeans in Antananarivo to be executed; others declared that the sentence of death had only been carried out on Mr. Lambert, and that the rest, including myself, had been sold as slaves; while another party maintained that we had been banished from the country, and murdered on the journey by command of the queen.

At last Pfeiffer was safe from the tanghin ordeal, bloodthirsty Malagasies and shipwreck. But she was not safe from the Madagascar fever. After a few days it struck her severely. It was feared she would not survive. Yet, even as she lay suffering from fever, her mind spun visions of new voyages. Perhaps she could visit Australia? Hearing of her illness, Dr Moon, with whose family she had stayed during her first visit, came and took her to his country house. He and Dr A. Perrot did all they could for her. By 9 October 1857 she was considered out of imminent danger. She wrote in her diary, "May God reward Dr. Moon and his wife, and Dr. Perrot, for all they did for me, a total stranger as I was to them!"[463]

And here Pfeiffer's travel journal ends. It was the last she would ever write. What happened to Lambert? He is not mentioned again after Madagascar. Was Pfeiffer just his dupe? In the end she expressed no disenchantment with or resentment of Lambert or the plot. As far as she was concerned, it was just. It was humane. It was necessary. The reason it had failed, the reason she had suffered and been banished was the evil Queen Ranavalona herself. Pfeiffer believed completely in the story she was told.

In two letters to the *Ost-Deutsche Post*, written in Mauritius in January 1858, Pfeiffer told a slightly different version of events than that given in her diary, which probably reflects her understanding when actually in Madagascar. From Mauritius she claimed that the English missionary William Ellis had heard of Lambert's plans and, fearing Madagascar would come under French influence and thus Catholic missionaries, had sought to interfere with Lambert's plan. According to these late letters, it was Ellis who had informed Queen Ranavalona of the plot.[464]

Queen Ranavalona did not live long after these events. She died in 1861 and was succeeded by Prince Rakoto, who took the title King Radama II. Lambert saw his chance and returned to Madagascar. King Radama now confirmed the charter and Lambert was even ennobled as the Duke of Merina. He did very well for himself in spite of the failed coup d'état. Did he ever spare a thought to the suffering and fate of Madame Pfeiffer?

Jean Laborde also returned. The French government appointed him its first consul and insisted that Radama compensate Laborde for the property losses he had sustained as a result of the banishment. This seems rather heavy-handed considering Laborde really did conspire to overthrow the government of Madagascar, and was therefore subject to the punishment of its authorities.

Even William Ellis, of the London Missionary Society, returned and spent three years in the capital as head of a renewed missionary campaign. But this was not the end. King Radama was assassinated in a palace coup in 1863. For many years accusations of involvement against Ellis arose again. But those lie outside our story.

Many years later the Lambert-Charter and letter by Prince Rakoto would be used to justify the Franco-Hova Wars, of 1883 and 1896, which resulted in the French annexation of Madagascar as a colony. The very thing that Queen Ranavalona had tried hardest of all to prevent ultimately transpired with the help of Lambert and her beloved son Prince Rakoto.

Pfeiffer continued through debilitating spells of fever and recovery on Mauritius. But her determination to travel was unabated. She wrote to her friend George Waterhouse in London on 19 November 1857 that she had brought nothing from Madagascar but "completely destroyed health".

The letter also reveals that she had written to the natural history agent Samuel Stevens to tell him how her trip to Madagascar went. This seems to strengthen the connection between Wallace's recommendation and Pfeiffer's plan. She told Waterhouse that if he could see her now, he would not recognise her. She was so thin that she looked like a skeleton and looked ten years older. But, she told Waterhouse, "I will not return to Europe, since I have not yet collected anything ... so I will go from here to Sidney, then New Zealand and possibly New Caledonia, I must and will make a beautiful collection."[465] Waterhouse was to direct his reply to Sydney.

At one point she even had her bags aboard a ship bound for

Sydney but a new outbreak of fever made it impossible for her to leave. As her health failed to return, she finally had to abandon all hopes of visiting Australia. The journey would be just too arduous. Perhaps in her frail and suffering condition she might have echoed Dr Johnson's biting quip about travel.

Boswell: "Is not the Giant's-Causeway worth seeing?"

Johnson: "Worth seeing, yes; but not worth going to see."[466] She would never see Australia. There was only one journey left in her, back home.

It was against Pfeiffer's nature to give up, even if she was gravely ill. But she could not shake off the fever. On 10 March 1858 she boarded the packet *Shannon* bound for London. On 15 May the readers of the *Athenaeum* were informed: "We learn from the Mauritius that Madame Ida Pfeiffer is on her way to England. She sailed on the 11th of March, and may be expected in London about the second week in June. She has fully recovered from her Madagascar fever, and is preparing her account of that wonderful island, together with a description of the Mauritius."[467] But the recovery was not to last. She arrived safely in London in early June and remained for a few weeks before sailing to Hamburg. There she was struck by a renewed outbreak of the fever.

In London, press reports were brief but frequent. The *Illustrated London News* noted on 3 July 1858: "Madame Ida Pfeiffer has just found a pillow in the hospital of Hamburg, where Dr. Tungel is treating her for chronic ague caught at Madagascar."[468] And a more serious note by *The Times* correspondent in Vienna reported on 6 July: "A literary man of note has called my attention to the fact that Mrs. Ida Pfeiffer, the traveller, who is now lying ill in the public hospital at Hamburg, receives assistance neither from the Austrian Government nor from her family. Now, Mrs. Pfeiffer is a woman of whom Austria has reason to be proud, and it is unpardonable that she should be left to subsist on the charity of strangers and foreigners."[469] And yet Pfeiffer had subsisted this way for years, not to mention countless thousands of miles.

After days of severe vomiting and diarrhoea she recovered somewhat and continued on to Berlin later in August. It was almost as if she was reluctant to return to Vienna, since this time she would not return in triumph having achieved unparalleled successes against incomparable perils. Once again the fever struck. One wonders if she tried again the American remedy. If so, it was no match for the Madagascar fever. During her spells of remission she was convinced she would be fine. But the severity of the subsequent attacks began to shake her confidence at last that her constitution would shake it off in the end, as it always had before. Her family, distraught with worry since she had returned to Europe, finally went to fetch her and bring her back to Vienna in a private railway carriage in mid September.

Pfeiffer was taken to the home of her brother Carl Reyer. He called on the most distinguished physicians in Vienna to help her. They all agreed that it was "cancer in the liver—a consequence probably of the Madagascar fever". Her suffering during the last days became so acute that she was given opiates to alleviate the pain. She died at midnight, 27 October 1858 in the home of her brother. She was 61. Her wanderlust had killed her in the end.

Her son Oscar later wrote, "Her funeral took place on the 30th of the same month. Besides a very numerous gathering of relations and personal friends, many scientific notabilities and other distinguished inhabitants of Vienna followed her to the grave."[470] It was Pfeiffer's last voyage. Her remains were interred in St. Marx Cemetery, just southeast of the city walls.

The news soon flashed through the electric telegraph networks of the world. Her death was almost simultaneously reported in newspapers and magazines around the globe from London to Berlin to Boston, Batavia to Perth, from Texas to Tasmania. News of her death was reported on the front page of the new illustrated magazines such as *L'Illustration* in Paris, the *Illustrated Times*, and the *Illustrated London News* on 13 November, which included an engraved portrait based on the oil painting by her relative Emilie Marie Schmück.[471] Her London promoter, the *Athenaeum*, wrote: "We grieve to state that Frau Ida Pfeiffer, the well-known traveller, after long sufferings, died at Vienna on the 28th of October."[472]

The final haul

Pfeiffer was gone, but she had succeeded in bringing the fruits of another voyage back with her. She had brought back her diary and a diverse collection of natural history specimens. It is curious that she called this no collection at all in her letter to Waterhouse. No doubt this meant that she made only a paltry collection compared to what she had hoped. Despite all that had happened, all of the restrictions, disease and sufferings, Pfeiffer somehow managed to send or bring from Madagascar a very diverse and important collection. The Natural History Museum in Vienna would eventually purchase 721 specimens she collected.[473] This collection included nine species of mammals, fourteen species of birds, twenty-three species of reptiles, three species of crustaceans, fifteen species of molluscs, ten species of spiders and 185 species of insects.[474]

A collection of live snails from Mauritius were "packed in paper and rags, in a tin pot with a lid" and survived the voyage to London. They were sold and one of them "lived for some months under a bell-glass with moss and ferns".[475]

Among the mammals were two news species of lemurs. One was the tiny wide-eyed brown mouse lemur, and a new species of bird was the diminutive brown-backed Madagascan pygmy kingfisher. The Royal Zoological Museum of the Netherlands purchased a new species of large shrew that she discovered.[476] The reptiles included several new species and even a new genus. Some of her new discoveries were named in her honour such as the Mascarene ridged frog (*Rana idae*). A water scorpion was called *Laccotrephes pfeifferi*.

According to Pfeiffer's wishes, her journal and papers were sent to her son Oscar who had been living in Rio de Janeiro since 1858 as a successful composer and pianist. Although at first too grief-stricken to go through them, he eventually performed his filial duty with great skill. He transcribed and edited her diary into a final manuscript, keeping it as unaltered from the original as possible. And at the front of the book he provided a brief preface explaining her death and his inheritance of the manuscript.

Also included was an unsigned memoir of Pfeiffer based on an autobiographical account she had left behind. Oscar is referred to in this memoir in third person. It is possible that it was contributed by him or by Trimmel as the writer understood Pfeiffer's lack of scientific education when she was young. The last five pages of the book, which take over from the point at which Pfeiffer's diary ends on Mauritius after her recovery, are also by Oscar. The book was published in Vienna in 1861 as *Reise nach Madagaskar* (Journey to Madagascar). An English translation appeared the same year in Britain and the USA. French and Dutch translations came out in 1862.

The reviews of Pfeiffer's last book were less enthusiastic than before. Of course this journey essentially only took her through Mauritius and Madagascar and very little else. *The Saturday Review* concluded that the book "cannot add much to Madame Pfeiffer's long-established reputation".[477] All of the reviews were more interested in the biographical introduction which at last provided more background on this inexplicable lady traveller. *The London Review*, for example, found the details fascinating as helping to understand "one of the most extraordinary women that ever lived" and ignored altogether the journey. The reviewer speculated that Pfeiffer's character had been shaped by never having known "the happiness of a home".[478] Her upbringing must have been the cause, allowing her to revel in the wildness of being a boy, the commandment that she must be a lady, the denial of her love, then her marriage to a man she did not love. *The London Review* proudly contrasted all of these unpropitious life events with the perfect home life and manner of child-rearing in England. The *Illustrated London News* used her book as a primary source for an article on the state of Madagascar and noted that Pfeiffer "set out on her 'last travels' with no other object than to get to this mysterious country, and, although she succeeded, it was at the cost of her life".[479]

Perhaps the most detailed and thoughtful review appeared in the *Athenaeum*. The writer was much less sympathetic for the late tourist-traveller than most. "Some demon seemed perpetually driving her forward" so that she felt she had no time to describe this or that important thing.[480] In particular the writer took exception to the fact that "she seemed to think it a sort of right" that she should be transported and housed "at other peoples cost". And as for her descriptions of Madagascar and its tyrannical queen, the reviewer pointed out that since Pfeiffer had her information from a conspirator against the queen, "one may be permitted to receive with grains of caution Madame Pfeiffer's minute hearsay statements of the horrible extravagance, superstition and cruelty of the wicked Queen of Madagascar". And so in conclusion, "We cannot regard [Pfeiffer] as one of the martyrs to science so much as of restlessness." She was a martyr to wanderlust.

THE END OF THE ROAD

"No one can hope to rival Ida Pfeiffer as a daring traveler,
for the reason that the dangers attending such an expedition
as hers are rapidly passing away."
Lilian Leland, 1890

By any standard and for any era of history, Ida Pfeiffer was an extraordinary person. Forced as a young woman to conform to the gender norms of her society, she was denied a life with her true love. She spent a decade and a half trapped in an unhappy marriage, forced to both struggle with unaccustomed poverty and to conceal it.

Everything changed with the advent of the second chapter of her life when she took the incredibly brave and daring decision – to leave the comforts and security of home and travel to distant lands alone. Her first trip was all the more intrepid because there simply was no precedent for such a long and unsupported journey by a woman.

Some mysteries remain. What happened to her husband, Dr Pfeiffer? Why didn't Pfeiffer marry or travel with her youthful love Trimmel, who never married and remained in Vienna until his own death almost a decade after hers? In his published collection of poetry, a few poems are dedicated to or refer to Pfeiffer.[481] Did she have an affair with Bartlett? Probably not, but we may never know.

Throughout her travels Pfeiffer displayed great personal courage, to the point in some cases of recklessness. She had prodigious determination in pursuing her goals. In addition, her skills as an observer of peoples and places was matched by her abilities as a writer. Her books remain a fascinating glimpse into a lost world. The places she saw and indeed many of the peoples and tribes she visited have changed beyond recognition or no longer exist. Like footsteps in the sand, they have otherwise left no trace.

Her zeal and diligence in collecting natural history specimens was comparable to that of some of the great male collectors who are now better remembered. Pfeiffer was no trained naturalist; nevertheless she was devoted to one of the new trends of her age: science and enthusiasm for the accumulative study of the natural world. As her unnamed biographer put it:

> For every kind of knowledge she showed the most profound respect, but particularly for the acquirements of people who had distinguished themselves in the domain of science. For Alexander von Humboldt her admiration amounted to perfect enthusiasm, and she never mentioned the great philosopher's name without testifying the respect she felt toward him. Nothing, perhaps, gave her so much pleasure in her later years as the appreciation for, and sympathy with her efforts manifested by Humboldt.

She felt strongly that slavery was a great evil and, often, that other races and cultures were no worse than her own; liberal views that make her more sympathetic to modern readers. On the other hand, she was a person of her time, as is everyone. So many of her remarks will strike a modern reader as racist or ethnocentric.

During her travels she often dressed eccentrically. Unlike the long hair then fashionable for women of her social class, she had hers cropped short. Her personal style was always plain and simple. Her biographer noted: "She was never seen to wear trinkets or jewels; and none of the lady readers who honor these pages with their perusal can show more simplicity in the adornment of her beauty, or greater indifference to the requirements of custom, than were displayed by this voyager round the world."[482] All other considerations were second to practicality in travelling. And since she was far out of sight of scrutinising society snobs of middle-class Europe, what did it matter?

At the same time she shocked and confused her contemporaries by travelling the world alone not just because she was a woman but for no better reason than that she just wanted to see and experience it. And she travelled in such an extraordinary "seat of the pants" way. She could be infuriatingly headstrong and stubborn. No doubt she exaggerated and perhaps even invented some of her exploits. The robber in Brazil certainly could not have had three fingers lopped off by her thrust of a pocket knife.

She become so accustomed to her international celebrity and the financial assistance of others that she came to expect these wherever she went and was not a little annoyed when they were not forthcoming. Her biographer noticed and confessed to this too.

At last she became quite accustomed to see her plan furthered in every possible way, and though she never failed to express her thanks, she seemed at last to receive the good offices of foreigners in all quarters of the globe as almost a matter of course. She even had to fight against little outbursts of wrath when she missed the sympathy for her efforts and herself to which she had become so accustomed. In later years especially, she was fully conscious of her own value, and showed it when people attempted to behave in a condescending or patronizing way to her. Persons of higher rank than herself were obliged to be very careful in their intercourse with her ... Hating all pretension, and all boastful self-assertion, she showed herself obstinate and self-willed wherever she met with such qualities. Antipathy or sympathy were quickly evoked in her, and it was not easy to make her swerve from an opinion she had once formed.[483]

For many she remained a heroine and explorer worthy of the highest accolades. After all she was called by contemporaries "one of the most remarkable women of modern times" and even "one of the strangest characters not only of our times, but in all of history". A writer in *The London Lady's Newspaper* in 1863 reflected on her contributions to science.

> She was thus, with the strong desire to be useful to science, really useful to it, though often she did not know to what extent. Surely the diligent collector, who, with immense trouble, and often at the peril of life, gathers together, has not less merit than the classifier who, at his student's table, allots to what has been collected its place in the kingdom of science.[484]

But for others she was a ridiculous old woman and an object of ridicule. She become a sort of stock comic figure, the eccentric old lady traveller.

Above all else, Pfeiffer was driven by wanderlust as the American missionaries at Urmia found in 1848: "A passion for travel is the ruling motive that carries Madame Pfeiffer so cheerfully and courageously through all her manifold hardships and perils."[485]

In 1892, thirty-four years after her death, the Viennese Verein für erweiterte Frauenbildung (Society for the Further Education of Women) instigated the transfer of Pfeiffer's remains to a place of honour in Vienna's central cemetery. She was the first woman to be admitted to the rows of honoured dead. A fine marble monument with a portrait medallion marks her grave.

She fell again into obscurity until around 1997, the bicentenary of her birth, when there was a resurgence of interest including two biographies in German. She was set to be portrayed on the 50-schilling banknote in 1995–1997 but this was never printed due to the introduction of the Euro. In 2000 a street in Munich was renamed after her as Ida-Pfeiffer-Straße and in 2008 a street in Vienna was named Ida-Pfeiffer-Weg. In 2018 an "Ida Pfeiffer Professorship" was established in the Faculty of Earth Sciences, Geography and Astronomy at the University of Vienna.

She may have been forgotten for generations now, but she had no aspirations to be a heroine or a feminine role model or to reform society or challenge stereotypes or gender roles. She wanted to see the world and experience as much of its incredible diversity for herself as she could. In this she succeeded beyond her wildest dreams.

Pfeiffer's followers

Pfeiffer's greatest impact was as an example of what women were capable of, she set a precedent that inspired female travellers everywhere. For the rest of the century she remained a heroine, especially for girls, who themselves dreamed of travel, adventure and freedom. The later reprints of Pfeiffer's books clearly show this use of her image.

Attitudes to travel were at any rate changing with modern transport like steamships, railways and omnibuses. One merely needed to buy a ticket and sit down and this could be done by anyone. In a provocatively titled book *Unprotected Females in Norway, or the Pleasantest Way of Travelling There* (1857) an anonymous English authoress declared:

> We two ladies, having gone before, show how practicable the journey must be, though we have found out and will maintain that ladies alone get on in travelling much better than with gentlemen: they set about things in a quieter manner, and always have their own way; while men are sure to go into passions and make rows, if

things are not right immediately. Should ladies have no escort with them, then every one is so civil, and trying of what use they can be; while, when there is a gentleman of the party, no one thinks of interfering, but all take it for granted they are well provided for. The only use of a gentleman in travelling is to look after the luggage...[486]

The book, and its sequel *Unprotected Females in Sicily* (1859) were written by Miss Emily Lowe who travelled in style with her mother to well-connected European tourist destinations. This was hardly Pfeifferesque, but it was a sign of things to come.

An exact contemporary of Pfeiffer was Fanny Loviot, who was described by newspapers in 1860 as "a kind of French Ida Pfeiffer, who lately returned from India and China".[487] In fact Loviot was nothing of the kind. A businesswoman resident in Hong Kong, she was kidnapped from a ship bound for San Francisco and held for ransom by Chinese pirates for a week before being rescued. Her book *A Lady's Captivity Among Chinese Pirates* (1858) made entertaining reading for those titillated by the idea of a European lady in the captivity of foreign races. But she was no solo traveller.

The English traveller and authoress Isabella Bird (1831–1904) visited America and Canada and later Australia, Hawaii, China, Korea, Malaya, Egypt and India between 1854 and the 1890s. Nellie Bly (1864–1922), the pen name of American journalist Elizabeth Cochrane Seaman, undertook to recreate the 1873 journey of Jules Verne's character Phileas Fogg who circled the globe in eighty days. Bly managed it in seventy-two but she made use of fast steamships, transcontinental railways and the Suez Canal. The young Englishwoman Fanny L. Rains travelled to southern Australia with a lady friend and then alone to Singapore, China, Japan and home via the USA. Her book was published in 1878.[488] Annie Brassey (1839–1887) travelled around the world between 1876 and 1877 but in a private yacht. This and her later voyages were recounted in best-selling travel books. The British authoress Mrs F. D. Bridges, although travelling with her wealthy husband, wrote *Journal of a Lady's Travels Round the World* (1883), which sounds almost identical to the title of Pfeiffer's travels and books.

The good-humoured and well-to-do Marianne North (1830–1890) was an English botanical artist and widely reckoned to be one of the most intrepid of the Victorian lady travellers. She travelled with her widowed father until his death in 1869 and thereafter around the world where she painted tropical plants. After Charles Darwin suggested she travel to Australia, she painted there and in New Zealand for a year. More than 800 of her paintings are now on display in a special gallery at Kew Gardens.

Lilian Leland (1857–after 1930) was an American imitator of Pfeiffer who undertook a two-year journey to Cape Horn, California, Japan, China, Singapore, Java, Ceylon, India, the Holy Land and throughout Europe. Her book was entitled *Traveling Alone: A Woman's Journey Around the World* (1890). Even the title of her book evokes Pfeiffer. Isabelle Eberhardt (1877–1904) was a cross-dressing Swiss writer who lived in and explored Algeria, converted to Islam, was attacked with a sabre and had her arm nearly severed. She became a popular writer in the 1900s.

The pioneering female cyclist Lillias Campbell Davidson (1853–1934) published a popular guide to a new generation of women willing and able to travel: *Hints to Lady Travellers* (1889). She seemed to find it a noble cause to help other women to travel: "If, by my endeavours, I have in any way assisted my sisters in their wanderings, or encouraged a single woman to join the path of travellers by land or sea, I shall feel that I have achieved the object of my labours, and that my task has indeed not been in vain."[489]

The African explorer Mary Kingsley (1862–1900) was like an 1890s version of Catherine Hepburn's character in the classic film

The African Queen (1951). She travelled alone in Africa several times and became famous for her adventures. She was said to be the first European to explore certain areas of the French Congo and Gabon. Despite her bold exploits, she was also against female emancipation. The subtitle of her 1957 biography by Olwen Campbell was *A Victorian in the Jungle*.

And perhaps one of the most famous lady travellers was Amelia Earhart herself, the celebrated American aviator who became the first woman to be flown across the Atlantic ocean in 1928 and then the first to fly it solo and nonstop in 1932. She was famously lost at sea in an attempt at the first around-the-world journey by air by a woman in 1937.

The ease, speed, safety and cheapness of mass travel that emerged after Pfeiffer's death meant that no one could ever repeat the feats of serendipitous and opportunistic travel she achieved as the Lilian Leland quotation above indicates. The adventures of Michael Palin, in his television travel series starting with *Around the World in 80 Days* (1989), may be the closest many people will have seen to Pfeiffer's mode of travel.

The English businessman Thomas Cook (1808–1892) took advantage of the new railways, steamer companies and a system of prepaid coupons to organise package tours of Italy, Palestine, Egypt and so forth. Mass tourism was born. By the latter part of the nineteenth century Cook's agency took so many British tourists to Egypt and up the Nile in their own steamers that the river was jokingly referred to as Cook's Canal.

What would Pfeiffer make of modern travel? She would no doubt wrinkle her brow at the appallingly slovenly way most tourists dress and behave. The informality of the modern world would disappoint and repel her. She would probably regret the enforced proximity and lack of personal space one is forced to endure in modern air travel. And she was a lone traveller. Visiting sites swarming with tourists would not have interested her.

The novelist Walter Besant wrote in the *Illustrated London News* in 1897: "Steam and electricity have conquered time and space to a greater extent during the last sixty years than all the preceding six hundred years witnessed. Think of the ocean greyhounds [steamers] of today, capable of crossing the Atlantic in less than five and a half days. The broad Atlantic has, indeed, become a mere pond."[490] We constantly hear renewed renditions of this supposed shrinking of the world with the advent of air travel, then jet aircraft and then budget airlines or the internet and social media. The latest communication technologies have supposedly transformed the world into a "global village". Yet it has been connected with arteries of international travel, transport and communication for many centuries. What we have in fact is a world that has been a global village for a very, very long time. But each generation keeps thinking it has just become so.

Further reading

There is no substitute for reading Madame Pfeiffer's delightful books themselves. These amount to approximately 2,700 pages. All were translated into English. Her translators were usually quite faithful to the original but of course if one compares the two, sometimes changes or omissions can be found. I have quoted largely from the contemporary English translations in order to preserve something of the period feel. All are still in print in one form or another and of course are available online. Project Sophie (http://sophie.byu.edu/) provides her works in the original German.

Pfeiffer has been of interest to local historians of the places she visited, anthologisers, historians of travel and particularly to writers interested in feminism and gender. All of the main books on her are in German, most centring around the 1997 centenary of her birth. The most substantive, in terms of originality of research and the vast quantity of new material presented and summarised, is Hiltgund Jehle's *Ida Pfeiffer: Weltreisende im 19. Jahrhundert* (1989). Gabriele Habinger has published Pfeiffer's surviving voyage correspondence: *Ida Pfeiffer: "Wir leben nach Matrosenweise": Briefe einer Weltreisenden des 19. Jahrhunderts* (2008) and other important studies of Pfeiffer. Other Victorian female travellers are discussed in Dea Birkett's *Spinsters Abroad: Victorian Lady Explorers* (1989). This is of course only the tip of the iceberg as far as the literature on lady travellers is concerned.

Bibliography

Allom, T. 1843. *China, in a Series of Views...* London: Fisher, vol. 1.

Anon. 1844. *Allgemeine Wiener Musik-Zeitung.* IV, p. 138.

Anon. 1854a. *Hints on Etiquette and the Usages of Society.* London.

Anon. 1854b. Ida Pfeiffer. *Der Sammler.* vol. 23 (27 Dec.): 394.

Anon. 1856a. *Men of the Time: Biographical Sketches of Eminent Living Characters.* London: Kent & Co.

Anon. 1856b. Ein Winter in Wien. Erster Brief. *Unterhaltungen am häuslichen Herd.* vol. 1, Nr. 15: 234–238.

Anon. 1861. [Review of] Ida Pfeiffer's last travels. *The London Review.* vol. 3, (3 Aug.): 153.

Anon. 1863. Ida Pfeiffer (part IV). *The London Lady's Newspaper and Pictorial Times.* (14 Feb.), p. 272.

Anon. 1880. Mme Ida Pfeiffer. *Journal des Voyages et des Aventures de Terre et de Mer.* No. 178 (5 Dec.).

Attenborough, David. 1961. *Zoo Quest to Madagascar.* London: Lutterworth Press.

Baker, D. B., 1995. Pfeiffer, Wallace, Allen and Smith the discovery of the Hymenoptera of the Malay Archipelago. *Archives of Natural History.* 23(2) 153–200.

Barber, James. 1850. *The Overland Guide-book: A Complete Vademecum for the Overland Traveller.* 2d edn. London: Allen.

Bartlett, William Henry. 1842. *Canadian Scenery.* vol. 1. London: Virtue.

———. 1844. *Walks about the City and Environs of Jerusalem.* London: Virtue.

———. 1850a. *Walks about the City and Environs of Jerusalem.* 2d edn London: Hall, Virtue & Co.

———. 1850b. *The Nile Boat; or Glimpses of the Land of Egypt.* London: Hall.

———. 1851. *Footsteps of our Lord and his Apostles in Syria, Greece and Italy.* London: A. Hall, Virtue & Co.

———. 1854. *The Danube, its History, Scenery, and Topography.* London: Virtue.

Berchtold, F. von and P.M. Opiz. 1836-1842. *Ökonomisch-technische Flora Böhmens.* Prague: Pospischil.

Besant, W. 1897. *Illustrated London News.* Diamond Jubilee number (June).

Bethune, D. 1847. *Views in the Eastern Archipelago.* London: McLean.

Bickmore, A. S. 1869. *Travels in the East Indian Archipelago.* London: John Murray.

Bleeker, Pieter. 1853. *Natuurkundig tijdschrift voor Nederlandsch Indië.* vol. 4, p. 298.

———. 1860. *De visschen van den Indischen Archipel.* vol. 2.

Boswell, James. 1791. *The Life of Samuel Johnson.* vol. 1. London: Baldwin.

Bougainville, Louis Antoine de. 1772. *A Voyage Round the World Performed by Order of His Most Christian Majesty in the Years 1766, 1767, 1768, and 1769.* Translated by John Reinhold Forster. London: J. Nourse and T. Davies.

Bradshaw, T. 1831. *Views in the Mauritius, or Isle of France.* London: Carpenter.

Brisson, Ulrike. 2013. Discovering Scheherazade: Representations of Oriental Women in the Travel Writing of Nineteenth-Century German Women. *Women in German Yearbook: Feminist Studies in German.* vol. 29: 97–117.

———. 2014. Inscribed in the Body: Ida Pfeiffer's *Reise in the neue Welt* (1856). In R. McFarland & M. S. James eds., *Sophie Discovers Amerika: German-speaking Women Write the New World.* New York: Boydell & Brewer, pp. 65–81.

Bryant, W. C. II & T. G. Voss eds., 1981. *The Letters of William Cullen Bryant.* vol. 3. New York: Fordham.

Buddingh, S.A. 1860. *Neêrlands-Oost-Indie.* vol. 2. Rotterdam: Wijt.

Burton, R. F. 1872. *Zanzibar: City, Island, and Coast*, vol. 1. London: Tinsley.

Butler, A. G. 1869. *Catalogue of Diurnal Lepidoptera Described by Fabricius in the Collection of the British Museum*. London: British Museum.

Campbell, G. 2012. *David Griffiths and the Missionary "History of Madagascar"*. Leiden: Brill.

Carne, J. 1836. *Syria, The Holy Land, Asia Minor, &c. Illustrated. In a Series of Views, Drawn from Nature by W.H. Bartlett, William Purser, &c.* London: Fisher, Son & Co.

Chartier, Henri Le and G. Pellerin. 1888. *Madagascar depuis sa découverte jusqu'à nos jours*. Paris: Jouvet & Cie.

Corner, [Julia]. [1847]. *The History of China & India*. London: Washbourne.

Creswicke, L. 1900. *South Africa and the Transvaal War*. vol. 1. Edinburgh: T. C. & E. C. Jack.

Dabak, Shubhangi. 1999. Images of the Orient in the Travel Writings of Ida Pfeiffer and Ida Hahn Hahn. PhD diss., Michigan State University.

Darwin, C. R. 1840. On the connexion of certain volcanic phenomena in South America; and on the formation of mountain chains and volcanos, as the effect of the same powers by which continents are elevated. *Transactions of the Geological Society of London* (Ser. 2) 5 (3): 601–631.

———. 1845. *Journal of Researches into the Natural History and Geology of the Countries Visited During the Voyage of H.M.S. Beagle Round the World, under the Command of Capt. Fitz Roy, R.N.*, 2d edn. London: John Murray.

———. 1847. [Review of] *A Natural History of the Mammalia*. [Vol. 1, Marsupialia] By G. R. Waterhouse, Esq., of the British Museum. *Annals and Magazine of Natural History*. 19 (Jan.): 53–56.

———. 1859. *On the Origin of Species by Means of Natural Selection, or the*

Preservation of Favoured Races in the Struggle for Life. London: John Murray.

———. 1871. *The Descent of Man, and Selection in Relation to Sex.* 2 vols. London: John Murray.

Darwin, Francis ed. 1887. *The Life and Letters of Charles Darwin, Including an Autobiographical Chapter.* London: John Murray.

Davidson, L. C. 1889. *Hints to Lady Travellers at Home and Abroad.* London: Iliffe & Son.

Dawood, N. J. trans. 1995. *The Seven Voyages of Sindbad the Sailor.* Penguin.

Denis, F. 1837. *L'Univers. Histoire et Description de tous les Peuples: Brésil.* Paris: Didot Freres.

Dickens, Charles. 1843–1844. *Martin Chuzzlewit.* London: Chapman & Hall.

Dickinson, 1854. *Dickinson's Comprehensive Pictures of the Great Exhibition of 1851; from the Originals Painted … by Messrs. Nash, Haghe & Roberts…*vol. 1. London: Dickinson.

Doleschall, C. L. 1857. Bijdrage tot de kennis der Arachniden van den Indischen Archipel. *Natuurkundig Tijdschrift voor Nederlandsch Indie.* 13 (3): 399–434, pls. 1–2.

Donner, Eka. 1997. *Und nirgends eine Karawane: Die Weltreisen der Ida Pfeiffer* (1797–1858). Düsseldorf: Droste.

D'oyly, Charles. 1848. *Views of Calcutta and its Environs.* London: Dickinson & Co.

Eberhardt, Isabelle. 1890. *Traveling Alone. A Woman's Journey Around the World.*

Ellis, William. 1838. *History of Madagascar.* 2 vols. London: Fisher.

———. 1858. *Three Visits to Madagascar.* London: John Murray.

———. 1867. *Madagascar Revisited.* London: John Murray.

FitzRoy, R. 1839. *Narrative of the Surveying Voyages of His Majesty's Ships* Adventure *and* Beagle*…Proceedings of the Second Expedition, 1831–36…* London: Henry Colburn.

Forster, E. M. 1908. *A Room with a View*. London: Arnold.

Foster, Barbara. 1975. The world as they saw it: memoirs of the travelling ladies. *In: Geography and Map Division. Special Libraries Association. Bulletin*. New York, Nr. 99: 49–58.

Fraser, George MacDonald. 1977. *Flashman's Lady*. London: Barrie & Jenkins.

Freeman, Joseph John. 1851. *A Tour in South Africa: with Notices of Natal, Mauritius, Madagascar, Ceylon*. London: Snow.

Gaimard, P. [1842]. *Voyage en Islande et au Groenland publié par ordre du Roi sous la direction de M. Paul Gaimard. Atlas historique*. Paris: Bertrand.

Gayette, Jeanne Marie von. 1856. *Die Wiener Elegante*. (20 Feb.): 42–43, 1 pl.

———. 1848. *Mädchenwelt. Gegen die falsche Frauenemanzipation*.

Gilbert, James. 1851. *Gilbert's Visitor's Guide to London*. London: Gilbert.

Gombrich, E. H. 2005. *A Little History of the World*. Yale.

Grandidier A. 1875. *Histoire Physique, Naturelle et Politique de Madagascar*. vol. 9, part 4, atlas. Paris: Nationale.

———. 1876. *Histoire Physique, Naturelle et Politique de Madagascar*. vol. 13, part 2, atlas. Paris: Nationale.

Gray, J. E. et al. 1847. *Nomenclature of Coleopterous Insects in the Collection of the British Museum*. Part I. Cetoniadae. London: British Museum.

Günther, Albert C. L. G. 1859. *Catalogue of the Fishes in the British Museum*. vol. 1. London: British Museum.

———. 1861. *Catalogue of the Fishes in the British Museum*. vol. 3. London: British Museum.

———. 1864. *Catalogue of the Fishes in the British Museum*. vol. 4. London: British Museum.

———. 1864. *Catalogue of the Fishes in the British Museum*. vol. 5. London: British Museum.

———. 1870. *Catalogue of the Fishes in the British Museum*. vol. 8. London: British Museum.

Gunow, A. 1873–1874. Algen der Fidschi-, Tonga-, und Samoa-Inseln. *Journal des Museum Godeffroy.* vol. 6, pp. 1–28.

Habinger, G. ed. 1995. *Ida Pfeiffer: Reise in das heilige Land: Konstantinopel, Palästina, Ägypten im Jahre 1842.* Vienna: Promedia.

———. 1997. *Eine Wiener Biedermeierdame erobert die Welt. Die Lebensgeschichte der Ida Pfeiffer (1797–1858).* Vienna: Promedia.

———. 2004. *Ida Pfeiffer: Eine Forschungsreisende des Biedermeier.* Vienna: Promedia.

———. 2008. *Ida Pfeiffer: "Wir leben nach Matrosenweise": Briefe einer Weltreisenden des 19. Jahrhunderts.* Vienna: Promedia- und Verlag-Ges.

Heidhues, Mary Somers. 2004. Woman on the Road: Ida Pfeiffer in the Indies. *Archipel.* vol. 68: 289–313.

Heine, Heinrich. 1826. *Die Harzreise.* Hamburgh: Hoffman & Campe.

Honsig, Markus. 2012. Die vortreffliche, kühne, erdumwandernde Frau Ida Pfeiffer. *Terra Mater.* (June): 132–146.

Howe, P. 1999. "Die Wirklichkeit ist anders": Ida Pfeiffer's visit to China 1847. *German Life and Letters.* 52:3 (July): 325–342.

Humboldt, Alexander von. 1819–1829. *Personal Narrative of Travels to the Equinoctial Regions of the New Continent, During the Years 1799–1804.* 7 vols. London: Longman, Hurst, Rees, Orme, and Brown.

———. 1858. Kosmos. *Entwurf einer physischen Weltbeschreibung.* vol. 4. Stuttgart: Cotta.

Imhof, Viola. 2001. Pfeiffer, Ida Laura. *Neu Deutsche Biographie.* https://www.deutsche-biographie.de/sfz95287.html

Jehle, Hiltgund. 1989. *Ida Pfeiffer: Weltreisende im 19. Jahrhundert: Zur Kulturgeschichte reisender Frauen.* Münster: Waxman.

Johnson, Samuel. 1775. *Taxation no Tyranny.* London: T. Cadell

Karsch, F. 1881. Neue Juliden des Berliner Museums, als Prodromus einer Juliden-Monographie. *Zeitschrift für die gesammten Naturwissenschaften.* 54, pp. 1–79.

Keynes, R. D. ed. 2001. *Charles Darwin's Beagle Diary*. Cambridge: Cambridge University Press.

King, P. P. 1839. *Narrative of the Surveying Voyages of His Majesty's Ships Adventure and Beagle... Proceedings of the First Expedition, 1826–30...* London: Henry Colburn.

Kipling, Rudyard. 1888. *The Man Who Would be King*. Indian Railway Library. A. H. Wheeler & Co. of Allahabad. 5. 1888.

Conrad, Joseph. 1899–1900. *Lord Jim*. New York: Scott.

Kneale, Matthew. 2000. *English Passengers*. London: Anchor.

Kollar, V. 1858. *Über Ida Pfeiffer's Sendungen von Naturalien aus Mauritius und Madagascar*. Vienna.

Laborde, L. de. 1848. *Le Parthénon: Documents pour servir à une Eestauration*. Paris: Leleux.

Lebzelter, F. F. 1910. *Die österreichische Weltreisende Ida Pfeiffer 1797–1858 mit besonderer Berücksichtigung der naturwissenschaftlichen Ergebnisse ihrer Reisen*. Vienna.

Lerner, Marion. 2015. Von der ödesten und traurigsten Gegend zur Insel der Träume: Islandreisebücher im touristischen Kontext. *Münchner Nordistische Studien*. München: Herbert Utz Verlag.

Lovell, Julia. 2011. *The Opium War*. Pan Macmillan.

Loviot, Fanny. 1858. *A Lady's Captivity Among Chinese Pirates*. London: Routledge.

[Lowe, Emily.] 1857. *Unprotected Females in Norway, or the Pleasantest way of Travelling There*. London.

[———.] 1859. *Unprotected Females in Sicily, Calabria, and on the Top of Mount Aetna*. London.

Mann, Thomas. 1901. *Buddenbrooks*.

Martens, E. von. 1867. *Die Preussische expedition nach Ost-Asien: nach amtlichen quellen. Zoologischer Theil*. vol. 2. Berlin.

Martin, Alison E. 2017. "Fresh fields of exploration": Cultures of scientific knowledge and Ida Pfeiffer's second voyage round the world (1856).

In: A. E. Martin, L. Missinne & Beatrix van Dam eds. *Travel Writing in Dutch and German, 1790–1930: Modernity, Regionality, Mobility.* Taylor & Francis.

Martin, R. M. [1857]. *The History of the Indian Empire.* vol. 3. London: London printing.

Mondain, G. 1929. *Rafaravavy Marie (1898–1848): une martyre malgache sous Ranavalona Ière.* Paris: Société des Missions Évangéliques.

Montagu, Mary. 1763. *Turkish Embassy Letters.*

Marryat, F. S. 1848. *Borneo and the Indian Archipelago.* London: Longman.

McLeod, Lyons. 1860. *Travels in Eastern Africa.* vol. 2.

Michaels, Jennifer. 2013. An unusual traveler: Ida Pfeiffer's visit to the Holy Land in 1842. *Quest. Issues in Contemporary Jewish History.* n. 6 (Dec.).

Miles, Pliny. 1854. *Norðurfari: Or, Rambles in Iceland.* New York.

Müller, Conrad ed. 2010. *Alexander von Humboldt und das Preußische Königshaus. Briefe aus den Jahren 1835-1857.* Severus Verlag.

Oliver, S. P. [1866]. *Madagascar and the Malagasy.* London: Day.

Perkins, J. 1848. Madame Pfeiffer. *Littell's Living Age.* vol. 19, pp. 307–308.

Petermann, Augustus. 1851. Madame Ida Pfeiffer in Africa. *Athenaeum.* 1258 (6 Dec.): 1281.

Pfeiffer, Ida. 1844. *Reise einer Wienerin in das heilige Land.* 2 vols. Vienna: Dirnböck.

———. 1846. *Reise nach dem skandinavischen Norden und der Insel Island im Jahre 1845.* 2 vols. Pest, Leipzig: Wigand Heckenast.

———. 1850. *Eine Frauenfahrt um die Welt: Reise von Wien nach Brasilien, Chili, Otahaiti, China, Ost-Indien, Persien und Kleinasien.* 3 vols. Vienna: Gerold.

———. 1851–1852. *A lady's Voyage Round the World: A Selected Translation.* Ed. and translated by Jane Sinnett. London, New York.

———. 1851. *A Woman's Journey Round the World, from Vienna to Brazil, Chili, Tahiti, China, Hindostan, Persia, and Asia Minor. An Unabridged*

Translation from the German of Ida Pfeiffer. Illustrated with Tinted Engravings. London: N. Cooke.

———. 1852. *A Woman's Journey Round the World: from Vienna to Brazil, Chili, Tahiti, China, Hindostan, Persia, and Asia Minor.* Unabridged. London: Illustrated London Library.

———. 1852a. *A Lady's Travels Round the World: Travels from Vienna to Brazil, Chili, Otaheite, China, the East Indies, Persia, and Asia Minor.* Translated by W. Hazlitt. London: Routledge.

———. 1852b. *A Visit to the Holy Land, Egypt, and Italy.* London: Ingram.

———. 1852c. *Journey to Iceland: and travels in Sweden and Norway.* Translated by Charlotte Fenimore Cooper. London.

———. 1852d. *A Lady's Voyage Round the World: A Selected Translation from the German of Ida Pfeiffer.* Translated by Mrs. Jane Sinnett. London & New York.

———. 1852e. *Visit to Iceland and the Scandinavian North.* Translated by H. W. Dulcken. London: Ingram, Cooke.

———. 1852f. *Reis eener Vrouw rondom de Wereld.* Gorinchem: Noorduyn.

———. 1853a. *Visit to Iceland and the Scandinavian North.* Translated by H. W. Dulcken. London: Ingram, Cooke, 2d edn.

———. 1853b. Letter to A. Petermann, 12 Sept. 1855, *Carinthia* Nr. 39 (14 May): 155–156.

———. 1853c. *Visit to the Holy Land, Egypt, and Italy.* 2d edn. London: Ingram.

———. 1855. *A Lady's Second Journey Round the World: From London to the Cape of Good Hope, Borneo, Java, Sumatra, Celebes, Ceram, the Moluccas, etc. California, Panama, Peru, Ecuador, and the United States.* London: Longman, Brown, Green, and Longmans.

———. 1856a. *A Lady's Second Journey Round the World.* New York: Harper.

———. 1856b. *A Woman's Journey Round the World from Vienna to Brazil, Chili, Tahiti, China, Hindostan, Persia, and Asia Minor.* 6th edn, London: Ward and Lock.

————. 1856c. *Meine zweite Weltreise.* 4 vols. Vienna: Gerold.

————. 1861a. *Reise nach Madagaskar: nebst einer Biographie der Verfasserin, nach ihren eigenen Aufzeichnungen.* 2 vols. Vienna: Gerold.

————. 1861b. *The Last Travels of Ida Pfeiffer, inclusive a visit to Madagaskar*, translated by H. W. Dulcken. London: Routledge, Warne and Routledge.

————. 1879, 1881. *The Story of Ida Pfeiffer and her Travels in Many Lands.* London.

————. 1885. *Voyage Autour du Monde de Mme Ida Pfeiffer.* Translated from the English by E. Delauney. Rouen.

Pfeiffer, L. 1856. Descriptions of fifty-eight new species of *Helicea* from the collection of H. Cuming, Esq. *Proceedings of the Zoological Society of London.* Part XXIV, pp. 324–336.

Plasser, Gerhard. 2009. Hubert Sattler und Ida Pfeiffer (1797–1858) *Salzburger Museumsblätter.* Nr 9/10 (Nov.): 5–7.

Rains. Fanny L. 1878. *By Land and Ocean; or, The Journal and Letters of a Young Girl who went to South Australia … New Zealand … Singapore* [&c.]. London: Sampson Low, Marston, Searle & Rivington.

Rhodes, E. 1824. *Peak Scenery; or, the Derbyshire Tourist.* London: Longman, Hurst, Rees, Orme, Brown & Green.

Riedl-Dorn, Christa. 2001. Ida Pfeiffer. In W. Seipel ed. *Die Entdeckung der Welt. Die Welt der Entdeckungen Österreichische Forscher, Sammler, Abenteurer.* Vienna: Skira, pp. 265–269.

Ritter, Karl. 1816–1859. *Geography in Relation to Nature and the History of Mankind.*

Rookmaaker, Kees ed. 2006. Darwin's Beagle diary (1831–1836). In John van Wyhe ed., *The Complete Work of Charles Darwin Online*, (http://darwin-online.org.uk/content/frameset?itemID=EHBeagleDiary&viewtype=text&pageseq=1).

Rupke, N. 2005. *Alexander von Humboldt: A Metabiography.* Chicago: University of Chicago Press.

Schlegel, Hermann. 1879. *Notes from the Royal Zoological Museum of the Netherlands*. Vol. 1.

Shepherd, T. H. [1856]. *The World's Metropolis, or, Mighty London*. London.

Sinnett, Jane. 1852. Translator's note. In: Ida Pfeiffer, *A Lady's Voyage*, pp. iii–iv.

Smedley, F. E. 1865. Gathered Leaves: *Being a Collection of the Poetical Writings of the Late Frank E. Smedley. With a Memorial Preface by Edmund Yates*. London.

Smith, Frederick. 1858. *Catalogue of Hymenopterous Insects in the Collection of the British Museum*. London: British Museum.

———. 1860. Catalogue of hymenopterous insects collected by Mr. A. R. Wallace in the islands of Bachian, Kaisaa, Amboyna, Gilolo, and at Dory in New Guinea. *Journal of the Proceedings of the Linnean Society (Zoology)*, 5 (17b) [Supplement to Vol. 4]: 93–143, pl. 1.

Smith, Murray. 1868 & 1873. *Round the World: A Story of Travel Compiled from the Narrative of Ida Pfeiffer*. London: Nelson.

St. John, Spenser. 1862. *Life in the Forests of the Far East*. 2 vols.

Speer, Albert. 1970. *Inside the Third Reich*. New York: Avon.

Stebbing, H. 1847. *The Christian in Palestine; or, Scenes of Sacred History, Historical and Descriptive. Illustrated from Sketches Taken on the Spot by W. H. Bartlett*. London: George Virtue & Co.

Stevenson, Robert Louis. 1719. *Robinson Crusoe*.

Stökl, Helene. 1920. *Die Weltfahrten der österreichischen Reisenden Ida Pfeiffer. Erzählt von Helene Stökl. Mit einem Bildnis der Weltreisenden und Bildern von Fritz Gareis*. Vienna: Österr. Schulbücherverlag.

Swinhoe, Charles. 1892. *Catalogue of Eastern and Australian Lepidoptera Heterocera in the collection of the Oxford University Museum: Sphinges and Bombyces*.

Taylor, Bayard. 1860. *At Home and Abroad*.

Thomson, J. T. 1864. *Some Glimpses into Life in the Far East*.

Thoreau, H. D. 1854. *Walden; or Life in the Woods*.

Tolkien, J. R. R. 1954. *The Two Towers.*

Trimmel, J. F. E. 1847. *Gedichte von Emil.* Vienna.

Walker, Francis. 1858. *List of the Specimens of Homopterous Insects in the Collection of the British Museum. Supplement.* London: British Museum.

———. 1861. *List of the Specimens of Lepidopterous Insects in the Collection of the British Museum.* part XXII. London: British Museum.

———. 1865. *List of the Specimens of Lepidopterous Insects in the Collection of the British Museum.* part III, supplement, part 2. London: British Museum.

———. 1868. *Catalogue of the Specimens of Blattariae in the Collection of the British Museum.* London: British Museum.

———. 1869. *Catalogue of the Specimens of Dermaptera Saltatoria… in the collection of the British Museum.* vol. 1. London: British Museum.

Wallace, A. R. 1868. Spiritualism in Java. *Spiritual Magazine* (n.s.) 3: 92.

———. 1869. *The Malay Archipelago: The land of the Orang-utan, and the Bird of Paradise. A Narrative of Travel, with Studies of Man and Nature.* 2 vols. London: Macmillan & Co.

Watt, H. S. 1991. Pfeiffer a 19th-century woman travel writer. *The German Quarterly.* Vol. 64, No. 3, (Summer): 339–352.

Werner, Petra, 2000. *Casanova ohne Frauen? Bemerkungen zu Alexander von Humboldts Korrespondenzpartnerinnen.* Berlin: Alexander-von-Humboldt-Forschungsstelle.

Westwood, John Obadiah. 1859. *Catalogue of Orthopterous Insects in the Collection of the British Museum, part 1.* Phasmidae. London: British Museum.

White, Adam. 1856. Descriptions of some Coleopterous insects in the collection of the British Museum, hitherto apparently unnoticed. *Proceedings of the Zoological Society of London.* part XXIV, pp. 8–17.

Wilberforce, E. 1856. *The Idler, A Treasury of Essay, Criticism and General Literature.* London: Houlston and Stoneman.

Woodbury, Walter. 1875. *Treasure Spots of the World*. London: Ward, Lock and Tyler.

Woodward, S. P. 1859. Note on Cyclostoma articulatum. *Proceedings of the Zoological Society of London*. Part xxvii, p. 204.

Wurzbach, Constant von ed. 1870. *Biographisches Lexikon des Kaisertums Österreich*. Vol. 22.

Wyhe, John van and Rookmaaker, Kees eds. *Alfred Russel Wallace's Notebooks from the Malay Archipelago*. Cambridge: Cambridge University Press (forthcoming).

———— and ———— eds. 2013. *Alfred Russel Wallace: Letters from the Malay Archipelago*. Foreword by Sir David Attenborough. Oxford: Oxford University Press.

Wyhe, John van ed. 2002–. *The Complete Work of Charles Darwin Online* (http://darwin-online.org.uk/).

————. ed. 2012–. *Wallace Online* (http://wallace-online.org/).

————. 2013. *Dispelling the Darkness: Voyage in the Malay Archipelago and the Discovery of Evolution by Wallace and Darwin*. Singapore: World Scientific Publishing.

————. ed. 2015. *The Annotated Malay Archipelago by Alfred Russel Wallace*. Singapore: NUS Press.

————. 2019. *The Conservation Expeditions 2016–2018*. Singapore: Tembusu College.

Zimmermann. E. A. W. von ed. 1802–1813. *Taschenbuch der Reisen, oder unterhaltende Darstellung der Entdeckungen des 18ten Jahrhunderts, in Rücksicht der Länder-, Menschen- und Productenkunde. Für jede Klasse von Lesern*. Leipzig.

Notes

1   von Gayette 1856, p. 43.
2   Smith 1868, p. v.
3   Anon. 1861.
4   Pfeiffer 1861, p. xxxiv.
5   Pfeiffer 1850, vol. 1, preface. Italics in the original.
6   Rhodes 1824, p. xiii.
7   Forster 1922, p. 37.
8   Foster 1975. Quoted in Jehle 1989, p. 4.
9   'The forfeit hand; a legend of Brabant' in Smedley 1865, p. 78.
10 See van Wyhe and Rookmaaker 2013, pp. 49, 78, 80, 98.
11 van Wyhe 2013, p. 38.
12 Pfeiffer 1861, p. x.
13 Gombrich 2005, p. 240.
14 Pfeiffer 1852e, p. viii.
15 Nicholas Rupke charted the changing image of Humboldt in Rupke 2005.
16 Pfeiffer 1861b, vol. 1, p. xiv.
17 Ibid., p. xvii.
18 Ibid., p. xvi.
19 Ibid., p. xv. In Pfeiffer's autobiographical memoir, Trimmel is referred to only by the letter T.
20 Pfeiffer 1861b, p. xvii.
21 Ibid., p. xxiv.
22 Anon. 1854b.
23 The letter is quoted in Jehle 1989, p. 27 and Habinger 2008, p. 61.
24 Anon. 1856b, p. 237.
25 Bartlett 1851, p. 128.
26 Anon. 1844.
27 Pfeiffer 1852e, p. ix.
28 Pfeiffer 1861, p. xxiv.
29 Pfeiffer 1852b, p. 18.
30 Ibid., p. 38.
31 Ibid., p. 40.
32 Ibid., p. 41.
33 Anon. 1854a, p. 21.
34 Pfeiffer 1852b, p. 50. On Pfeiffer in this region see Michaels 2013.
35 Plasser 2009, pp. 5–7.
36 Pfeiffer 1852b, p. 76.
37 Bartlett 1851, p. 128.
38 Ibid., p. 122. Of course another explanation is that the later account is inaccurate.
39 Bartlett 1850a, p. 227.
40 Pfeiffer 1852b, p. 80.
41 Ibid., p. 90.
42 Ibid., p. 91.
43 Ibid., p. 92.
44 Ibid., p. 105.
45 Ibid., p. 107.
46 Ibid., p. 109.
47 Ibid., p. 127.
48 Bartlett 1850a, p. 227.
49 Pfeiffer 1852b, p. 135.
50 Bartlett 1850a, p. 175.
51 Ibid., p. 227.
52 Pfeiffer 1852b, p. 139.
53 Ibid., p. 165.
54 Ibid., p. 174.
55 Ibid., p. 207.
56 Ibid., p. 210.
57 Ibid., p. 231.
58 Ibid., p. 243.
59 Ibid., pp. 257–258.
60 Ibid., p. 259.
61 Ibid., p. 316.
62 Ibid., p. 328.
63 Preface to Pfeiffer 1844. Lebzelter 1910 refers to the existence of "the original diaries" of Pfeiffer then in the possession of friends of Pfeiffer living in Waidhofen. He was not given permission to use them in his work. It is unclear if these included the notebook from the first world journey found by Jehle.
64 Jehle 1989, p. 73.
65 Burton 1856, vol. 1, pp. 16–17.
66 Pfeiffer 1852e, p. viii.
67 Ibid., p. 18.
68 Ibid., pp. ix–x.
69 Pfeiffer 1852c, p. 175.
70 On Pfeiffer as collector see Riedl-Dorn 2001, Baker 1995 and Lebzelter 1910.
71 Pfeiffer 1852e, p. 41.
72 Ibid., p. 60.
73 Ibid., p. 72. See the map of Pfeiffer's route through Iceland in Jehle 1989, p. 43.
74 Ibid., p. 75.
75 Ibid., p. 69.
76 Pfeiffer 1852c, p. 143.
77 Pfeiffer 1852e, p. 121.
78 Ibid., p. 109.

79 Ibid., p. 150.
80 Ibid., p. 179.
81 Ibid., p. 189.
82 Ibid., p. 201.
83 Ibid., p. 202.
84 Ibid., p. 270.
85 *Salzburger Constitutionelle Zeitung*, 28 Aug. 1849, vol. 3, p. 1020.
86 *Morgenblatt für gebildete Leser*, vol. 40, Issue 3, 1846, p. 884.
87 Jehle 1989, p. 71 and Habinger 2008, p. 41, note 2. The daguerreotypes survive in a private collection but are reproduced, without the images being clearly discernable, in Honsig 2012. They depict houses with people standing before them. I am grateful to Hiltgund Jehle for sharing details of these from her own research.
88 *Blätter für literarische Unterhaltung*, 15 May 1847, p. 540.
89 *Spectator*, 25, 1851, p. 375.
90 *Dublin Review*, 33, 1852, p. 341.
91 Miles 1854, p. 123. For a recent discussion of Pfeiffer in Iceland see Lerner 2015. With thanks to Hiltgund Jehle.
92 This was suggested by Jehle 1989.
93 Honsig 2012.
94 Pfeiffer 1852, p. 10.
95 Ibid., p. 13.
96 Ibid., p. 15.
97 Ibid., p. 34.
98 Perkins 1848.
99 The handle survives in a private collection. According to Hiltgund Jehle (personal communication) the handle had a small note in Pfeiffer's handwriting attached to it that stated that she had beaten off an attacker in Brazil with it. The note has since been lost.
100 Pfeiffer 1852, p. 39.
101 *Entomologische Zeitung*, vol. 8, 1845, p. 270.
102 Ibid., p. 43.
103 Ibid., p. 44.
104 Ibid., p. 45.
105 Ibid., p. 48.
106 Ibid., p. 49.
107 Ibid., p. 59.
108 Ibid., pp. 61–62.
109 Keynes 2001, p. 249.
110 Pfeiffer 1852, p. 64.

111 Darwin 1840, p. 611. Available in John van Wyhe ed. 2002 – *The Complete Work of Charles Darwin Online*: http://darwin-online.org.uk/content/frameset?pageseq=1&itemID=F1656&viewtype=text.
112 Pfeiffer 1852, p. 70. The captain's name was misspelled as Jurianse by Pfeiffer.
113 Ibid., p. 72.
114 Ibid., p. 74.
115 Darwin 1845, p. 416.
116 Gunow 1873–1874, pp. 25, 26, 39, 47.
117 Pfeiffer 1852, p. 78.
118 Ibid., p. 81.
119 Ibid., p. 87.
120 Ibid., p. 88. On Pfeiffer in China see Howe 1999 and Dabak 1999.
121 Pfeiffer 1856a, p. 99.
122 Pfeiffer 1852, p. 89.
123 Ibid., p. 90.
124 Ibid., p. 92.
125 Ibid., p. 94.
126 Ibid., p. 104.
127 *The Lamp: a Weekly Catholic Journal*, Sept. 1852, p. 482.
128 Pfeiffer 1852, p. 97.
129 Ibid., p. 99.
130 Pfeiffer 1852, p. 89.
131 Pfeiffer to Marie, 24 Oct. 1847, in Habinger 2008, p. 53.
132 Pfeiffer 1852, p. 117.
133 Ibid., p. 118.
134 Ibid., p. 120. On Pfeiffer in Southeast Asia see Heidhues 2004 which has excellent references.
135 *The Singapore Free Press*, 9 Sept. 1847, p.3.
136 Pfeiffer 1852, p. 118.
137 Ibid., p. 120.
138 Ibid., p. 122.
139 Ibid., p. 124.
140 Ibid., p. 129.
141 Ibid., p. 166.
142 Ibid., p. 211.
143 *Blackwood's Edinburgh Magazine*, vol. 70, July 1851, pp. 86–102, p. 95.
144 Pfeiffer 1852, p. 207.
145 Ibid., p. 208.
146 Ibid., p. 216.
147 Ibid., p. 217.
148 Ibid., p. 218.
149 Ibid., p. 225.
150 *The British Indian Gentleman* 28 March

1848. Quoted in *Carinthia*, 11 Nov. 1848, p. 151.

151 Pfeiffer 1852, p. 245.

152 Ibid., p. 246.

153 Ibid., p. 333.

154 Pfeiffer 1856b, p. 259.

155 Ibid., p. 264.

156 Perkins 1848, p. 307.

157 Pfeiffer 1856b, p. 270.

158 Ibid., p. 279.

159 Pfeiffer 1852, p. 281.

160 Perkins 1848, p. 308.

161 Ibid., p. 307.

162 Barber 1850, p. 59.

163 Pfeiffer 1852, p. 290.

164 *California Farmer and Journal of Useful Sciences*, 24 May 1855, p. 164.

165 Pfeiffer 1852, p. 299.

166 The relief head is now in the Antikensammlung of the Kunsthistorisches Museum in Vienna.

167 Pfeiffer 1852, p. 302.

168 Pfeiffer 1856b, p. 306.

169 Ibid., p. 307.

170 Pfeiffer 1852, p. 327.

171 Ibid., p. 329.

172 Ibid., p. 336.

173 Bougainville 1772, pp. 300–301. Available in the *Beagle* Library in John van Wyhe ed. 2002- *The Complete Work of Charles Darwin Online*: http://darwin-online.org.uk/content/frameset?pageseq=1&itemID=A745&viewtype=text.

174 *Athenaeum*, No., 1232, 7 June 1851, 602–604, p. 602.

175 *Economist*, vol. x, 31 Jan. p. 123.

176 *Blätter für literarische Unterhaltung*, vol. 2, 29 Oct. 1857, p. 801.

177 Review of *Lady's voyage around the world*. *The Foreign Quarterly Review*, vol. 56, p. 249.

178 Thoreau 1854, p. 26. Thoreau cited from the Sinnett translation, Pfeiffer 1852d, p. 265.

179 Sinnett introduction to Pfeiffer 1852d, pp. iii–iv.

180 Emma Darwin's diary for 1851 is available in John van Wyhe ed. 2002- The Complete Work of Charles Darwin Online: http://darwin-online.org.uk/content/frameset?itemID=CUL-DAR242%5B.15%5D&viewtype=image&pageseq=1

181 *Men of the Time: Biographical Sketches of Eminent Living Characters*. London, 1856, p. 902. The letter was addressed to A. Petermann, 12 Dec. 1852, Surabaya, and was first published in the *Athenaeum*, 7 May 1853, p. 562.

182 Review of *Lady's Voyage Around the World*. *The Straits Times*, 13 Jan. 1852, p. 5.

183 Review of *Lady's Voyage Around the World*. Sinnett translation. *Eliza Cook's Journal*, vol. 6, 1852, p. 297.

184 Dawood 1995, p. 12.

185 Habinger 2008, p. 60.

186 Cited in Jehle 1989, p. 80.

187 An 1850 letter from Pfeiffer to Breunig is in the Schotten Gymnasium Stiftsarchiv (Scr. 206 Nr. 37). It is unknown if any items were purchased from Pfeiffer. With thanks to Hiltgund Jehle.

188 Darwin to J. D. Hooker, 6 Aug. 1881, in F. Darwin 1887, p. 247, in John van Wyhe ed. 2002 – *The Complete Work of Charles Darwin Online*: http://darwin-online.org.uk/content/frameset?pageseq=1&itemID=F1452.3&viewtype=text.

189 "daß er mehrmalen ausrief: 'Sie haben Unglaubliches durchgesetzt.'" quoted in Jehle 1989, p. 30. On Humboldt and Pfeiffer see Werner 2000.

190 Pfeiffer 1855, vol. 1, p. 2.

191 Ibid., p. 12.

192 Ibid., p. 6.

193 *The Times*, 12 Apr. 1851, p. 8.

194 Pfeiffer 1855, vol. 1, p. 5.

195 Ibid., p. 7.

196 Ibid., p. 8.

197 Pfeiffer to Frau von Schwarz, 29 July 1851, in Habinger 2008, p. 74.

198 Pfeiffer 1855, vol. 1, p. 10.

199 Pfeiffer to Frau von Schwarz, 29 July 1851, in Habinger 2008, p. 74.

200 Shepherd [1856], p. 61.

201 Gilbert 1851, p. 87.

202 Pfeiffer 1855, vol. 1, p. 15.

203 Ibid., p. 16. [Darwin] 1847, in John van Wyhe ed. 2002- *The Complete Work of Charles Darwin Online* http://darwin-online.org.uk/content/frameset?itemID=F1675&viewtype=text&pageseq=1.

204 Petermann 1851.

205 Bartlett 1851, p. 182.

206 Freeman 1851, p. 14.

207 Pfeiffer 1855, vol. 1, p. 38.
208 Ibid., p. 42.
209 Petermann 1851.
210 Pfeiffer 1855, vol. 1, p. 41.
211 Ibid., p. 46.
212 Freeman 1851.
213 *The Singapore Free Press and Mercantile Advertiser*, 21 Nov. 1851, p. 2.
214 Pfeiffer 1855, vol. 1, p. 49.
215 Ibid., p. 50.
216 Ibid., p. 52.
217 Wallace 1869, vol. 2, p. 37. See van Wyhe 2015, p. 86 and van Wyhe 2013, pp. 83–86.
218 Pfeiffer 1855, vol. 1, p. 51.
219 NParks Flora & Fauna Web. (https://florafaunaweb.nparks.gov.sg/Special-Pages/animal-detail.aspx?id=374).
220 Wallace to Samuel Stevens, 12 May 1856, in van Wyhe and Rookmaaker 2013, p. 80.
221 Quoted in Habinger 2008, p. 84.
222 Quoted in Riedl-Dorn 2001, pp. 265–269.
223 *Straits Times*, 16 Dec. 1851, p. 7.
224 Quoted in Habinger 2008, p. 87.
225 Pfeiffer 1855, vol. 1, p. 59.
226 Ibid., pp. 59–61, 63.
227 St. John 1862, vol. 1, p. 152.
228 Wallace to F. Sims, 25 June 1855, in van Wyhe and Rookmaaker 2013, p. 49.
229 Pfeiffer 1855, vol. 1, p. 66.
230 St. John 1862, vol. 1, p. 153.
231 Pfeiffer 1855, vol. 1, p. 68.
232 St. John 1862, vol. 1, p. 155.
233 Pfeiffer 1855, vol. 1, p. 74.
234 Ibid., p. 77. I have borrowed the title of this section from the eponymous book by Redmond O'Hanlon (1984).
235 Ibid., 80
236 Ibid., p. 84. At Canton Pfeiffer had observed "I once happened to go near the place of execution, and to my horror beheld a long row of still bleeding heads exposed upon high poles." Pfeiffer 1852, p. 99.
237 Pfeiffer 1855, vol. 1, p. 90.
238 Ibid., p. 92.
239 Ibid., p. 94.
240 Pfeiffer 1856c, vol. 1, p. 105.
241 Taylor 1860, p. 25.
242 Wallace to Samuel Stevens, 27 Sept.
1856, in van Wyhe and Rookmaaker 2013, p. 98.
243 Pfeiffer 1855, vol. 1, p. 106. The translator mistakenly rendered this as a bamboo hat "which I had got in the island of Bali." Pfeiffer never visited Bali and in the German original she merely stated that the hat was from Bali. I have therefore modified this passage.
244 Ibid., p. 108.
245 Petermann 1851.
246 With thanks to Gerrell M. Drawhorn.
247 Pfeiffer 1855, vol. 1, p. 128.
248 St. John 1862, vol. 2, p. 166. Pfeiffer's name was removed from the 1863 edition.
249 Pfeiffer 1855, vol. 1, p. 142.
250 Ibid., p. 155.
251 Pfeiffer to Ritter, 3 June 1852, quoted in Habinger 2008, p. 96.
252 Karsch 1881.
253 van Wyhe 2015, p. 256.
254 Pfeiffer 1855, vol. 1, p. 159.
255 Ibid., p. 161.
256 Ibid., p. 162.
257 Ibid., p. 167.
258 Ibid., p. 168.
259 Ibid., p. 176.
260 Pfeiffer 1856a, p. 283.
261 Pfeiffer 1855, vol. 1, p. 185.
262 Translated in Martin 2017, p. 10.
263 *Straits Times*, 13 July 1852, p. 4.
264 Pfeiffer 1855, vol. 1, p. 220. The American Baptist missionaries were Samuel Munson and Henry Lyman. They were killed and reportedly cannibalised in 1834.
265 Ibid., p. 223.
266 Pfeiffer 1855, vol. 1, pp. 227–228. Pfeiffer called the village Kotto-Godong, now spelled Koto Gadang. The Batak of Lake Toba call these rice barns *sopos*.
267 *Straits Times*, 3 July 1855, p. 8.
268 Pfeiffer 1855, vol. 1, p. 249. This was not strictly accurate as there were shamans called *datu* who performed various rituals and divinations.
269 Ibid., p. 260.
270 Ibid., p. 268.
271 Ibid., p. 270.
272 Letter to A. Petermann, 12 Dec. 1852, Surabaya. *Athenaeum* (7 May 1853), p. 562.

273 Pfeiffer 1855, vol. 1, p. 275.
274 Ibid., p. 285.
275 Ibid., p. 286.
276 Pfeiffer to A. Petermann, 12 Sept. 1852, in Ein Schreiben der Frau Ida Pfeiffer, gerichtet an Herrn Petermann in London. *Carinthia*. 43, Nr. 39 (14 May), 1853, pp. 155–156. Reproduced in Habinger 2008, pp. 99–106.
277 Pfeiffer 1855, vol. 1, p. 303.
278 Ibid., p. 292. See a different version of these events in Pfeiffer's letter to A. Petermann, 12 Dec. 1852, *Athenaeum*, 7 May 1853, p. 562.
279 Pfeiffer's words are quoted by von Humboldt in Müller 2010, p. 255.
280 Pfeiffer 1855, vol. 1, p. 293. However a different speech is reported in Pfeiffer to A. Petermann, 12 Sept. 1852, *Carinthia*. 43, Nr. 39 (14 May) 1853: 155–156.
281 I am grateful to Gerrell M. Drawhorn for this suggestion.
282 Pfeiffer 1855, vol. 1, p. 294.
283 Ibid., p. 298.
284 Ibid., p. 304.
285 Ibid., p. 314.
286 Bleeker 1860, pp. 98, 358.
287 Bleeker 1853, p. 298.
288 Translated in Martin 2017, p. 11.
289 Pfeiffer 1855, vol. 1, p. 326.
290 Ibid., p. 321.
291 Ibid., p. 333.
292 Ibid., p. 357.
293 Wallace, *Journal 2*, pp. 133–134. In van Wyhe and Rookmaaker, *Alfred Russel Wallace's Notebooks from the Malay Archipelago* (forthcoming).
294 van Wyhe 2015, p. 344.
295 Pfeiffer 1855, vol. 1, p. 375.
296 Ibid., p. 383.
297 Smith 1858, p. 80.
298 Pfeiffer 1855, vol. 1, p. 390.
299 Ibid., p. 393.
300 Ibid., p. 396.
301 *The Perth Gazette*, 1 July 1853, p. 3.
302 Smith 1860.
303 Günther 1859, pp. 202, 223, 241, 405; Günther 1864, vol. 4, p. 23; Günther 1870, p. 216; Swinhoe 1892, p. 140.
304 Gray 1847, p. 341.
305 Günther 1861, pp. 22, 152; Günther 1864, pp. 11, 43, 128; Walker 1868, pp. 20, 126, 138; Walker 1861, p. 610; Walker 1858; Walker 1869, p. 85; Butler 1869, pp. 88, 97, 206; Swinhoe 1892, p. 139.
306 Walker 1865, p. 342.
307 Wallace to Henry Walter Bates, 30 Apr. & 10 May 1856, in van Wyhe and Rookmaaker 2013, p. 78.
308 For more detail see van Wyhe 2013, pp. 205–217.
309 van Wyhe and Rookmaaker (forthcoming).
310 This fact has been disputed by various conspiracy theorists and those influenced by their writings over the years. However the mundane and unavoidable historical evidence confirming the traditional date of receiving Wallace's letter is given in van Wyhe and Rookmaaker 2012 and van Wyhe 2013, pp. 221–227, 358, note 692.
311 Pfeiffer 1855, vol. 1, p. 411.
312 See van Wyhe 2015, p. 344.
313 See Martin 2017.
314 Wallace 1869, vol. 1, p. 349. Wallace reproduced the passage in his book. Bickmore 1869, p. 36.
315 Pfeiffer 1855, vol. 1, p. 444.
316 Thomson 1864, p. 25.
317 Pfeiffer 1856a, p. 276.
318 Walker 1858; Walker 1869, p. 87; Walker 1861, p. 555; Butler 1869, p. 262.
319 Pfeiffer 1855, vol. 1, p. 325.
320 White 1856, pp. 16–17.
321 Ibid., p. 277.
322 Ibid., p. 279.
323 Ibid., p. 285.
324 Wallace 1868. See van Wyhe 2015, p. 23.
325 Pfeiffer 1856a, p. 286.
326 Ibid., p. 288.
327 Pfeiffer to A. Petermann, 30 Oct. 1853, in Habinger 2008, p. 117.
328 Pfeiffer 1856a, p. 297. On Pfeiffer's visit to the USA see: Brisson 2013.
329 *California Farmer and Journal of Useful Sciences*, 24 May 1855, p. 164.
330 Pfeiffer 1855, vol. 2, p. 59.
331 Ibid., p. 66.
332 *Sacramento Daily Union*, 8 Oct. 1853.
333 Pfeiffer 1855, vol. 2, p. 94.
334 Ibid., p. 97.
335 Keynes 2001, p. 348.

336 Pfeiffer 1855, vol. 2, p. 152.
337 Ibid., pp. 147–148.
338 Ibid., p. 155.
339 Ibid., p. 160.
340 Ibid., p. 140.
341 *Athenaeum*, March 1854, p. 344. The letter was also printed in *Die Gartenlaube*, 1, 1854, p. 12 and Habinger 2008, p. 116.
342 Pfeiffer 1855, vol. 2, p. 166.
343 *The Times*, 3 Apr. 1854, p. 9.
344 Pfeiffer 1855, vol. 2, p. 177.
345 Ibid., p. 178.
346 Ibid., p. 193.
347 Ibid., p. 194.
348 Rookmaaker 2006.
349 Pfeiffer 1855, vol. 2, p. 204.
350 Ibid., p. 207.
351 Ibid., p. 209.
352 Ibid., p. 230.
353 Ibid., p. 235.
354 Ibid., p. 236.
355 Ibid., p. 242.
356 Pfeiffer 1856c, vol. 4, p. 4. The 1855 English translation omits the word "coloured" which is used in the German original.
357 Pfeiffer 1855, vol. 2, p. 243.
358 See Race & Slavery Petitions Project (https://library.uncg.edu/slavery/petitions/details.aspx?pid=16528)
359 Pfeiffer 1855, vol. 2, pp. 250–251.
360 Johnson 1775, p. 89.
361 Pfeiffer 1855, vol. 2, p. 269.
362 Ibid., p. 271.
363 Ibid., p. 278–279.
364 Ibid., p. 281.
365 *The St. Louis Directory*, 1821. Pfeiffer's quotation was translated into German, Pfeiffer 1856c, vol. 3, p. 51.
366 Pfeiffer 1855, vol. 2, p. 289.
367 Ibid., p. 303.
368 Ibid., p. 311.
369 Ibid., p. 315.
370 Ibid., p. 333.
371 Interview in the *Sun* (New York), 20 Aug. 1882.
372 Pfeiffer 1855, vol. 2, p. 339.
373 Ibid., p. 347.
374 Bryant and Voss 1981, vol. 3, p. 345.
375 Pfeiffer 1855, vol. 2, p. 361.
376 Ibid., p. 367–368.
377 Ibid., p. 370.
378 Pfeiffer 1861, p. 248.
379 Pfeiffer 1855, vol. 2, p. 370.
380 *Friends' Intelligencer*, 1857, vol. 13, p. 202.
381 *Harper's New Monthly Magazine*, 1856, vol. 12, p. 837.
382 Pfeiffer 1855, vol. 2, p. 388.
383 Ibid., p. 392.
384 Manuscript in private collection. A photograph is reproduced in Honsig 2012. With thanks to Hiltgund Jehle for sharing this with me.
385 Pfeiffer 1855, vol. 2, p. 403.
386 Günther 1864, vol. 5, p. 223.
387 Ibid., p. 421.
388 Ibid., p. 423.
389 See Pfeiffer to Rose, 2 Aug. 1855, and Pfeiffer to Paetel, 22 July 1855, in Habinger 2008, pp. 134, 132.
390 See Heidhues 2004, p. 313.
391 'Ida Pfeiffer', *Carinthia*, 46, Nr. 18, 3 May 1856, pp. 69–72. The review includes some apparently first-hand recollections of Pfeiffer's parents before they moved to Vienna.
392 *Didaskalia*, 15 Dec. 1855.
393 Die Reiseberichte der Frau Ida Pfeiffer. *Abendblatt zur Neue Münchener Zeitung*, Nr. 175, 23 July 1856, p. 697.
394 *The Edinburgh Review*, Apr. 1855, p. 337.
395 Review of second journey, *The Criterion: Literary and Critical Journal*, 1856, vol. 1, p. 407.
396 *Putnam's Monthly Magazine*, 1856, vol. 7, p. 551.
397 *Athenaeum*, 16 Dec. 1854, p. 1525.
398 *The Rambler*, 1856, vol. 5, p. 159.
399 *Punch*, 5 Jan. 1856, p. 8.
400 [Wilberforce] 1856, p. 34.
401 Westwood 1859, p. 44
402 *Catalogue of the Bones of Mammalia in the Collection of the British Museum*. London, 1862, p. 2.
403 Wallace to H. W. Bates, 30 Apr. and 10 May 1856, in van Wyhe and Rookmaaker 2013, p. 71.
404 Doleschall 1857, p. 406. Thanks to Kees Rookmaaker. See van Wyhe 2013, p. 191.
405 Darwin 1871, vol. 2, p. 347. This, like all of Darwin's published work, and almost all of his manuscripts, is available in John van Wyhe ed. 2002 – *The Complete Work of Charles Darwin Online* (http://darwin-

online.org.uk).

406 Jehle 1989, p. 32.

407 Detailed in Habinger 1997, pp. 79–80.

408 Riedl-Dorn 2001.

409 See the many Pfeiffer specimens listed in Martens 1867.

410 Wallace to Frances Sims, 25 June 1855, in van Wyhe and Rookmaaker 2013, p. 49.

411 Ein Winter in Wien. Erster Brief. *Unterhaltungen am häuslichen Herd*, 1856, vol. 1, Nr. 15, pp. 234–238, p. 237.

412 I am grateful to Hiltgund Jehle for confirming my suspicions that this is not a water bottle as described in the text by Gayette.

413 von Gayette 1856, p. 43.

414 Ibid., "die keiner Gattung angehoert."

415 Pfeiffer 1861b, p. 48.

416 Quoted in Jehle 1989, p. 33.

417 "Ich bin mit dieser Reise- und Wanderlust geboren worden." [In an interview] *Unterhaltungen am häuslichen Herd*, 1856, vol. 1, p. 237.

418 Ibid.

419 Humboldt 1858, vol. 4, p. 575 citing Pfeiffer's observation of the eruption of Cotopaxi.

420 The four letters of Humboldt to Pfeiffer are given in the appendix to Pfeiffer 1861a, vol. 2, and the French translation but were not included in the English translation.

421 There are two brief July 1855 letters from Pfeiffer to Barth in Habinger 2008, p. 152.

422 Imhof 2001.

423 *The Times*, 14 Aug., 1856, p. 10.

424 *Association Medical Journal*, 27 Sept. 1856, p. 842. An undated thank you note by Pfeiffer is reproduced in Habinger 2008, p. 136.

425 Pfeiffer 1861b, p. 93.

426 Ibid., p. 95.

427 Fraser 1977. Speech to the Chamber of Deputies, Paris, 1884. Quoted in Fraser 1977, Appendix C.

428 Pfeiffer 1861b, p. 210.

429 Speer 1970, p. 238.

430 Darwin 1859, p. 393.

431 Quoted in Jehle 1989, pp. 99–100.

432 Reprinted in *Portland Guardian* (Aus-

tralia), 8 Apr. 1857, p. 3.

433 Pfeiffer 1861b, p. 123.

434 Gunow 1873–1874, p. 27; Walker 1869, p. 108.

435 See Pfeiffer to anon., 27 Dec. 1856, in Habinger 2008, p. 156.

436 Pfeiffer 1861b, p. 118.

437 Ibid., pp. 110–111.

438 Ibid., p. 130.

439 McLeod 1860, p. 199. See Habinger 2008, p. 158.

440 Pfeiffer 1861b, p. 154.

441 Ibid., p. 155.

442 Ibid., p. 248.

443 Ibid., p. 171.

444 Ibid., p. 172.

445 Ibid., pp. 186–188.

446 See Ellis 1838, vol. 2, pp. 410ff.

447 Ibid., pp. 136–137.

448 Ibid., p. 201.

449 Ellis 1858. Ellis's account of the Lambert coup attempt is in Ellis 1867, p. 58.

450 Pfeiffer 1861b, pp. 226–227.

451 Ibid., p. 237.

452 *Athenaeum*, 14 Nov. 1857, p. 1425.

453 Pfeiffer 1861b, p. 243.

454 Ibid., p. 250.

455 Ibid., p. 255.

456 Ibid., p. 264.

457 Pfeiffer to *Ostdeutsche Post*, 22 Jan. 1858, reproduced in Habinger 2008, p. 167.

458 Pfeiffer 1861b, p. 265.

459 Ibid., pp. 268–269.

460 Pfeiffer spelled the village 'Beforn' (Pfeiffer 1861a, p. 173) but in the English translation this was changed to 'Befora.' Pfeiffer 1861b, p. 268.

461 Barbié du Bocage, Ambassade anglaise à tananarivou (madagascar). *Bulletin de la Société de Géographie* 5.3 (1862), p. 169 quoted in Campbell 2012, p. 882–883.

462 I am grateful to Hiltgund Jehle for sharing a copy of the report with me.

463 Pfeiffer 1861b, pp. 276–277.

464 The letters are reproduced in Habinger 2008, pp. 160–168.

465 Quoted in Jehle 1989, p. 34 and Habinger 2008, p. 169.

466 Boswell 1791, vol. 1, p. 340.

467 *Athenaeum*, 15 May 1858, No. 1594, p. 626.

468 *Illustrated London News*, 3 July 1858, p. 3.

469 Austria. (from our own correspondent.).
    The Times, 10 July 1858, p. 9.
470 Pfeiffer 1861b, p. 280.
471 Madame Ida Pfeiffer. *Illustrated London
    News*, 13 Nov. 1858, p. 444.
472 Austria. (from our own correspondent.)
    The Times, 2 Nov. 1858, p. 8. *The Ath-
    enaeum*, 1858, Issues 1601–1626, p. 589.
473 Habinger 2008, p. 156, note 1.
474 See Kollar 1858.
475 Woodward 1859.
476 Schlegel 1879, p. 85.
477 *Saturday Review*, 24 Aug. 1861, p. 206.
478 Anon. 1861.
479 *Illustrated London News*, 30 Nov., p. 557.
480 *Athenaeum*, 22 June 1861, pp. 823–825.
481 Trimmel 1847. See Jehle 1989, p. 257,
    note 28.
482 Pfeiffer 1861b, p. xxxvii.
483 Ibid., p. xxxvi.
484 Anon. 1863.

485 Perkins 1848.
486 [Lowe] 1857, p. 3.
487 *The Sydney Morning Herald*, 19 March
    1860.
488 Rains 1878.
489 Davidson 1889.
490 Besant 1897, p. 45.
491 Private collection. See Jehle 1989. The
    literature on Pfeiffer always lists the
    painting as presumably by Schmück. But
    the author of the biographical entry in
    Wurzbach 1870, p. 184, knew Pfeiffer
    personally and had access to others who
    knew her, and states that the painting is
    by Schmück.
492 Available online at: https://web.archive.
    org/web/20120112062827/http://aes.
    iupui.edu/rwise/banknotes/austria/
    AustriaP153B-50Schilling-(1995)-
    donatedmjd_f.jpg

Index

A

Adolf, 22
adventurers, 1, 251
Agassiz, Arthur, 80–1
Agassiz, Louis, 80, 233
Aidid, Sultan Abdul Kadir Moh, 196
air passengers, 64
Alfred, 19, 23
Alfuros of Seram, 159, 185–6
Allandale (sailing ship), 133
Amboyna (steamer), 182–4
"American" term, for US citizens, 200
Anglo-Burmese war, 140
antimony, 146
Athenaeum (British literary journal), 59, 116,
    128–9, 155, 161, 182, 208, 238, 275, 277, 279
Attenborough, David, 258
Zoo Quest to Madagascar (1961), 258

B

Baedeker, Karl, 5
Balbiani, Giuseppini, 28–9, 31, 113
Banda (Cores de Vries steamer), 182, 196–7
Baret, Jeanne, 114–15
Barnum, P. T., 228
Baron Kübeck (steamer), 114
Barth, Heinrich, 248
Bartlett, William Henry, 31–6, 38, 130–2, 280
on Pfeiffer, 32
Bates, Henry Walter, 51, 127, 240
Battista, Mr, 34
Battle of Ctesiphon (363 CE), 98
Battuta, Ibn, 2
Bauer, Dr, 178
Bayerbach, Philipp, 74
Bedouin tribe, 34, 37, 44, 115
Behn, Frau, 86
Behn, Herr, 87, 137, 140
Behn, Meyer & Co., 86
Behn, Theodor, 86
Belfast (paddle steamer), 218–19
Bell, Captain, 72
Bellingshausen, 1
Bentinck (P&O steamer), 88
Bentinck, Lord William, 88
Bergner, Captain, 165
Berlin Geographical Society, 245
Bertha, 20
Bescke, Carl Heinrich, 68

Beske, Herr, 68
Bhosle, Pratap Singh, 90
Biedermeier society, 14
Bik, Pieter Vreede, 194
Bird, Isabella, 285
Black Hole of Calcutta, 89, 118
Black Minstrels, 228
Blackwood's Edinburgh Magazine, 91, 116
Blätter für literarische Unterhaltung (Leaves for
    Literary Entertainment), 58
Bleeker, Pieter, 163, 179, 194
Bly, Nellie, 285
Bolivia (steamer), 205
Bornean jungle, 148
botany of Bohemia (1836–1842), 62
Braganza (P&O steamer), 88
Brassey, Annie, 285
Braun, Karl, 203
Breunig, P. Ferdinand, 119
Bridges, F. D., 286
British Indian Gentleman, The (newspaper), 95
Brodie, Captain, 133
Brooke, James (Rajah), 139–40, 145, 147, 151,
    155
Brooke, John (Captain), 140–3, 145, 147–50,
    152–3, 155–6
Bryant, William Cullen, 227
Buddhist monument, 181
Sewu temple complex, 182
budget travel, 7, 28, 49, 62
Burdon, Captain, 90–1
Burton, Decimus, 128
Byrne, Charles, 127

C

California State Telegraph Co., 202
Canton (Guangzhou), 78–81, 83, 123, 233
Carinthia (Austrian magazine), 237
Caroline (Danish brig), 62–3
carriole (two-wheeled carriage), 56
Cassolani, Robert, 107
Castilla, Ramón, 207
Cherokee Indians, 221
Chevallier, Henri, 179
Chippewa Indians, 224
chopsticks, 79
Christiaan Huygens (Dutch ship), 160
Christian VIII (steamer), 51
Clarendon, Lord, 252